SYNCHRONICITY

The Compleat Schroeder

PART II

BILL SCHROEDER

PUBLISHED BY FIDELI PUBLISHING, INC.

© Copyright 2017, Bill Schroeder

All Rights Reserved.

No part of this book may be reproduced, stored in a retrieval system, or transmitted by any means, electronic, mechanical, photocopying, recording, or otherwise, without written permission from the author.

ISBN: 978-1-60414-985-2

Published by
Fideli Publishing, Inc.

www.FideliPublishing.com

DEDICATION

This book is dedicated to my friend
ALLEN W. HICKS

Dear Allen,

    Much of the content of this memoir is directly connected to our friendship that began in 1990. Were it not for your advice and personal support, I might well have spent much of the last twenty years at Walmart.

    I am proud to call you my friend and the most influential person in my adult life.

Sincerely,
Bill Schroeder, 10/10/17

Contents

Dedication .... *iii*
Introduction .... *ix*
Prologue .... *xv*

1958-1963 — Westinghouse Defense Center 1
Enter Pat Christopher, January 1960 5
Eulogy 6
Pat's Memorial Service — November 5, 2008 7
Pat's Poem 9
Poem for Pat 9
Widowed Mother at Fells Point 10
Telling Helen 12
Bay Belle 13
1932 14
Bochenski Family 15
1900s — Christopher family 16
1933 — Howard 18
1930s — Photographs taken of Pat as she grew up 20

1950 — Pat's autobiography 22
    Prologue 24
    Chapter One 25
    Chapter Two 29
    Chapter Three 34
    Chapter Four 37
    Chapter Five 38
    Chapter Six 46
    1940S 54
    Girl In Profile (Circa 1948-1949) 57
    Oh, Promise Me 61
    Graduation — June 1950 63

1952	65
1952 — Ocean City	66
1954	67
The Third Floor	70
Richard	71
Robyn	72
Chris	72
Myself	74
Joan	75
March 1960	79
July 3, 1960	79
July 4, 1960	85
Fishing trip at Thoma's, Summer 1960	88
Cooking	90
1961	91
First House	91
Technical Training Consultants	92
June 9, 1961 — Margaret Rose is born	95
December 1961 — Pippin's Old Book Store	108
1961 Began *The Innocent Assassin*	111
May 31, 1963 — William Richard, Jr. is born	116
August 1963–May 1966 — Chrysler	127
The haunted house	134
October 16, 1965 — Melissa Robin is born	142
1991	152
1964	155
1966 — Xerox	157
For the first time I knew what copywriters really do	158
June 19, 1967 — Melanie Ruth is born	159
Lipton Transition	165
1968	165
February 6, 1969 — Howard Christopher is born	169
2007 Urban Challenge	176
Credit Where Credit's Due	177

1967 — Meanwhile, back at Lipton 183
1969 185
Spartanburg Synchronicity 187
Spartanburg Sewing School 192
Olympia Mills 195
    May 1970–January 1971 — Community Relations
Director, Allegheny General Hospital 200
July 28, 1971 — John Patrick is born 205
Theater Roles 1981–1987 214
1984–1990 217
1988 225
Sam Smith Park Pratt and Light Street 237
Harborplace Market 237
Pat's Later Work 240
40th Wedding Anniversary 249
Harry Potter 251
Siberian Huskies 251
Official Press Release—
    Pat Schroeder the Nightknitter 253
Star Island Remembered 255
Telephone Tarot reading 259
eBay, Etc. 260
Schroeder Scientific 261
    Archeological and Anthropological 261
    Natural History 262
    Antique and Historical 263
Flea Markets & Ebay 264
New Age 265
Tomato Harvest 1996 267
Prison Uniforms 2002 268
Playing Card Collecting 269
Local Recognition 2005 275
    Holocaust Memorial Lecture Series 277
    Carroll County Farmers' Market Writer's Day 277
    Baltimore's Enoch Pratt Free Library 277

FDR Deck 2010	278
FDR and the ALL	280
2010 Fake Flags	285
2013 Dielman Inn Project	288
Friends	290
Allen Hicks	291
Marcia George	304
November 2008	312
Epilog	315
Loose Ends	318
Truth	320
Serenity Prayer	323

PART II

1960–2017

INTRODUCTION

Several readers of *Synchronicity, Part One* have remarked on my ability to recall details. This is a mixed blessing. Time is telescoped in my mind so that things that happened 60 or 70 years ago are as clear as though it was last month. ... In fact, sometimes they are clearer because the equipment was in better shape.

All the while I have not lost sight of a vital guidepost: "If you don't write it down, it didn't happen." There were scores of people who were part of the stories I have told in this book (maybe even you, the reader)... but *I* wrote it down.

Part One was dedicated to Dr. Rich Herink in recognition of the role he played in constructing some of the foundations of my life. He continues supporting me in various ways to the present day. The dedication of *Part Two* is to another friend of the past 20 years, Allen Hicks.

Every time I sit down in front of my computer, it seems I promise myself it is the last book I will write. This time I mean it. I'd like to spend my last days reading and listening to music. Since I am obviously in love with words, my greatest problem is reining them in. Stories do not always reveal themselves in a logical, sequential order. That's why there seems to be quantum jumps in my writing. If I don't act on it, it might not become visible again until much later (if at all). Please bear with me when chronology gets intertwined with thought clusters.

But, as I have said, I write to feed my ego ... feel free to just move on to another page.

During the period of time from when I wake up and finally get out of bed (at least an hour) I review what I intend to write that day. Most recently I sought to find a unifying thread between and among my previous books. My answer is, they explain varied perceptions of *consensus reality* (it's there whether you believe it or not).

Even then, humans do not fully understand or agree upon the nature of being, becoming, or existence. What I seek to illustrate in my books is how two individuals may be part of a situation, but have diametrically opposed perceptions of its nature.

In *The Innocent Assassin*, (ISBN: 9781604145090) Charles Guiteau and his death-row spiritual advisor, William W. Hicks, both believe in Divine Guidance. However, neither can persuade the other to move toward his perception of how it works.

John Frum, He Come (ISBN:9781604144956) pits a modern, 20th Century Christian missionary against a Stone Age South Pacific Island shaman. Because of their cultural heritages, each is focused on a different final objective, even though both are embroiled in a war with the Japanese near Guadalcanal.

The Rub (ISBN: 9781500978204) introduces us to two 21st Century commercial media entities … One a Professional Pessimist; the other a Professional Optimist. There is no real resolution to their conflict.

In der Fuehrer's Face (ISBN: 9781604144864) is ostensibly an historic account of World War II. But it opened my eyes to the fact that each of the events discussed had so many reported variations, I could have written another book using "alternative facts."

In *Synchronicity: Parts One* (ISBN 978-1-60414-961-6) *and Two* I offer a first-person memoir of my own perceptions of reality over an eight decade period. During its writing I discovered my sister, Elsie, saw the same period quite differently. We both drew on our personal experiences although we were in basically the same timeline.

What follows in *Part Two* is my best recollection of the world — to use Guiteau's phrase, "as I am given light."

In October 2011, I published *Seven Decks You Will Never Play Poker With* (ISBN: 9781604144826). It is a purely non-fiction book as an homage to my playing card collecting hobby.

 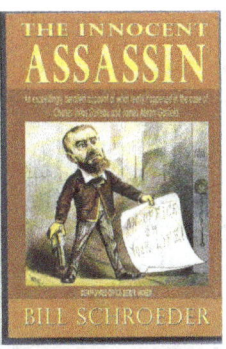  
 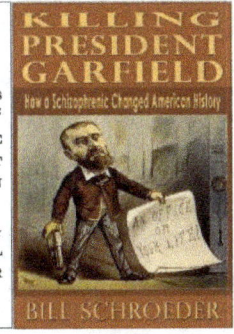  
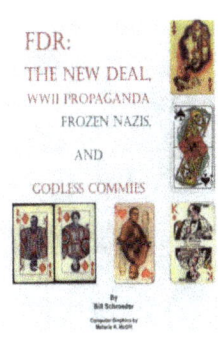 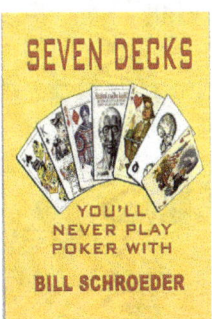  

The first thing that comes to mind as I approach telling "the rest of the story" in *Part Two* is an old Chinese curse: *"May you live in interesting times."*

Discussing the past eight decades with some of my contemporaries, we agree that they were, indeed, interesting times. But since you are already thinking about it, I can't avoid quoting the obvious from Dickens's *A Tale of Two Cities;*

"It was the best of times, it was the worst of times, it was the age of wisdom, it was the age of foolishness, it was the epoch of belief, it was the epoch of incredulity, it was the season of Light, it was the season of Darkness, it was the spring of hope, it was the winter of despair, we had everything before us, we had nothing before us, we were all going direct to Heaven, we were all going direct the other way — in short, the period was so far like the present period, that some of its noisiest authorities insisted on its being received, for good or for evil, in the superlative degree of comparison only."

My personal opinion is that <u>it was great.</u> It was great because I lived it ... I didn't just watch it from the sofa on the CBS News with a six-pack on my lap.

Curiously, there is one entity that has had a singular influence on almost all the jobs I have had and the places my family has lived ... *The Wall Street Journal.* You will see it repeatedly throughout the pages that follow. I don't know why, except that it has always worked when I needed it. I never looked at a copy of the paper before 1960.

I almost unwittingly achieved one of my goals ... I had gotten a job in advertising (even if I wasn't quite sure what it was all about). Some of the people I met at the Grey Advertising Agency, (who had the Westinghouse TV account) were as phony as a three-dollar bill.

One of the extremes was our junior account executive, John Matzy. He fit the description of guys who wore silk suits and couldn't afford underwear.

He made me aware of the fabric of the industry. For one thing, everything was a billable expense. He took, me to lunch at the Four Seasons, a well-known restaurant in New York, and billed the cost of it back to Westinghouse, with a 15% agency commission. At that point my boss, Russ Johnson, told me I was not to accept any more "free meals" from him.

When he had a cocktail party at his apartment he apologized in advance to Russ for the fact that he might see an expensive Bogen hi-fi speaker at his house (instead of a cheap Westinghouse model), explaining that he had bought it before he was assigned to our account.

It was that same cocktail party that caused me to stop talking to him. He apologized to me for not inviting me to the party (Actually, I understood it was really only for executive types and I was only a lowly copywriter). He took me aside in the conference room and said, "I'm sorry I can't invite you to the party, but we're not taking on any new friends at this time."

I was truly stunned at the remark. I waited a minute and said, "Do you have any Applications for Friendship forms with you that I might fill out?"

He didn't know what to say. I turned and left the room. I moved to Baltimore the next month.

PROLOGUE

As with *Part One*, the **synchronicity** of events continued to be a major element in the development of our lives. In case you have forgotten, synchronicity is a concept, first explained by psychologist Carl Jung. It should not be confused with serendipity. Google's comparisons are: *Synchronicity* is the experience of two or more events that are apparently causally unrelated occurring together in a meaningful manner. *Serendipity* is a propensity for making fortunate discoveries while looking for something unrelated.

As a result, the work that started as *The Compleat Schroeder* is now titled "*Synchronicity, Part One (1900 — 1959) and Part Two (1960 –2017)*."

Essentially, Jung said that some events are "meaningful coincidences" that can be neither planned nor anticipated ... They just happen and have a major influence on everything that follows.

For example, in 1956 I met a guy named Jim Hudson in a diner in Metuchen, NJ. He set up a meeting for me and two Westinghouse executives to try to settle a local strike. Our car was assaulted by Teamster Union goons on the way to the meeting, sending us all to the hospital. My involvement identified me as a *Corporate Commando* resulted in my being rewarded with a good job in Maryland.

My boss at the Baltimore Defense Center sent me to a meeting in Washington where I met Pat Christopher. She was sent to the same meeting by her boss, which began a new round of events in both our lives.

Meanwhile back in NJ, Jim Hudson died in an auto accident. I never saw him again after he arranged the meeting that sent me to encounter Pat, 200 miles away.

I have looked forward to this time when I could begin assembling Part 2 of *Synchronicity*. I was, in fact, sick of reading and proofing *Part One*. It was only about me, and I felt I wanted to talk about Pat. *The Compleat Schroeder* would not be complete until I brought her into the picture. The Schroeder family today is a direct extension of her influence.

My first step was to strategize my actions as how to tell the story. The plan includes significant events that shaped our lives from 1960 to 2017.

The one constant factor I employed throughout my adult working life was subscribing to *The Wall Street Journal*. I make no pretense of understanding the worlds of Finance and the Economy. The only parts of the paper I read were the Want Ads and the daily feature story on the front page. It was enough to cause pivotal changes in my life course.

My narrative follows a rough chronology of what happened when, but I reserve the right to toss in a thing or two I forgot to include in *Part One*. In some cases (like biographical descriptions) it makes better sense to cluster certain events by topic for better continuity of thought.

1958-1963
WESTINGHOUSE DEFENSE CENTER, BALTIMORE, MD

When I was promoted to the job as Editor of the *Westinghouse Circuit (Westinghouse News)* at the Baltimore Defense Center, I took it as my first step to becoming a member of management. In 1958, the practice at the time was for companies to pay the moving expenses of certain new employees or transfers, so I lucked out. They paid my way to move from New Jersey to Maryland.

The job was officially categorized as Management and Professional. The new job included an office; as opposed to the desk in the open office area I had at the TV and Radio Division. My mindset was that I was obliged to follow the expected behavior of a Young Executive.

There was a paradigm of correct behavior for that role. I devoted my efforts to meet the challenge. My old friend, Synchronicity, did not let me down. The same day I started work, so did the perfect model of what I wished I was ... Harry W. Smith, Jr. He was the son of a Westinghouse Corporate Vice-President. The kind of job I had struggled to get was his because Daddy wanted him to get some experience in the trenches.

His assignment was relatively undefined. On paper he reported directly the Human Resources Manager as a management trainee. His primary job was to observe how things worked in the personnel field. In the meantime,

I observed *him*. After a year or so he was made the Employee Insurance Administrator.

Harry had found an apartment complex where several young guys already lived ... appropriately named Maiden Choice Lane.

It did not take me long to find out how sheltered I had been from the expenses of real life by living with my parents. I suddenly found that I had no pots and pans. The fridge was empty ... no milk, no ketchup, no nothing. If I wanted a sandwich, I had to buy a loaf of bread and some ham.

Synchronistically, it turned out that years before, my friend Dave Vargo had gone to the St. Charles Seminary, literally up the street.

Harry acquainted me with a dating site ... The Stars and Bars Club. It was originally a serviceman's club for WWII military officers (hence the name). It was just off the lobby of the once glamorous Belvedere Hotel. Unfortunately, as the city itself declined, so did the hotel. But it will always remain in my memory as the place I discovered Crab Imperial, the signature dish in their restaurant. I ordered it at least once a week.

When Baltimore lost its military connections, Stars and Bars made itself available to young college grads. That meant anyone who would pay a buck to enter their lounge. Women hunting for husbands were admitted free.

Harry went crazy for the place. It was his first time away from home, with the exception of a Jesuit college he had attended. Here he met a girl named Connie Stack (nee: Constance Stakowski). He asked me to attend one of their sessions when he had to go home to Pittsburgh one weekend. My job was to see if she left the club with anyone. I left before she did so I never knew.

A couple weeks later she spent Saturday night in his apartment. Up to that point Harry was a virgin.

But he did not fully enjoy the event. He told me the following Sunday afternoon that he was expecting the police to break down the door at any minute during the night. Catholic priests had provided his sex education. He was a nervous wreck and needed someone to discuss the happening with. I was the nearest friend he could confide in.

"Well?" I asked. "How was it?"

His answer amuses me to this day. He thought a minute and then said, "Messy, isn't it?"

Her weekend visits were regular from then on. They came over to my apartment one afternoon to make our introduction formal. I had a large, full bookcase. Connie looked at it and said, "Did you *read* all these books?"

I told her I did, but I don't think she believed me.

Meanwhile, back at the office, conversations with Harry revealed that his connections with Pittsburgh Headquarters were even stronger than I thought. He mentioned that his family used to go to the home of Gwylim Price (Uncle Bill), the Westinghouse CEO, for Christmas. Little could I ever anticipate that my path would cross Gwylim Price's indirectly ten years later when I became the Community Relations Director for Allegheny General Hospital.

My career blossomed at the Defense Center, and I wound up making a program presentation to the President of Westinghouse on one occasion (that really puffed up my ego).

The Westinghouse Defense Center was headed by B.M. (Buford Mason) Brown. He was titled "President of the Defense Center" to give him the paper title he needed to deal with Generals and big-time Washington politicians. Other divisions were headed by General Managers and Vice Presidents. Apparently, Vice Presidents were a dime-a-dozen in Washington, and could not get audiences with anybody higher than a Colonel. His Presidency opened doors to negotiating with Generals and Admirals who controlled multi-million dollar contracts.

Brownie was a brilliant engineer who had invented the F-16 Radar, found in virtually every military jet aircraft in the world. As a reward, they made him the President of the division.

However, he had no administrative talents or people skills. They appointed Edward Benoit as his personal consultant and assistant. Brownie could not make any decisions without his concurrence (*read approval*). His daughter was married to Larry Lipschitz who became the Manger of Engineering, as soon as his name was legally changed to Larry Parker.

One of the jobs of Community Relations was to keep Brownie from making an ass of himself in public and with employees. We wrote all his speeches and public utterances. However, at a press conference, my boss planned to have him say something like, "It's always a pleasure to talk to members of Fourth Estate. ... But," he said "I'd like to welcome visiting members from the Fifth Dimension." When they all laughed, he thought he had said something clever.

Since my Spanish had improved somewhat since my troopship adventure in Colombia in 1954, part of my job was as company interpreter. When we had visitors from The Westinghouse Commercial Sales office in Madrid, Spain, I acted as Brownie's representative. These people spoke no English at all. I took them on a tour of the facility, including our health and safety department.

Their reaction was surprising and unexpected. They said, "You must have some terrible accidents here to justify such an expense. Our town in Spain doesn't have clinical facilities such as these!"

I had to explain that it was a model showplace demonstrating the use of Westinghouse Micarta panels to build the rooms. I told them that the walls were made of Micarta *plastico* (plastic). There was a flurry of discussion among the three visitors. They were greatly impressed, as I pointed out many office areas made of the same material.

We had an appointment with Mr. Brown next. This is where my language skills provided laughs for everyone. The big wall facing his desk was carved walnut and they examined it closely. "Es Plastico?" one asked.

"No," I answered. "Es mierda." They roared with laughter. I meant to say *madera,* the word for wood. Instead, I said *mierda,* which means shit.

We were obviously in the main office, so they inquired who used the beautiful office connected to it. I did it again. I said, "El *conejo,* del Presidente." More raucous laughter. Meaning *consejo,* the President's counselor. I said, "The President's rabbit." We were all fast friends now.

At that time, Brownie arrived, and I introduced him, explaining to him they understood no English. We all settled in around his conference table, and he told me, "Make this short and sweet. I have other things to do. We have time for one story, then get out of here. Tell them I am a hunter."

Then he launched into a pointless story, which wasn't funny in English.

I said, "El Presidente es un cazador (hunter)."

"What does he hunt?" they asked.

I did not know the Spanish word for duck. The only word I knew for bird was *pajaro*." So *I* said, "He hunts *pajaros*." I did not know that in slang it can mean homosexuals.

They were so amused, that they were pounding their fists on the table.

Brownie was delighted. He thought they were laughing at his story. So he dredged up another inane tale. They were sympathetic to my problem, so I told them, "The President thinks you are laughing at his story. I have to admit that I cannot translate what he is saying ... so when I tell you to laugh out loud, please do so and pretend you think he's is hilarious."

They performed on cue, so I told Brown they had to leave to catch a plane, and we all got up and shook hands with him. They were chuckling all the way back to the lobby, and I am sure they are still telling their friends what a marvelous time they had in America.

ENTER PAT CHRISTOPHER, JANUARY 1960

In January 1960 my boss, Don Poland, thought it would be a good idea if I got to meet other people in my business. He sent me to a meeting of the Middle Atlantic Association of Industrial Editors in Washington. As it turned out, Pat's boss made the same suggestion to her. Thus we experienced another synchronistic event that changed both our lives forever. Our world took off in a new direction.

Pat came with a friend named Jeeter Pritchard (center). One of my prime motivators was to check out the women who belonged. I don't know who the girl is in the picture, but I was using Jeeter to meet the gorgeous girl in the blue knit dress that he came with. I pretended I wanted

to sit opposite him at the dinner table for conversation's sake, but I knew the shapely blonde would sit next to him. She did, and I got an introduction. She was Miss USF&G in the statewide beauty contest.

She accepted my invitation for lunch some time in the next few days. However, she admitted later that she did not remember my name and had to ask Jeeter who the talkative guy was at their table. By the same token, I wasn't sure I would recognize her if she were dressed differently. I was competing with another guy named Bob McNally, who fortunately was a jerk.

EULOGY

Odd or unusual as it may sound, my best plan to lay the proper foundation for what happened since 1960, is to start at the end.

Only since she died (October 31, 2008) have I realized that there was so much we could have talked about. She supported my dreams far more than I did hers.

A recurring theme of this book is largely Pat's contribution to all our lives. If I don't write it, who will? No one knows as much about her as I do, and when I die that leaves nobody.

A constant topic of thought for me is how to format the story… Simply doing a chronology isn't enough? I want the reader to know at the onset how extraordinary she truly was.

I start with the premise that "The Past is Prologue." In this case, the prologue is the eulogy I gave for her memorial service at the Carroll County Ag Center where she had spent so many hours.

PAT'S MEMORIAL SERVICE
NOVEMBER 5, 2008

Thank you all for coming. Pat would be overwhelmed at the turnout. She never realized how well loved she was by so many people.

We talked about this day often in recent months, except she believed I would be the first one to leave. I wish I had lost that argument.

We both agreed on how to handle the last illness and the graceful exit from this world. We shared a great dislike of the Funeral Culture. We do not shed tears for the departed — our tears are for those of us left behind to deal with a loved one's absence. That does not mean we don't weep — it means we know why we weep.

Pat's life was full of emotional and physical pain from childhood on. Her last months were a painful struggle, until she finally gave herself permission to let go. It can be summed up in the Old Negro Spiritual *"Free at last! ... Free at last! ... I thank God, I'm free at last."*

When I was in college one of my friends said he thought true love was to find yourself in the opposite sex. Fortunately, I thought I deserved better than that — <u>another me</u> would have been a real pain in the ass.

Let me read you a piece I wrote for one of my writing groups that tells the story:

When Pat appeared on the horizon, I couldn't believe my luck. She met virtually all my physical requirements with no problem. She was tall (In 1960, five feet seven inches was tall for a woman). She was blonde. She had a knockout figure (She was USF&G's candidate in the Miss Maryland Competition). She had green eyes (Blue was the ideal color of choice, but green was the default). She appeared to be healthy (Though health turned out to be an ability to cope with severe adversity, rather than an absolute).

Now, the mental part is where she really had me beat. I had known my IQ since the 8th grade, and made it a point of steering the conversation around to the matter when I believed it would be to my advantage. I was summarily cured of the practice when I found Pat's score was 153 — the top of the old Wonderlic chart. Like that was it. Measurement ended at 160.

Aha, I thought, but I know the names of all the major composers of classical music, and can even recognize some of their works. So could Pat. I discovered that when I took her to the Baltimore Symphony on a date. But not only could she recognize classical pieces, she could play them on the piano. (in one instance, during one of her recitals in High School, she lost her sheet music and improvised in the style of Franz Liszt for five minutes).

Unlike the Schroeder in the Peanuts cartoon strip, I couldn't even play the toy piano. One of the prizes Pat won when she graduated from the Institute of Notre Dame was a music scholarship to the Peabody Institute of Johns Hopkins. She was a musical <u>*wunderkinder.*</u>

Shortly after the symphony date, I took Pat to the art museum. After all, I was from New York. I used to spend my Saturdays and Sundays at the Whitney Museum of Modern Art, and the Metropolitan Art Museum. I knew all the buzzwords and a bunch of stories about Jackson Pollack. So, I demonstrated my wisdom in the art field. Then Pat took me home to her mother's apartment where I saw some paintings on the wall she had done when she was 15 years old. They were better than stuff done by people three times her age. It was then I found out that she also won a scholarship to The Maryland Institute of Art.

Being an unpublished writer, but a writer nevertheless, I was earning my living as the editor of the Westinghouse News. Pat was the editor of the USF&G Insurance Company's Employee Magazine. We met at a meeting of the Middle Atlantic Association of Industrial Editors. I was cajoled and deluded into thinking that she needed help with her publication. But you guessed it; she did that as well as everything else. It was just a ploy to deprive me of my bachelorhood. (Did I tell you that she won a scholarship to the University of Maryland to study English?)

Somehow, I was selected to help this remarkable woman to fulfill her <u>*real*</u> life's work — the production of remarkable children. We met in mid-January (1960), we were engaged in March, and married by the 4th of July.

Pat once remarked to me at a restaurant that when we had children, there would be six of them in all. When we went to a restaurant they would file in gracefully, make their selections from the menu, and sit quietly while they were served. I laughed it off. I should have known better.

During the next eleven years we had a new baby every two years until her goal was reached. Then she had her tubes tied, and went on to become a ceramic artist and the best knitter in the State of Maryland with a large following.

... At least she was wrong about how the kids would behave in a restaurant.

I tried to sum up my love in a poem, but it merely scratches the surface in measuring the impact of my love for her.

POEM FOR PAT

You left without me ...
I never guessed you planned to go!
Somehow, I guess I thought we'd leave together.
You even let me think I'd go ahead and clear a space.

At the very last, I thought I'd see you in the A.M.
I said, "Good night, I love you," and kissed you
With a promise to bring you coffee in the morning.
Who could think there was no tomorrow?
Mornings always came. Why not now?

The phone rang.
We wept!
We cried because you weren't there...
We wept because you left us all alone ...
We cried because now there was no one to ask!
You always had a word of strength to help us through the storm.
Which way was west? There was no Sun.
We tried to remember how to row to shore.
How could you leave us without a valid compass?
You always knew which way was North?
The rest of us could only guess ...
None of us would move until our navigator read the charts.
We were simply adrift ...

Then one day last week, just before I woke,
You told me of the truth about those mornings

Full of "sinus" pains and daily aches that only needed
A real stiff cup of morning brew, two orange-coated aspirins,
    and a long drag on a couple Virginia Slims.
"Caffeine — Aspireen — and Nicotine!"

Suddenly, The Alchemist's magic spell no longer worked.
Even Harry Potter and Dr. Who were helpless!
A frantic effort to get hot chocolate into your system
    never reached completion.
At one-thirty the burden became too great —
The walls of the dam collapsed.
Frantic chickens ran in all directions — to no avail.

With the dawn your soul had earned its just reward —
Free at last! Free at last! Free at last!

WIDOWED MOTHER AT FELLS POINT

Getting back to our first dinner date, Pat told me she lived with her widowed mother, but forgot to tell me that she was the Wicked Witch of Fells Point. However, the first time I picked her up at home she had to tell me about the bar.

That's when I made my first big mistake with Helen. McNally had a few beers with the old lady while he waited for Pat. But I thought she would be pleased that her daughter's date would not drink and drive. Instead, she decided I was a cheap bastard. After all, she made a living by getting men to drink more than they should.

She saw me as effeminate because I was not a macho tugboat captain-type.

She asked me what I was driving. Thinking she would be impressed, I said it was a 1956 Jaguar Mark VII (I saw it as a poor man's Rolls Royce).

She responded, "Well, we have a brand new 1960 Dodge Convertible!"

We went to dinner and Pat told me that after her experience as an only child she planned to have a large family.

I laughed off Pat's picture of a large family as a joke, never dreaming that she was not kidding. About kid Number Four (Melanie) I realized that she was serious. I wonder if she psychically glimpsed the picture I took in 1979.

Family Tree, 1979

TELLING HELEN

This led to the biggest breach in relations between Helen and me. Both Pat and I dreaded telling her about our marriage plans. We were both 27 years old and I certainly didn't see any necessity of asking anybody's permission to marry. Nevertheless, one Saturday afternoon I took a Valium tranquilizer and we broke the news to Helen in the back room of the bar.

Her response was, "You're not asking my permission ... you're telling me what you plan to do!"

I said, "That's right. We just want to fix the date."

Helen responded, "I think Pat should marry someone in her own social class."

Without giving it a second thought I said, "If she can move up, I think she should!"

Pat was shocked, but Helen was outraged. "Your father's only a grease monkey, and your parents aren't even married."

"And you're a bartender," I nearly shouted.

The disagreement had its roots in the fact that my father was a Catholic as a child and he married my mother in a Lutheran church. In Helen's eyes that was not a valid marriage, making me and my sister bastard children. Her self-identification as a leader of the community didn't hold up to the Schroeder lens of gauging values.

My mother's German background involved viewing Polish people as inferiors. In fact, when the house was messed up my mother would say, "This place looks like a bunch of Pollacks live here." My Lutheran catechism class taught that Catholics were idolaters who worshiped the Virgin Mary instead of Jesus.

As far as occupations were concerned, as long as I could remember, my father did not approve of bar owners. Working men would drop a big chunk of their paychecks on payday at the bar; then look to buy gasoline on credit. He considered himself a proprietor of a small business who kept cars running during the shortages of WWII.

BAY BELLE

The next round came when we were planning to get married on the 4th of July. Helen objected since that was a big sales day at Fells Point: "That's the day the Bay Belle comes in!" (One of the biggest sales days at the bar).

After intense haggling, we settled on July 3rd, so we would always have our anniversary on a holiday. I would just as soon have gotten married in the City Hall, but Helen needed to have a big Polish Wedding for her daughter to underscore her position in the community.

Her self-concept was reinforced by occasional feature stories about Fells Point in the local newspapers.

HELEN'S CORNER—Standing by the dockside at the foot of Broadway, the quaint, Olde English bar, presided over by Helen Christopher extoles turn of the century charm. The building has been used as a tavern since 1914 when Helen's father assumed ownership. Prior to that it is known to have been named the Dreamland Café, dating back to the late 1890s.

FRIENDLY CHAT — And the right place for it ... the English bar, with Helen tending her customers, is filled with Edwardian bric-a-brac.

1932

But we are sort of coming in when the movie has been running for quite a while. Let's back paddle here and take a look at the previous 27 years or so. We'll start with Pat's direct ancestral predecessors.

She was born into a very dysfunctional and unhappy family on July 27, 1932.

BOCHENSKI FAMILY

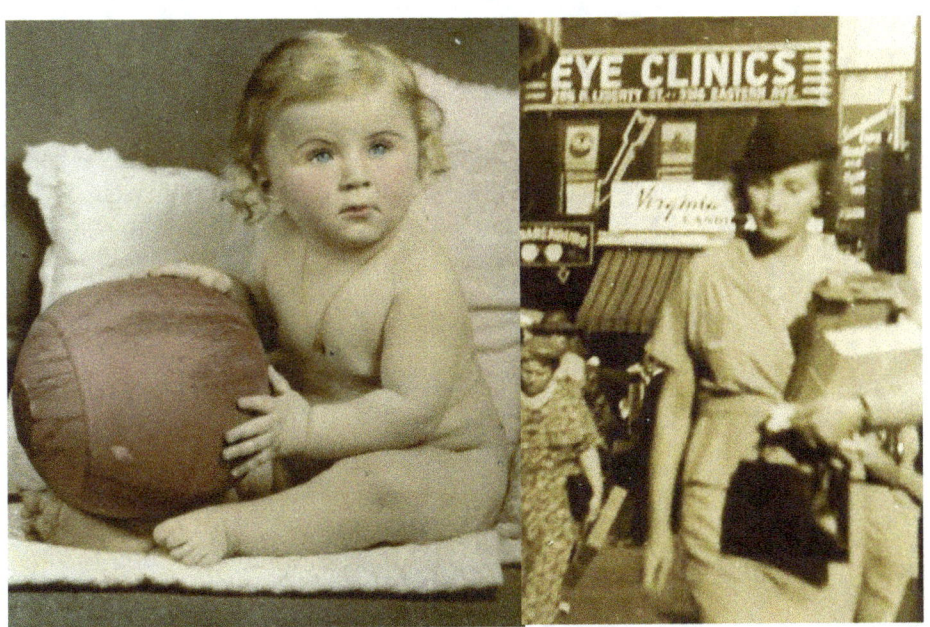

Her mother was Helen Bochenski (born 1909).

Pat's father was Howard Christopher, slightly younger than Helen.

Her grandfather was Jacob Bochenski (died 10/11/64).

He opened a bar in the corner of 1647 Thames Street and Broadway, Fells Point, Baltimore in 1917. Pat's Grandmother was Mary (Cleo) Bochenski (nee Pawlak). Cleo was the nickname she got for seeing herself as the Cleopatra of Fells Point. I don't think she ever got the joke.

Cleo's earliest reference was working in a fish-packing warehouse at Fells Point in 1912.

In local Polish-American community culture, the bar-owner was at the top of the food chain. He could extend credit for alcohol until payday. Pat said that Jake owned many properties at Fells Point, but through excessive drinking and mismanagement he lost most of it during WWII. Pat recalled making the rounds for rent collection when she was a kid and was instructed by Cleo to carry the rent money to keep Jake from spending it on drinks. He kept a portion of the money secret from his wife and hid it in the hollow bedpost of his massive brass bed. Pat said when he died, there was money stashed in there, quite possibly a goodly sum of cash. Helen and Cleo disposed of the bed after his death, never aware that they lost a large sum of cash.

The bar eventually became Helen's Corner. She titled herself "the Mayor of Fell's Point" but there is no evidence anyone else regarded her as such.

1900s
CHRISTOPHER FAMILY

The Christopher Family were Irish Catholics of what they considered the "Lace Curtain" variety (as opposed to "Shanty Irish.") They considered themselves of higher status because Grandpa Christopher was a Firefighter Captain in the Baltimore Fire Department who moved here from Philadelphia. They lived on Walbrook Avenue and Grandpa served at the Walbrook Station. Merle said that his Brigade assisted in fighting the Great Baltimore Fire.

Having a job in the Police or Fire Department was a badge of accomplishment in the Irish immigrant community at the turn of the 20th Century. The Polish community held them in low regard. Irish were among the lowest classes in the WASP hierarchy, competing with Negroes for jobs. It was

In his teen years he was in trouble frequently, due to what was euphemis-

Great-grandpa Christopher lived in Philadelphia. We know nothing about him.

not uncommon when advertising available jobs for signs to read "Irish need not apply."

They had six children; Emma, Mayble, Florence, Myrle, Eugene and Howard. Emma married into the Ellicott Family, who once owned most of what is now Ellicott City. Mayble married a successful realtor, Gaylord Brooks. Myrle married a successful CPA, Walter (Boots) Wannen. (Margaret lived with her for much if her time at Towson). Gene was an affected gay and was often protected from the world by his sisters. Florence died of TB when she was 12. Howard was very fond of her and sat vigil with her casket in the house the night before she was to be buried. Myrle said he had to keep chasing Florence's pet cat away from the casket.

1933 — HOWARD

When Howard married Helen he was a male clothing model who travelled with his employer to major cities.

tically called "a drinking problem".

His most colorful antic was to get arrested for riding George Washington's horse *naked*. He earned himself a visit to the Maryland Training School for Boys (M.T.S.B).

I believe Will has a bunch of letters Howard wrote to Helen while he was on the road modeling. A diary he kept for a while is in the possession of Howard Christopher Schroeder, his namesake. It illustrates how he was trying hard to improve himself through reading and vocabulary building. Unfortunately, there was no one to act as his mentor and point him in some profitable direction.

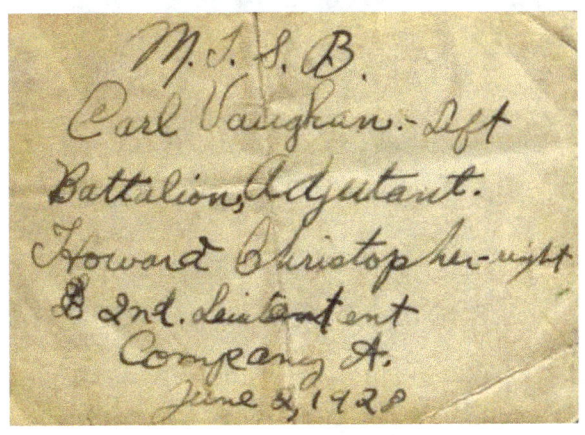

What became of Howard was the subject of much conjecture. There was general agreement that he got a job as a deckhand on a ship. It was never decided if it was on the Great Lakes where he was washed overboard in a storm, or if he went to South America. There was speculation that he jumped ship at a South American port. Pat dreamed of him often, and believed he was alive in a foreign country. For many years, when she went to sleep she dreamed of flying through the sky and meeting him on a beach somewhere. Myrle's family told her that her brother was reportedly serving as an officer's assistant on a Merchant Marine ship that had a mutiny. When the ship returned to

Helen and Captain Bill

Baltimore for trial, Howard was not aboard.

When Howard never came back, Helen took up with Captain Bill Campbell as a live-in lover. I don't know when it started, but he was a fixture at the bar when I first met Pat. I was never sure what he had been a Captain of, but he had a lot of money which Helen claimed upon his death.

1930S
PHOTOGRAPHS TAKEN OF PAT AS SHE GREW UP

As was the practice of the period, Helen had professional photographs taken of Pat as she grew up.

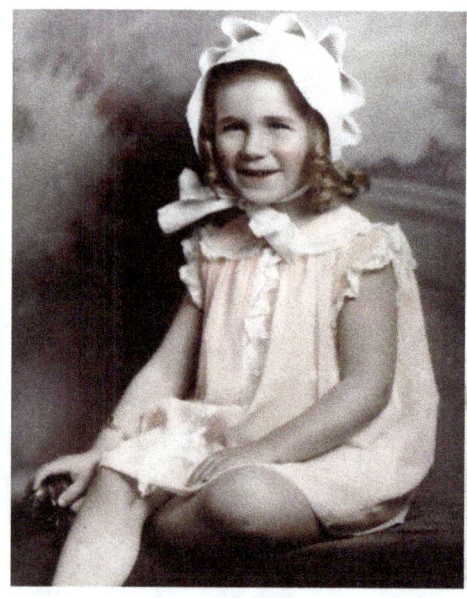

Age 4, 1936

Age 5, 1937

Pat's hair began to be noticeable as platinum, colored.

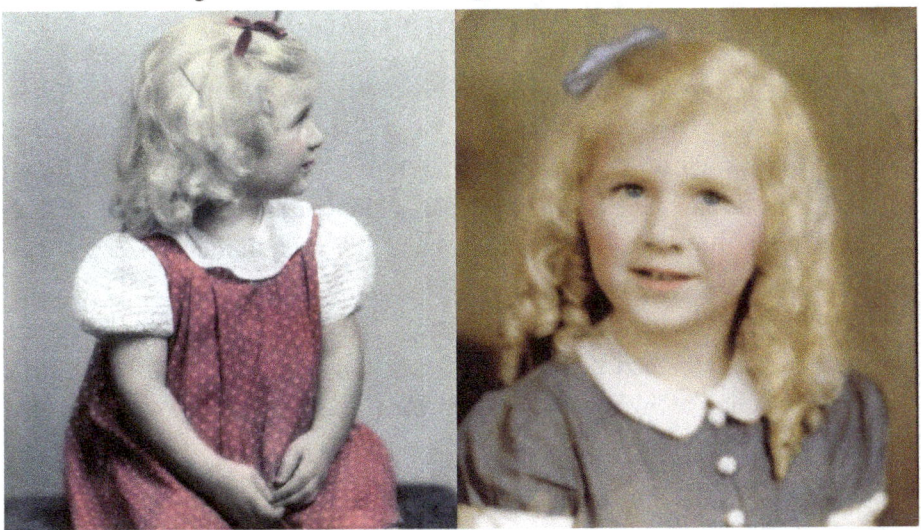

Age 6, 1938   *Age 7, 1939*

Responding to neighborhood women's gossip, Helen held a public hair-washing to prove that the child's hair was naturally platinum and not artificially bleached as some had implied.

Age 10, 1940

Pat grew to hate her pigtails, and much to Helen's horror she took a pair of scissors and cut the braids off at ear level.

1950
PAT'S AUTOBIOGRAPHY

In 1950 Pat had to write an autobiography in her Senior year at The Institute of Notre Dame. To avoid the scorn of her class-conscious classmates, she used to give her home address as Shannon Drive, a good neighborhood, where her grandparents owned a house. Nowhere in her autobiography does she directly mention Fells Point or the bar ("her grandfather's place of business" is the closest it comes).

When she gave it to me to read the first time, it was with the strong caveat that the story had to pass two severe censors — her mother and the nuns at the school. There was no room for the true story (growing up in a waterfront bar). It was what we call in the public relations and political world a *campaign biography*, written consciously avoiding negative connotations.

Following is the book as she wrote it. There may be gaps or misalignments of the pages. I have taken the liberty of inserting *(Editor's Notes:)* where I think clarification might be in order, based on things Pat said when I read the book for the first time. One element of the text worth noting is the remarkable vocabulary she uses so easily. I can honestly say I could not write so colorfully when I was only 17 years old.

I did not include all the photographs from the original in the interest of space conservation. The chapters have line drawings or cartoons she drew to capture the essence of that portion. She drew cartoons much later in life to illustrate personal notes, and even a comic strip which I will cover later on. She omitted Chapter Four without explanation or comment.

FOREWORD

I write this foreword with the fear of someone who cannot do justice to her subject. This is, after all, a foreword to the life of my daughter, Joan, who has, I think, a passionate love of all beautiful things as was ever in the heart of anyone and with whom I have taken as much care in forming her morals as improving her understanding. She is a girl knowing, and yet unknowing, to whom false culture and smug sophistication simply will not adhere. This book is the truth and the whole mess of detail that actually happened. In preparing this book she has only made use of real happenings both known and unknown.

Mrs. Helen Christopher

PROLOGUE

When I first learned that our class was assigned to write an autobiography of our very own lives, I was filled with feelings of dismay and apprehension. My immediate thought was that nothing really important enough to write about had ever happened to me, but then Mother and I talked it over, and we recalled a whole flood of reminiscences, some funny some tragic to me' at the time of their happening; which I shall attempt to set down as best as I can.

CHAPTER ONE

To begin with, my appearance in this world was a bit belated, since the old stork had promised to deliver me on the First of July, Mother hoped that he would deliver me with the firecrackers by the Fourth. But that was not to be. In one of the hottest months in years, I waited until the twenty-seventh to meet the world. Imagine my mother's shock and surprise. Instead of receiving the bouncing baby boy she so confidently expected, to receive a black-haired, blue-eyed baby girl who bounced in at exactly nine pounds.

At nursing time, the nurses gaily walked in holding the tiny babies, two on each arm, but I was always presented to mother as one on two arms.

Mother always thought the nurse was some sort of prophet, for in spite of the black hair with which I was born, she predicted that I would turn into a fair-haired blonde child. Her prediction came true, for by the time I was two years old, next to Jean Harlow, the original platinum blonde actress for that era, I had the most platinum blonde hair in the United States.

When I was brought home from the hospital, our family, composed mostly of women, were very pleased and happy with me, since it is a well-known fact that most women favor girl babies.

My mother supposed that the men (my daddy and Grandpop) hid their disappointment, because they smoked their new cigars. However, as the days went by they gave in, and admitted that they could have been wrong because after all, all new babies are wonderful.

Then a little less than one year old, I took my first step and have been walking ever since. My first word next to "Mama" was "more." I was never at all satisfied with one bottle of milk, and when Mother tried to substitute water in the second bottle, I invariably threw the bottle out of the crib. I was not a baby who believed in afternoon naps, and Mother always said that she looked forward to my growing up so that she could get some sleep.

Of course Mother had me all to herself since my father died when I was three months old. Being in such close association with her, I never wanted anyone but her to hold me and be near me. Even today Mother is still tired from the days of my childhood. Blond hair fascinated me and they tell me that whenever I saw a head of blond hair, I just had to put my hands on it and pull. I would rub noses with the owner of the blonde hair and scream and pull at the same time.

Mother never dared to turn in her bed for fear of awakening me in my crib. And unfailingly when she did, she would see me standing there with my arms outstretched to be with her. I suppose she spoiled me because she gave in most of the time. Mother claims that she would be sleeping soundly and then heard my gurgling and cooing, and would awaken to find me staring at her. I never slept. Mother said she tried fennel tea and a bit of paregoric, the usual baby sleep inducers. But they never had the desired effect, only gave me more pep.

One day Mother left me in the care of her mother-in-law who had raised nine children of her own. On her return, about two hours later, she found an almost frantic woman, who said she had never heard a child scream for her mama so much. She was greatly relieved to see Mother and be rid of me at the same time.

An instance of my early life when I narrowly missed death was the time when Grandmother was giving me an airing in the carriage. *(Editor's Note: Always known as Grenma in direct address, and Cleo in the third person.)* She stopped to talk to a neighbor and while she was talking she kept the carriage moving, until without realizing it, it reached the edge of the curb and turned over with me in it. Mother was washing windows at the time, and was complacently gazing down upon me until I toppled over. She and Grandmother both screamed at the same time, and one would think the end of the world had come. Providence was with me, because my little mattress and myself were thrown clear. And by some miracle I landed on it. Grandma still says today that if anything had happened to me she would never have forgiven herself.

In spite of the large family on Daddy's side, I was the only grandchild on their side, and all their Christmases revolved around me. I suppose I was too young to realize then that they bought almost everything the toy shops had to offer. One year I insisted on taking home the miniature railroad under the tree, which of course was part of the tree.

We were all prepared to go out there the following year when I fooled them all; they had to bring Christmas to me since I very inconveniently fell heir to chicken pox on Christmas morning. Mother says that there was nothing I did not have a touch of when I was small. The only reason I did not get smallpox was because she had me inoculated against it at the age of six months. Still, I enjoyed being sick because it was like having a picnic to me with all my relatives bringing me gifts. I always made a quick recovery when I got tired of the medicine.

It seems I was always getting into mischief when I was not being watched. Mother often speaks of the time she got the scare If her life. I was about three when I was left in the kitchen with a little boy playmate of mine, just six months older than myself. Tired of playing, we decided to explore the kitchen cabinet. The lower part held nothing of interest, so I climbed upon a chair and looked farther. Candy at that time was the love if my life and I could not get enough of it.

As I peered into the cabinet, what did my eyes behold but a tiny box of candy, or so I thought. My little playmate was smarter than I and cautioned me against it, as he evidently knew what it was for, but I did not heed his warning. I ate fifteen tablets of a chocolate laxative called Ex-Lax. Mother came into the kitchen some time after that and noticing the chocolate smear on my lips, asked where I had gotten the candy. If it had not been for that little chocolate smear I might not be alive today, writing this autobiography.

My little playmate told on me, and amid great excitement and trepidation, Mother called Dr. Little, our family physician, and explained the situation. She did not get much consolation from him, for upon her query of "Doctor, what shall I do?" all he said was, "You can pray to God."

He told Mother to rush to the drugstore and get some syrup of Ipecac, and give that to me alternately with hot water, which would cause me to be nauseated. I do not know much understanding a child of that age would have, but Mother says she looked at me very seriously and told me that if I did not do as the doctor ordered I would die. I must have realized that to die would be a terrible thing, and I took my medicine without protest. And it was not long before it worked and relieved myself of most of the chocolate.

I was prayed for and watched fearfully all of that night. But I have lived lots of days and years since then. What a worry I must have been, but I still like candy in any form.

CHAPTER TWO

Much to my regret, I hazily remember that we travelled extensively in my early years. Luckily, we had relatives living in various parts of the United States whom my mother just had to visit, and she would always take me along.

On one particular visit to New York, when I was about four years old, Mother and Aunt Emma, whom we were visiting for the Easter holidays, were invited to a gala affair, beginning with a cocktail party at the Waldorf Hotel and ending with dinner at the Stork Club, which was being given by the vice-president if a New York stock brokerage firm,

Mother was greatly excited, and wanted very much to go, since New York was new to her and she had never been to either of these places. But since my aunt lived alone, there was the question, "What do we do with the baby?" They debated pro and con and finally telephoned the party who was holding the affair, explaining the situation. Mother said he sounded a little dumbfounded at first, but then suggested they bring me along. So I was dressed in my best and off we went to the Waldorf.

Upon our arrival we zoomed way up high in an elevator. And then we were ushered into a gigantic room situated in the Waldorf Towers. It was filled to overflowing with people, all adults, except for me. The first thing that caught my eye was a huge table at the other end of the room with a beautiful centerpiece on it, full of canapés, sandwiches, and hors d'oeuvres of all descriptions.

The host caught me in time and asked Mother what I liked best to eat. And she said chicken soup, as that had always been a favorite with me. I was taken into a small private room adjoining the large one to be served. Mother said she was never more embarrassed than when the waiter brought the soup in a silver tureen and all the splendor a hotel of that type affords. I flatly refused to eat it and demanded instead a cheese sandwich! The host was very obliging in giving me what I wanted but I am willing to bet he wished I was not there.

Mother was glad when the cocktail party was over and we proceeded to the Stork Club for dinner. Quite a few eyebrows were raised when we entered, as Mother says, she thinks I was the first child ever to be in there, even if it was called the Stork Club. She said I had a grand time, and almost everyone in the place that passed by our table paused and spoke to me. Shirley Temple had just made the song "Polly-Wally-Doodle All The Day" famous for little children and the orchestra leader played it especially for me. Then he took me by the hand, gave me his baton and had me lead the band.

The next day we went shopping, and I was presented with my first New York Easter outfit, which came from Lord and Taylor, a beautiful store on Fifth Avenue. We went to New York quite often after that, at least once or twice a year. I got quite familiar with the gorgeous shops, theaters, and interesting sights New York has to offer, but more of that later.

My Aunt Stella, (Mother's sister) married an Army man, and by visiting her at each new post they were sent to, we got to see quite a bit of the country. I especially remember Fort Sill, Oklahoma, mainly almost because of the red ants.

My uncle had a car and he often took us sightseeing. Oklahoma is full of barren stretches of land and very little of it fertile, as it is sandy. At a little town called Lawton, about 20 miles from the Army post, I saw my first real Indians. It is not surprising there to go through the streets and see an Indian mother with her papoose strapped to her back, just as we have read in books and seen in pictures. This town was having some sort of carnival at the time we were there, and saw many of the Indians dressed in full regalia. The men looked very fierce and frankly I was terrified.

They drove by in giant Packards and Cadillacs, those who were made rich through oil. Speaking of oil, we once drove to Oklahoma City and saw how oil was actually drilled for on front lawns and back yards. It was truly something to see and remember.

Oh yes, I almost forgot to tell you about the red ants. My cousin Paul (who is six months younger than I) decided we should go exploring one day. So we walked and walked for what we thought were miles. We were pretty tired and thought we would sit down and rest a while. There seem to be no convenient place to sit upon outside of two little mounds of sand, so down we sat. It was not long before we were greatly distracted by a burning, itching sensation in our sitting region, and quickly headed for home. Our panties were full of red ants which, believe me, can cause quite a bit of havoc! We were greatly relieved to be rid of them. That was my one and only experience with red ants, and as far as I am concerned they can keep them in Oklahoma.

Another time the soldiers were preparing for maneuvers, and my uncle warned us specifically to stick close at home while they were practicing. To us that was an open invitation, and on the appointed day my cousin and I left early and wound our way to the shooting grounds. We thought we were safely away from danger, but we reckoned wrong. The men were using some real ammunition that day, and my cousin Paul still has some shrapnel in his leg and arm from that experiment.

The next Army camp we went to was Fort Bragg, NC. The nearest town to that was Fayetteville, to which we did not go very often, since mother said there was a lot of race hatred there. They often had trouble between black and white soldiers. It was not a place to feel safe in. We always left plenty of time to get back to the base before dark.

PAUL, PAT, BOBBY
FAYETTEVILLE, N.C.

As a little girl, I was especially fond of horses, and they had a lot of them at Fort Bragg since it was a field artillery unit. It was the height of my ambition to ride one, and my uncle promised me that I could. He came home one day with three horses in tow, one for each of us. I was filled with joy when he mounted me on my horse, an old nag named Maggie. I was so proud.

I wanted all the world to see, but my joy was short-lived. We were merely riding around and around the yard in back of the house. But to me it was tremendous open space, and so much that I did not see, (and obviously neither did the horse) the line that Aunt Stella had strung up for her washing. She forgot to take it down. In less time than it takes to tell, the horse walked right into the line and reared up. I was thrown down and knocked out. Mother, as usual, was anxiously watching, and saw the accident when it happened. She must have had a lot of worrisome moments with me, since Fate decreed that she should witness all the bad things that happened to me.

She was a frantic, nervous wreck by the time I came to, and we did not stay longafter that. I think she was really afraid that I would try it again. Even so, I have never lost my love for horses. I have ridden often since then and was thrown many times. But thank goodness, never in the presence of my mother.

(Editor's note: Pat told me she went riding Saturdays secretly as a teen-ager. She pretended to be visiting her grandparents at Shannon Drive, but went riding as soon as they left for the Fells Point bar. One morning she slammed her head into a low-hanging tree-branch and was knocked senseless. The next thing she remembers was suddenly finding herself in a Broadway movie theater at about 5:30 in the afternoon. She had no idea how she had gotten there or what had preceded it. She experienced time distortions for years afterward. She never told her mother about the incident for fear of not being able to ever go riding again).

Later on we visited two other posts, Fort Benning, Georgia, and Fort Meyers, which is, I think, in Tennessee. But nothing happened at either of them that I can remember. Then Uncle Phil was transferred to Schoefield Barracks in Hawaii. He wanted us to come there too, but Grandmother was worried about our going so far away. So to keep her happy we did not go. It probably would have been a wonderful experience though. Because my Aunt Stella says it is truly a land of beauty and never to be forgotten scenery. She also said it almost broke her heart to leave after being there for two years, as the natives throw leis of flowers on the water to say farewell, and sing sad, poignant songs, especially "Aloha."

Grandma tried to make up for my missing that Hawaiian trip by taking me with her on a trip to Manistee, Michigan, to visit some of Grandfather's relatives. They lived a very rural life and were simple people. They had a little boy, my cousin Donnie, that I played with while I was there. I liked it very much since farm life was something very new to me, especially jumping up and down on the haystacks, and watching the animals on the farm. One thing I remember is that I would not drink any milk while I was there after I saw where it came from. Grandma was worried but I promised her faithfully I would drink my milk when we got home again where it came in a bottle.

So much for my travelling reminiscences from early childhood. My only wish is that I may be able to travel and see what I would like to. It is my ambition to really to see Americas first, the Giant Redwoods in California and Yellowstone National Park, Boulder Dam and the desert of Arizona, the Great Lakes and Niagara Falls, to mention but a few. Who knows that but one day I will have put away a tidy little sum and my dreams will come true.

Maybe if I had been the little boy my mother expected I could see all these places because it is my contention that life is far more simple for boys.

CHAPTER THREE

I do not know whether these circumstances in my life as I have related them are very coherent to anyone but me, because for every remembrance that I recall, a myriad others cross its path. I am lost in a maze of memories. Each little thing recalls a dozen others and I hope that the memories that I have set down are at least interesting to others, so I shall bravely but timidly continue.

At the age of five I was reluctantly pushed into a new world, namely kindergarten. I was not alone in crying for being placed in a room full of strange children because most of them were crying too. But my strangeness soon wore off when I realized the paper and crayons were there for our use and I was soon drawing to my heart's content. Even then, as now, I loved paints and crayons, and Mother tells me I was very imaginative. She used to buy every coloring book sold in the stores. When I tired of them I cut out my own paper dolls, and colored them myself to suit my fancy.

Perhaps that was the beginning of my love for art. I but vaguely remember little boys being in that class, but I was much to busy to pay them much attention. But it is my only recollection of being in a coed school, because the following year I was placed in St. Patrick's parochial school, which had separate buildings for boys and girls.

My first years were not particularly eventful outside of the fact that one of the nuns sold foreign stamps and I became an avid stamp collector. I have dabbled in just about everything in my time, and cannot understand why Mother got so angry saying I was just finding more ways to spend money. In my third year I received our Lord in Holy Communion and was as good as any little girl can be.

HOLY COMMUNION

It is custom among people of Polish descent, to have the little communicant visit all his or her relatives on that day. As I remember, I had a perfectly glorious time, as you do not leave anyone's home empty-handed. I did not look as virginal at the end of that day as I did at the beginning. I can still show you the chocolate stains in my dress which mother has kept to prove it. As I recall, I was an awful worry to my mother. *(Editor's Note: A situation, Pat said, Helen reminded her of at least once a week.)*

Much of real joy was going down to Grandpop's place if business. It is situated on the waterfront, facing Baltimore Harbor and caters to seagoing men. Grandpop, like me, is a great lover of animals. The sailors knew this and often brought him something alive. At one time he owned a groundhog, an American eagle, an anteater, a parrot and a rabbit, besides our own collection of three Pekingese dogs.

The animals were kept in cages on the floor, and the dogs slept on a shelf above them. The place was being turned into a veritable zoo; until Grandma put a stop to it.

The sailors were all very kind to me and brought me gifts from all over the world. They would often join me in my childish games, and I had lots of fun with them. We lived privately on Bel Air Road, where we had a police dog to guard the house. He was chained to an apple tree to ward off intruders, but he got so fierce and vicious, that Gramps *(Editor's Note: She never called him Gramps in real life)* decided to get rid of him. So he put him in the car and drove him away out to the country and let him out. Imagine his consternation, when he got home to find the same dog he left out in the woods waiting for him on the lawn. He did not have the heart to take him out again, so he found him a home with some friends who had a house in the country.

Having inherited my Grandfather's love for animals, I was forever bringing home whatever creatures I could find or trap. Stray kittens or hurt birds were not the only thing I presented to my family. We were all gathered at my Aunt Stella's house. It was after dinner and my cousin Paul and I were restless. So while my younger cousin Bobby wasn't looking we wandered off to the brook at Herring Run Park. We did not want him with us because the last time we took him he fell in. But that is another story.

The fishing was very good and besides the minnows and tadpoles, we proudly presented my mother with a jar of slimy black lizards. She did not seem to appreciate them, even after I explained every detail of their capture. For Bobby we captured a toad, but for some reason my Aunt Stella wouldn't let him keep it. I have always had a weakness for turtles and frogs. It got so that Mother forbade me to bring any more into the house. But one day I found myself with fifty cents and I bought five new turtles at Woolworth's five and dime store.

I was afraid to bring them into the house where Mom could see them, so I

left them outside on the steps until dark when I could sneak them into the house. Someone found them crawling around and brought them in. Mother knew at once they must be mine. She, however, forbid taking turtles to bed with me, as she awoke one morning with a turtle on the pillow beside her.

All of my animals had names. I had a chameleon from the circus named Elizabeth, a giant grasshopper named Hitler, and a mouse I called Popeye. Mother suspected that we had a mouse in the house and wondered why it did not fall for the bait she had set in a trap. Then she found out that I had tamed it and was feeding it myself. I still think it was cute the way it used to come to me to be fed.

Paul and I once caught a wild rabbit, and even after we let him go he would come to the back door for lettuce leaves. Grandma said if she left Gramps and me alone we could charge admission to see the creatures we had at our house. When I started to bring home bees and insects in a jar, she said one of us would have to go. So, of course, I stayed.

The fourth, fifth and sixth grades at school were just time that passed in my estimation. Nothing very eventful happened. I was in the seventh grade when it dawned upon me that the boys' class for the same grade was directly opposite ours on the court. Oh, the crushes and dreams I had then, It was then we used to leave our classes after school and surreptitiously apply lipstick and try to look nonchalant as the boys went by.

I then had my eye on the cutest blonde boy I had seen. He was shy and so was I, and we never talked outside of saying hello, but one night he went to a birthday party at which I was also present and he took me home. We never became really friendly, but I worshipped him from afar. He rode me around on his bike a few times, and I used to go and cheer for him at ball games. It was taken for granted by the others that I was his girl. I was so proud of him at graduation when he won the medal for attendance for all eight years. But mother said he was too dumb to do anything but probably get into the Navy. He did.

Then there was Francis, the poetic type, the dreamer. But he was already claimed by one of my girl friends, Gloria, who became my bitterest enemy when she became aware of my interest in him. He liked me; I knew because he used to tell all his friends to tell me so. Finally, when Gloria became aware of this she gave up in despair; but not easily because she was the jealous possessive type, hardly the type for him.

Francis was the second boy who kissed me. We parted ways shortly after that; his family moved away. But he lingered in my mind for a long, long time afterward.

I had made quite a few friends among the girls at St. Patrick's. But after graduation our lives drifted into different channels. Two of the girls married not long afterward. They were a little bit closer than I.

Some went on to business college; a few to Seton Hall High School, and the majority to Catholic High ... but I was left to stand alone.

CHAPTER FOUR

(There was no Chapter Four. No explanation.)

CHAPTER FIVE

It was always taken for granted that I would go to the Institute, as did my mother before me. Certainly we had heard that the schools were overcrowded, but we did not realize how much until Mother called the Institute and found their quota was full.

It was not until Mother explained to Sister Maurelian that she herself was an alumna that Sister agreed to find room for me. Before this, Mother had written a letter to the school which was read by two of her old teachers, Sister Vitalia, who is now secretary of the Institute, and Sister Dolorette whom she had in the fourth year. It was mainly through their kind instigation that I was allowed to enter.

At that I almost did not get in, but not though any fault of my own. While I was being measured for my uniform, Sister Maurelian had neglected to tell me that I would be required to take an entrance exam, so I 'was not there on the appointed day. Sister Maure1ian telephoned and sounded very angry, because this meant that I would have to be given a separate exam, and she was greatly pressed for time.

Mother and I both breathed a sigh of relief when we finally got everything straightened out. What a wonderful memory Sister Vitalia has! While I was being fitted for my uniform, she recognized Mother after all of those years and even called her by her first name.

It was in my first year that I became one of a trio. We called ourselves D1zzy, Daffy and Dilly. I was Daffy. Am I? It consisted of Doris Anderson, who came from New York, Joan Keneal and myself'. We were always in trouble, so that we spent many a late afternoon at school. Mother never could understand. Despite the fact that I took both Music and Art, why I should be late coming home from school every day. We had real friendships and such wonderful times together that I know I shall never forget them as they made my first year at the Institute a very happy one. Although Joan went on to Commercial, and Doris moved back to New York, I have kept up our old habits faithfully,

Freshman initiation was a day to be feared. We had all been receiving threatening notes from the Juniors, sprinkled with cross-bones and skulls of thing that would happen to us on that day. We were prepared for almost anything. And what happened? We went back to being babies, dressed in baby bonnets and bibs, which we had to wear all the way home under threat of punishment. We had lots of fun laughing at ourselves about the way we looked.

Then there was Freshman-Parents day, of which I was a little afraid. It was my first public appearance at the piano. I was not only accompanied by Mary Jane Marringer with her violin, but also played a solo. Sister Benitia must have had a great deal of confidence in me because in spite of all our fears, we did beautifully. I could not help thinking that Sister Chrisara of St. Patrick's, my first music teacher, would have been proud of me then. She had a natural love for the piano that she tried to instill in all her pupils, and I thank her for it.

Since I had, even as a little girl, I had a great love for drawing and painting, It was only natural that I should wish to study it. I started drawing as soon as I was able to grasp a pencil and have passed many long afternoons away sketching to my heart's content. Perhaps I was not satisfied with cut-out books so dear to a little girl, I because I stubbornly persisted on my own creations, even if at first they appeared very crude.

The Institute offered an Art Course, and I could not wait to begin. Sister Sabina was a challenge to me with the first lesson I had. She has the gift of genius, and to look at her paintings and comparing them to mine was like comparing a puddle to an ocean.

Her studio on the fifth floor is enjoyed by all, and is quite a busy place since. There are lots of people wandering in. Sister makes all of her students feel immediately at ease. And in her own characteristic way wins their favor, The hours I spent talking and painting with Sister and occasional teasing of one another offered a pleasant relief of the daily routine of school work.

Trouble, of course followed me everywhere, and this made the school day not only exciding, but very adventurous. I was always a great talker and Sister Germaine, our homeroom adviser, said she would warn my future sisters not to seat me next to anyone who would talk with me. Her biggest mistake was to seat me in front of Mary Ann Panuska. Here was a girl after my own heart. We sat in back of the room and chattered incessantly. Whenever there was a low mumble or a muffled giggle, Sister knew who to blame.

In my Sophomore year, I missed a part of my Freshman trio, Doris Anderson, very much. I was broken-hearted when I heard that she had moved back to New York permanently. The term "Sophomore" has been interpreted to mean "a wise fool." There were no wiser fools than me and my friends. The only advantage I had over them was that I can stop laughing as quickly as I began. Detention would not be Detention without us present.

One of my greatest friends was a girl the whole school knew and admired. Her name was Eleyse Gervaise, and she had come from her home in Canada to study one year at the Institute in order to learn the English language more thoroughly. She was placed in the fourth year and I was only a Sophomore, but she came often to see Sister Sara who taught French, her native language. That was how our acquaintance began.

She could only speak French when she arrived, and it was fun to listen to her trying to speak English. I am afraid, though, that I have done worse to French than she ever did to English. She possessed the natural warmth and understanding of the French, so that she made a great many friends. She did not understand my French very well. But she always pretended that she did, and that made me feel we were getting along very well, for which I liked her very much.

She had to return to Canada at the end of the year. Though, as I remember, several of her Senior friends and I, feeling very much out of place in their presence, bade her a tearful farewell at the station. Eleyse begged me to go with her and spend the summer with her family, but unluckily Mother would not consent to my going. She did promise to return for my graduation, since she sneaked me into hers.

She would not go up on stage with the other graduates to receive a diploma because she said she did not deserve it, Although Sister and I tried to convince her that she did. Tickets were very scarce to the graduation. Underclassmen were not allowed at the ceremony. as it was only for relatives and close friends. Eleyse had only one ticket and this she had given to the doorman. She wanted me to come with her, so she went to the doorman and asked for her ticket back, saying she would rather sit downstairs.

There was no standing room. He saw me stranding there but gave us two tickets. We did not stop to argue, but ran downstairs and got into our seats. Now, as in the case of Doris Anderson, our letters are the only links between us. There is an old saying that all good things come to an end, but I sincerely hope that is not the case with my friends as I would very much like to see them again.

I must not only have been a worry to my mother, but also to my teachers. Mother was to meet me at the school to take me to the doctor's for some minor ailment. I, as usual, was in Detention although Mother did not know this. When she tired of waiting, she went on up to my classroom. Sister Sara did not seem to have a very complimentary opinion of me, for when she heard that I was going to see the doctor, she calmly suggested that Mother take me to see a psychologist, as she thought there was something seriously wrong with me. I am afraid she did not know me very well. It seems funny though, that the following year Sister Thomas Aquinas and Sister Bernadette made the same suggestion but not in the same manner. *(Editor's Note: Pat said they were really quite serious about it.)*

Then it was June again, the end of the school year, and then July, and I was sixteen. In my sweet, silly youth I always envisioned sixteen as some magical year when a girl's whole life would suddenly change and a whole new world would open up before her. Nothing very different or dramatic happened that had not happened before. And now I realize that I am no different from thousands of other girls whose dreams are made of stardust.

In our Junior year we were five: Rose Marie Beres, Dorothy Poeta, Maria Droney, Mary Clampett and I. Rose Marie is a quiet, reserved sort of person. That is, until she met us. She likes to have everything to the point of perfection, and she is the one who methodized our madness. Dottie is an exceptional girl. Many times I have wished I could be as carefree as she. She is lots of fun to be with and makes a very true friend. Marcia is the quiet one. She has more poise than any one of us, and wears sophistication like a cloak. She is, although I hate to admit it, more capable of acting her age. She is the oldest of our crowd and maybe that accounts for her manner. Mary is the type of girl who makes friends everywhere she goes. A Sister once warned her mother that Mary had a mischievous twinkle in her eye. She is liked by all the girls in our class, and there was not much trouble that went on or scrapes we did not have a part in. She is my best and closest friend.

As juniors we were allowed to initiate the Freshmen. When the call came for volunteers we were among those who answered. For the initiation, our class had planned a spectacular circus. We wanted it to be a wonderful and never-to-be-forgotten event for the Freshmen. We connived and worked together secretly on our plans. I do not think the Freshmen had even an inkling of what was coming, because for them to know would be inviting disaster. We would have to plan something else.

Threatening notices were posted in every available corridor, classroom, and even lunchrooms. Every bulletin board and every nook and cranny was filled with warnings to the Freshmen. We enjoyed ourselves and secretly laughed at the looks on the faces of the Frosh.

I shall never forget how she looked when she got her assignment. She was chosen to be the Fat Lady in the circus. But as she is naturally fun loving and gay, she got over her consternation and got fully into the spirit of the circus. We had to stuff pillows underneath her dress until she was twice or even three times her own size. It truly took a magnanimous spirit.

Rose Marie was to be the Magician, and she was into it heart and soul by practicing on us for the next few weeks until she had even us convinced of her magical powers.

Mary, Jeanette Wajer, Pat Gellerman and I had volunteered to do a dance. We decided to dance to the tune of "You Better Watch Out." I had written some new words, which were about I.N.D's circus instead of Santa is Coming to Town.

Our act was the first on the show because we prepared the way for the circus to follow. What a messy sight we were that day! Having to dress as tramps, we spared no detail. Charcoal was smeared over our faces and arms, and lipstick highlighted our shiny red noses. Our shirts were torn and bedraggled, sleeves pushed up from charcoaled arms, and no ties to support our collars.

The others wore pants belonging to their fathers or brothers, but I had to wear a pair belonging to Gramps. And as they were a very large size I had trouble trying to look carefree and to keep my trousers up at the same time. His hat was quite large and most of the time was balanced on my nose. We took pictures of ourselves, but for the life of me, I cannot find my face on them.

We carried the usual knapsacks and paraphernalia of the road. Pat had a long keychain and walking stick; Mary a torn, dated newspaper; and I had a cane and a very glamorous copy of the *Police Gazette*. Jeanette looked the cutest with her white kerchief, five o'clock shadow and jeans rolled up to her knee. We made quite a hit, imitating the clumsiness of the tramps in our dance and singing in low-pitched voices which would suddenly go off tune.

All the girls were successful in their acts and greatly appreciated by the little Frosh. Of course, the show was for them, but I secretly think we had the most fun laughing at ourselves. After we entertained them, it was their turn to act. They were wonderful sports and in the beauty-pact and scooter contests, besides others we had prepared for them. At the end of the day, Juniors and Frosh alike, eating candy and ice cream and drinking cokes, voted it a fun day for all.

This year we received our class pins. I, like the rest of the Juniors, had been pining for it, and I was never so proud as the day I received mine. It made me feel I was a real part of the Institute, wearing it like a banner.

I had a social treat, too, in my Junior year. Mother decided to go to New York and take me along. And this time I was grown up and could look with new eyes at what I had seen in my childhood. Of course we had a hectic time just getting ready to go. Our suitcases would not close; they were packed so full. The zipper on my new suit would not budge, and millions of other things happened that never should have happened when one is going on a pleasure trip.

Finally, we were there at the Hotel New Lexington where Mother had reserved a room. This was Easter Sunday, so naturally we had to go out at once to see the Easter Parade, and what a parade it was! I have never seen anything so fantastic in my life. It seemed that millions of people were crammed between Madison, Park and Fifth Avenues, all bent on one purpose, to see and to be seen. The crowds were thickest around St. Patrick's Cathedral, where newspaper photographers were stationed to photograph the elite, the saucy models, and the bizarre, and believe me, most of them were mostly bizarre.

We saw pale blue furs, live birds perched on top of hats, men in formal day attire playing nursemaid to fancy dogs dressed as formally as they. The cutest, I thought, were the French poodles as most of them had their topknots tied in a ribbon, and little ruffled dresses about their bellies. It seemed so funny to see these very, very elegant men escorting very seriously their ultra-ultra dogs.

At the same time, horse-drawn vehicles, highly decorated, were going up and down Fifth Avenue. They were filled with people dressed in Easter finery of bygone years. The streets were so crowded we could barely move. We saw in the newspapers the next day that 100,000 visitors had come to New York for Easter. I, for one, know I was so.

We walked and walked for what seemed like endless hours until we realized that our feet hurt and that we were hungry. New York has thousands and thousands of cabs but not that day. It seems that some sort of strike was going on, and those that were available were already filled. So we walked some more until we came to Ruby Foo's, a famous Chinese eating place. It must be too famous, because the meal cost my mother nine dollars, besides the dollar tip for the waiter *(Editor's note: This is 1949)*. I guess that is why they let you have a souvenir menu gratis, carefully placed in an envelope.

After that, we went to a much-heralded movie playing in New York at that time. When we came out, we walked about three blocks and found ourselves on Broadway. We were still walking. Then we found a theater that had a Sunday show, and we decided to go and see that and rest our feet at the same time. Our feet hurt so badly that we took off our shoes to ease the pain. After the show we could hardly get them on again. The play we saw was called "High Button Shoes", and did not amount to very much. But the comedian, Phil Silvers, kept me in stitches.

By that time we were both so tired that we went back to the hotel to get some rest. After we got settled in our beds we found we were hungry again, so Mother called Room Service and we ordered two chicken sandwiches and milk. No sandwich ever tasted so good, even if they each cost a dollar and fifty cents *(Editor's note: 1949 again)*. Mother is a brave soul and took everything in her stride.

We awoke the next morning, to find that it was still raining. And although our suitcases were crammed, we neglected to bring an umbrella or galoshes. So we decided to go shipping. We went to Saks Fifth Avenue where my Aunt Emma used to work. We purchased a lovely umbrella and a few other incidentals, such as compacts and three lovely dresses for me.

That took most of the day, and we went to Rockefeller Center and looked around a bit and had something to eat. While there, we purchased tickets for a play called "The Madwoman of Chaillot." I enjoyed it more than any other play I have ever seen.

We had to see the glamorous places such as the "Club 21" and the "Stork Club" before nine o'clock at night. Believe it or not, New York has a curfew law that states that women without escorts were not allowed after that hour. We did not care about that too much, as we had enjoyed ourselves so much at the play. Anyway we were too tired and were still walking. It was still raining. We stayed another day, which too, proved to be a dismal one. But New York is exciting to me, even in the rain.

We were so tired from the walking that Grandma said we looked much better when we left than when we returned. After such an exciting vacation as I never imagined, I returned to school and was faced with the dreary prospect of facing so many beautiful, balmy days struggling with French pronunciation and Algebraic theories.

Upon awakening one morning, I glanced at the calendar and discovered I was face to face with exams. Once again I was faced with rushing to cram into my head all the things I had neglected to learn within a few days. Exams came and a few gray hairs later I learned that I had again made the grade and passed.

The summer of 1949 was an idyllic phase of my life. The week before our annual cruise on the Chesapeake, Mary, Marie Anne and I paid a visit to the Cahill Teenage Center. I had gone out with other boys before and there were some that I really liked, and some I only liked as friends. But this was different. Even in a group he stood out ... at least to me. His name was William Highland and Boston was his home. I liked his clipped manner of speech and this is how I met him.

I had been dancing with a boy who was a very good friend of the boy from Boston. After the dance we went over to the side of the room where our pals were sitting. As we were laughing and talking, I heard a voice that sounded different and out of place in Baltimore since native Baltimoreans have a tendency to draw out their words. I turned quickly to see who possessed this voice, and turned into a tall boy with hazel eyes and crisp black hair. The boy I was with took the hint and introduced us. For the rest of the evening we danced together. We both promised to be there again the next week.

This was the day of our boat ride and I sunburn easily. I was as red as a lobster from the trip. In my green and white print dress, I looked like an Indian, but since Mary was as red as me I didn't mind it too much. He was there and did not seem to mind that I outshone a stoplight. He comforted me with words that in the dim light of the dance hall I merely looked as though I was blushing. We went out quite a bit after this and I really blushed when he told me he really liked me quite a lot.

Yet, as what happens in most sad cases, his stay was not long. He had to return to Boston and continue college at Harvard. Maybe someday he will return again, and perhaps we will continue where we left off. Oh, the stuff that dreams are made of.

CHAPTER SIX

For all of three years I had looked forward to the day I would become a Senior. Naturally, being a Senior meant being someone highly respected and loaded with prestige. I neglected, however, to realize that that I was the only one who continued to think so.

To begin with, I did not look very much like a person with prestige. I had outgrown my uniform and its utility value was very low. In the early Fall of 1949, the short, new look haircut came into fashion, and I had to be one of the first to get one.

It did not add much to my poise. The day my hair was cut, my mother greeted me with the remark that I looked more like a shorn lamb than the new "look." Grandma was even more emphatic, saying I had lost all my womanly dignity and beauty, and that my hair looked more like the fur of a wet cat. I was greatly hurt by this abundance of praise from my own family. I gracefully retired within my shell. Even now that it has grown more than an inch, Grandma has a disgusted look on her face when she looks at me. *(Editor's Note: Typical.)* This combined with my worn-out uniform doesn't add to my dignity as a senior.

Mary and I wanted very much to be in the same classes together, and although we were in the same homeroom, we were separated in most of our classes. Particularly, I remember teasing Mary that she would probably have Sister Aloysius for English. She is the one who believes in discipline, strict discipline. Mary said that she would rather do almost anything than face all that homework and memorizing she would be sure to have. As it turned out I was assigned to Sister Aloysius, and now Mary teases me.

To me homework is misery in itself, and with so much English homework to do in addition to our other subjects, I am certainly suffering. Then too, I have the added work of my music and art, to which I have devoted many, many hours. Yet, in spite of all this I am able to recite more poetry than any of the other girls in the group. *(Editor's note: All the English homework helped her win a Maryland State University Scholarship.)*

Sister Eleanora, whom we had for homeroom, is a wonderful person. I have never had a teacher whom I liked so much. One of the classes she teaches is "Problems of Democracy." We usually spent this period in fast moving discussions that really bring one up to date on world affairs.

One of my hardest classes is Chemistry ... the plague of my life. I have a constant struggle to keep endless formulas in my head. Though I like it very much, it presents one of my biggest troubles. My favorite subject still remains the same. It is lunch.

One afternoon after the first quarter, seniors are told if they have passing marks enough to get their rings. Everyone looked forward to the ring ceremony. For months, the rings had been our only topic of conversation. The girls who were not going to get their ring felt bad, of course, and so did we, as we would have preferred to wait until they could improve their marks. So they could receive theirs too. Sister Girard, our principal, also thought the seniors should get their rings together. So she set a date just before Christmas, and finally the big day arrived.

The Christmas Tree had been set up in the auditorium, and our rings were in gaily wrapped in little boxes under the tree. Each was destined for its particular owner. While the orchestra played, the seniors began to line up and march onto the stage. There Sister Girard awaited us and gave each the coveted box, which we unwrapped and presented to our homeroom advisor, who placed the rings on our fingers.

I was among the last to go up for mine as I played the piano in the school orchestra. The little girl who took my place at the piano when I went up to the stage did very well. Although Mary Jane, who plays first violin, Mary McDonald who plays second, and Joan

Williams who plays trumpet, all left at the same time, leaving the orchestra very weak indeed. I may be prejudiced, but I believe our rings are the prettiest of any I have seen. I know they mean more to us because of the way we received them. I, for one, will never forget the occasion.

So many things happened in my senior year that I can hardly get the events in my head in the order they occurred. One of these was the Curtis Magazine Drive. The man who explained the Drive at the school said a certain percentage of all the money brought in would be given to the school. Besides that, the girls selling the most subscriptions would be given prizes. If the school achieved its goal, duplicate prizes would be awarded.

The prizes were a grand assortment of pretty things, and I had my eye on one of them, a Parker 51 pen and pencil set. I put too much energy into my project and wound up being the first prize winner. I received a beautiful little watch, together with a trophy for super-salesmanship. I had never dreamed I would win, and was greatly surprised to hear my name being called as the first prize winner ... all I really wanted was the pen and pencil set. But the watch seemed to be the more valuable of the two.

Basketball season arrived soon after and although I cannot play very well, I can cheer loud and long. We usually had our pep rally right before a game, that is, all except one. This rally was of such an unusual nature, that it can be regarded as something special. The Sisters gave us this one. We marched into the auditorium as usual and thought that it was strange that we did not see anyone. We wondered what was going on. Suddenly, the music started and the curtains opened. On the stage were the Sisters lined up singing, "We are very proud of you." That was the most heart-warming and best rally I had ever attended.

The Retreats held at the Institute were always very beautiful and serious. This year it seemed even more so because it was our last and I shall hold on to it for a long, long time. It always seemed to me that in these days of prayer, I was so much closer to God, and fully recognized the meaning of life.

One of the highlights of 1950 was the Mount St. Joseph's Senior Prom. Mark Hunt, a very handsome dark-haired boy asked me to go during the most exciting part of a Bob Hope movie. He looked so worried that I wondered if he saw any part of the show at all. I quietly answered that I thought I might go, but I was already planning what to wear.

I was in real trouble in that I had nothing to wear. My last year's dresses did not fit. I would have to approach Mother for a new dress. She finally succumbed because I would need a new dress for my own school dances anyway. We shopped and shopped, and finally found a dress that is truly a dream. It has the appearance of a fluffy white cloud and yet it has a very modern look at the same time, if you know what I mean. I had it shortened to the new ballerina length and with it I wore sky blue satin slippers to match the blue sash. The date of the dance was February tenth, which was on a Friday, and also a school day, which did not leave me too much time to do things with myself. This was one time I rushed home immediately after school to put my hair up in curlers and begin my glamorizing process.

About two weeks before this, "LOOK" had published an article dealing with a series of pictures of a young girl getting ready for a dance. I owned a flash camera and talked my mother into taking a series of pictures of me getting ready.

The first picture was of me in my bath, into which I had dumped a half a bottle of a bubble bath I had received for Christmas, to make sure that I was fully covered. The second was a picture of me in my slip applying lipstick in a mirror and the third and final picture of me putting on my dress. I felt like a queen and Mother got some really good shots of me in my queenly regalia. I was dressed and ready way before time, and just getting more and more nervous by the minute.

A few minutes before, I had felt confident that I looked beautiful, but now my tensions increased as to whether I look like anything at all. My tension spread to my mother, and then to my grandmother, until even Cornelia, my dog, caught it and would not stop barking. We were all worn out by the time Mark arrived.

His arrival, with two other couples, brought on a flurry of excitement. The wrist corsage he brought me was made up of little roses and blue forget-me-nots, held together with a blue ribbon. So after some pictures together, off we went to the

NIGHT OF ST. JOE PROM

prom, or so we thought. When we were about eight blocks from the Emerson Hote4l, where the dance was being held, the car broke down. No attempt could make it move, so while the boys got out and pushed, one of the girls steered the car and we wound up on the pavement. It finally started, and off we went to the prom again. This time we got there.

The biggest event of the evening was the Senior Promenade. After which the boys got together and sang their alma mater song. As a favor all the girls got sliver bracelets engraved with the school's seal. I enjoyed myself more than I ever thought I could. There were lots of familiar faces from the Institute and that only added to my enjoyment.

After the band played the last dance, we bid farewell to the Emerson, and went in search of a place to eat. There were four couples of us in the car, including my cousin Paul and Gloria his girl. We found a spot where we had some more of a wonderful time. At four o'clock in the morning I stumbled up the steps, tired but happy. Mark is such a quiet, shy boy, that when it go out in school that instead of kissing me he missed and kissed the door, a poem on the occasion was printed in the "Quill," the school paper. Poor Mark became the laughing target of the school.

The next dance that I went to was the *Mardi Gras,* on February twenty-first, which was held at the Maryland Yacht Cub. I asked Frank, a freshman at Loyola College. He also brought me a wrist corsage, consisting of two beautiful camellias. I was so disappointed that neither Mary nor Rose-Marie went, but Marcia and her date, Gene, went together with us. It took us a little longer to get there than we expected, so we arrived a bit late. Nevertheless, we arrived in time to receive the flaming red *Mardi Gras* programs which one of the seniors had designed. I made and trimmed one into a large fan, which looked lovely on the wall and was hoping to get it back as a souvenir when the dance was over, but somebody else had the same idea.

I had my flash camera along, and got some very nice group pictures, which I shall put in my scrapbook. I wanted a souvenir of the dance, so I asked Frank to get me the huge *Mardi Gras* mask hanging over the door. He got not only the mask, but a vase full of flowers from the table.

We went out to eat afterwards and once again I wearily returned home, not only with souvenirs, but with happy memories as well.

I did not expect to have a visit to New York right the year after I had been there with Mother. Fifteen seniors on the yearbook and newspaper staff had been given the privilege of attending press conferences and discussions at Columbia University as representatives of the Institute. Since the meetings extended Thursday through Sunday afternoon, we were excused from school on Thursday and Friday.

It was a chattering, excited group that met in the B&O Railroad station early that Thursday morning. We had a special car at the end of the train, which was just for Notre Dame students, including those from Notre Dame of Maryland and their chaperones. Sister Eleanor's mother, as in previous years, kindly consented to act as our chaperone.

During our ride on the train we made so many plans, that it would have been impossible to fulfill them all with even a month in New York. Since I had arranged to stay at the home of Marcia's aunt in Flushing, Long Island, we two did not take the same bus as sister and the girls, but went to the Pennsylvania station to check our bags. After we had checked our bags we went to Columbia University to meet the girls.

Either they were lost or we were, for they were nowhere to be found. So Marcia and I attended three of the conferences, and then stopped and went home to Long Island.

After we had refreshed ourselves and had a bit of dinner, we took the subway to Rockefeller Center, where we expected to see a television show. Our guide-sheets instructed us to be at Radio City at eight-thirty. But when we inquired what floor the Kay Keyser Show was on, we found it was to be held at the International Center. Where that was we did not have the slightest idea, so we hailed a cab and when we arrived, it was only few minutes past eight-thirty yet the usher would not let us in. You can imagine our disappointment then.

The show would not be over until ten o'clock. So we strolled up Fifth Avenue and looked in all the beautiful shop windows, something I enjoy very much. At a quarter to ten we came back to the studio, and to our surprise there was a different usher on duty. We explained our dilemma and he sneaked us in for the last few minutes of the show. At least we can say we say we saw Kay Keyser.

The second day, instead of going all the way back to Long Island, after the meetings I remained at The Hotel Vanderbilt with the girls. That afternoon, Marcia, Rose-Marie and I went to Romeo's for spaghetti and ravioli, but as it was Friday we could not sample the delicious meatballs for which they are famous. I can still see the steaming platters of spaghetti, and the rich *Tortuni* we had for dessert, not to mention the fresh-baked Italian rolls. *(Editor's note: At the time, Catholics considered eating meat on Friday a sin.)*

That night Barbara, Reds, Maryanne, Mildred and I visited Radio City and what a wonderful show we saw! The first selection was an organ solo, followed by the Music Hall Symphony Orchestra which played the "Sabre Dance," and the "Dance of the Rose Maidens" by Khachaturian, among their repertoire. Next on the program was a medley of songs and dances which included the Corps de Ballet, the famous Rockettes, and the Music Hall Choral Ensemble. The movie we saw was *Stage Fright* and that too was very good. We had a pajama party that night and I did not get back to Long Island that night until 3:30 a.m. *(Editor's note: I have no idea what happens at an all-girl pajama party that justifies staying awake.)*

Saturday afternoon we met at the Waldorf Astoria to have a luncheon and hear General Eisenhower speak. We had chicken with wine and cherry sauce. It was very delicious. But I was very disappointed, because from where we sat we could hardly see General Eisenhower, much less hear him.

After the luncheon I went shopping and bought Mother a beautiful slip at Saks, a scarf for Gramps, and Rosemarie candies for Grandma, besides a few little things for myself. The scarf, sad to say was pure silk, and was stolen from me in the in the hotel lobby.

The night before, we had fried shrimp at Toffenetti's, and today we had an appetite for more spaghetti. We found a little place near the hotel and the food was very delicious. The waitress there was very friendly, and when we asked her where we could go, she suggested Bop City. We had wanted to see Bop City anyway, and were glad we went as we had so much fun. All you do there is sit and listen to Be Bop music by famous Boppers.

We had another pajama party that night and this time I did not get to bed until four-thirty. Marcia went to Mass in a little church in Flushing: so did I. Then we rushed home to pack our bags, and we just made the bus as it pulled away from the front of the Vanderbilt Hotel. I was feeling sad because I had lost Grandpop's' scarf, and I did not have anything for him.

On the train going home we again had our own private car, and Reds and I had the most fun walking from this last car to the first and back again. We did a lot of singing and joke-telling and even danced. We formed a rumba line and rumbaed down the aisle. Sister Aloysia even learned how to do the "Hokey-Pokey" although she will not demonstrate it now.

We were all glad to get back home again, and personally, I think the best part of any trip is coming home to your loved ones.

I have now reached the end of my seventeen years of remembrances, and all I have now is the ambition to keep them as good as they were. I shall keep this book and perhaps many years from now it will refresh my mind with happy memories. This is a big year for me as I am facing Graduation, and perhaps a completely new world. There are so many things I would like to do with my life, but as yet I have not decided just what. All that I hope is that with the help of God, I make the right choice.

Finding pictures of Pat growing up was not too difficult. However, the reality of what her life was like is another story. She was not eager to share her childhood with anyone, but through patient (often painful) discussions she told me small parts of it after we were married.

The Bochenskis despised Howard Christopher. He wasn't Polish ... and he certainly wasn't macho. A man who modeled men's clothing had no claim on manhood. I can empathize with him since I had failed those tests myself.

They were German Poles (Prussian) and classified themselves as "narrow-faced" Pollacks, as opposed to the inferior "round-faced" variety. Jake approved of my German name, but was disappointed that I could not converse with him in German. I had enough trouble understanding his heavily accented English. I had no idea of what to talk with him about. He made an effort to engage me the first time I met him. He asked me if I liked to hunt.

I stretched the truth a bit and said I hunted squirrels (back on Uncle Henry's farm in NJ when we were building our log cabin).

He said, "I like shooting dogs."

My God, I thought, *what kind of a guy am I talking to that likes killing dogs?*

Since I was speechless, he added, "Sometimes I am shooting geese."

I breathed a sigh of relief when I realized he was saying, "I like shooting *ducks!*" We hardly ever spoke again ... it was a strain on both of us.

Pat said she loved him in spite of himself. She later admitted that the thing they shared most was the personal disapproval by Cleo and Helen. He treated Pat better than either of the other two.

However, in a weak moment she told me that he was alleged to have kicked Helen in the belly to induce her to have a miscarriage. Then she defended him by saying he was drunk at the time, but by Schroeder Family values, drunkenness was never a defense of vile behavior

The family situation was at such a low ebb when Pat was delivered that she did not even have a name when she was born. Her birth certificate simply read "Baby

Girl Christopher." She did not become Joan Patricia until she was christened several weeks later.

[Birth certificate, Health Department—City of Baltimore, Certificate of Birth D98242, for Baby Girl Christopher, born July 27, 1932. Father: Howard Christopher, Salesman, age 23, residence 1647 Thames St. Mother: Helen Bocheynski, age 33, residence 1647 Thames St. Date issued: SEP 29 1980.]

1940S

She grew up in the Fells Point Polish community, and went to their Catholic school. When she finished 8th Grade they enrolled her in the Institute of Notre Dame, an all-girls private school. For four years she kept her Fells Point connection secret from her wealthy classmates.

Certain nuns provided her with the love she was so sadly lacking in her life. They encouraged her natural artistic and musical gifts. She became the chosen pianist for all school events and auditoriums. She said that the only time she did not play the piano was when she graduated herself. Even then, she was  relieved at the Grand Piano by the music teacher only while she accepted her diploma. The nuns told her that she was good enough to pursue a career as a classical pianist.

At one point she considered becoming one of the nuns, but decided that getting married and having a large family would be more life fulfilling. That explains the six-children dream.

Helen was **not supportive** of her musical aspirations. She complained that Pat's incessant practicing of scales and the perfection of small portions of Liszt's work were annoying the customers. She wanted Pat to play complete melodies to provide a sort of ambience for the bar.

While Helen contended that the piano was the best available, the opinion of a piano tuner we called shortly before we gave it away was quite to the contrary. He said that it was of such poor quality that it did not justify the expense of having it tuned.

When we were discussing the scholarships Pat won, she

This portrait imortalzes a Pekingese, named Chinny. I am not sure of the present location of the original.

told me that the reason she did not take any of them was it meant living at home for four more years. Instead, she took a Maryland State competitive exam and won a University of Maryland scholarship in College Park. She majored in English.

Once she got into college life, she found numerous reasons for not being able to go back to Baltimore on weekends. She joined the Sigma Kappa sorority and lived there on campus.

One of the things that drew her back to Fells Point was her love of pets. She had a string of dogs throughout her teen years.

Since Pat's whole story has so many intricacies, chronology is not my only guideline. However, this might be a good point to discuss Pat's paintings, and her growth as an artist while she was only a teenager at the Institute.

The nun who was her art teacher recognized her talent right from the beginning; Sister Sabina, and enforced a work discipline on her that paid off. She had an eye for detail, and an innate spatial concept she converted into pictures others could not match.

I do not know the actual sequence in which she painted her works, but I will attempt to put them into what I believe that they may have been done. There may be others, but these are the ones I have actually seen.

These still life pastels were done about 1946 on drawing paper as a beginner's project. Based on these, the teacher saw a talent that could be developed. I do not know the whereabouts of these pieces, but I did rescue them from the basement about 2007. They were on dry, brittle cream-colored paper.

This painting, at right, hung on the wall of Helen's bedroom as I recall. I believed I had seen the original of this in an art survey book, but cannot remember where or when. I did a Google survey from many angles with no leads.

Margaret recalls a conversation with her mother at which time she said it was an original piece, rather than a copied detail. Also, Margaret thinks there was a companion piece hung next to it, but may have been stolen by one Helen's visiting "friends." Pat's favorite artists were the Impressionists, especially Renoir, which influenced her style.

Location of Pat's original is unknown at this writing. If you (the reader) know, please share the information.

Sometime during Pat's art training (1947-1950) she did a charcoal drawing based on this painting by Sir Thomas Lawrence (British, Bristol 1769–1830 London) in 1823. The girls have been identified as The Calmady Children (Emily, 1818–1906, and Laura Anne, 1820–1894).

It is a very similar drawing; with the exception that the child's left hand appearing behind the head of the other was omitted by Pat in the interest of better composition. Pat's original charcoal and a copy are in the possession of Melanie McGill for the sake of preservation.

The most impressive piece of artwork Pat did was her copy of a *Roman Girl at a Fountain* by French artist Léon Bonnat (1833–1922). She was only 15 years old when she painted it while under the supervision of Sister Sabina at The Institute of Notre Dame. The original artist was 47 years old when he painted it in 1875. The difference between the original and Pat's version is a matter of brightness. Her interpretation is a much lighter and brighter.

I took a color transparency of each painting and overlaid them on a light box. Form-wise they almost identical in size, shape and proportion. Yet she used no artificial aids, like a pantograph, to position the elements of the picture. She told me she eyeballed it all the way. It was a large factor in being awarded a scholarship to the Maryland Institute College of Art.

The original hangs in the NY Metropolitan Museum of Art. (Oil on canvas. Dimensions: 67 x 39 1/2 in). Pat's version was first placed in her mother's apartment. When we were married she gave it to me and we hung it with pride wherever we lived. It now is under the care of Melanie McGill for preservation.

Pat Christopher

Léon Bonnat

Art teachers at the Institute did not encourage students to pursue individual or personal interpretations of subjects. The focus was on reproduction of established works in a near photographic manner. This painting was traditionally believed to be The Virgin Mary with the Infant Jesus. However, Google recently uncovered a contrary background story. The original artist, Roberto Ferruzzi, who won an award in a prestigious 1897 exhibition in Venice, called the painting Madonnina (little mother). It is better known today as Madonna of the Streets.

Until recently, I thought Pat's Girl at the Well was her premier work, and probably the last painting that she did. However, in writing this memoir I discovered that I had forgotten about Madonna and Child. It was hung at Helen's house and somehow found its way into John's possession. It is now safely in Melanie's home along with many of Pat's other works.

Once I had a copy of it for closer inspection, I had a cascade of memories going back fifty years. I believe it shows Pat's technique reaching a closer finalization, and was probably done in her Senior year at Notre Dame. From a motivation and inspiration angle it illustrates her deep-seated identification with motherhood. Her obsession manifested itself in how highly she held the love of her family in spite of personal pain and anxiety.

Pat Christopher, 1950

Roberto Ferruzzi, 1897

Jesus (circa 1949)

I rediscovered this original painting on Valentine's Day weekend in February 2016. It was an unusual experience. Someone brought a piece of furniture in from the front porch that I did not know existed. It had been sitting for months, maybe years, being part of Helen's stuff. It was a 78-RPM electric phonograph console that belonged to Pat during her high school days, circa 1946–1950. I knew there were some records in its storage area, but for one reason or another it sat in my room for several weeks before I examined it closely. On Friday night (2/12/16) I was listening to a "Big Bands of the 1940s/50s" program on NPR, and decided to see what records were in the phonograph the next morning, Saturday.

My bedroom used to be Pat's workroom for many years. I often felt as though I could still feel her presence there. I dream of her often. Margaret uncovered our wedding pictures while clearing out the small bedroom. I had not seen them for twenty years and had some of them converted from 3D color slides. They appear further on.

About the same time another phenomenon took place. Every night, while changing for bed, the first two lines to the song "Oh Promise Me," ran through my mind. I could not fall asleep until I said them out loud. It was the song sung at our wedding. In case you are not familiar with it, here is what Google reports:

OH, PROMISE ME

Copyright, 1889, by G. Schirmer.
Words by Clement Scott. Music by Reginald De Koven.

Oh, promise me that some day you and I
Will take our love together to some sky,
Where we can be alone and faith renew,
And find the hollows where those flowers grew.

Curiously, the concept is theologically foreign to my view of the nature of the afterlife, but I still find it a comforting piece of music.

But, returning to my narrative: Saturday morning I opened the doors in the case and found several albums of 78-RPM records. That's right, you guessed it; the top record in the stack was "Oh Promise Me." If it had not happened to me, I would not have believed it.

But the best is yet to come! Wedged in between the albums was a picture frame. I have been aware of the fact that there are one or two missing paintings done by Pat in her teenage years. One in particular hung in her mother's bedroom … the face of the un-risen (but somewhat grisly) Jesus. We never knew what became of it. Now here it was! It is in oils on canvas about eight by ten inches in a gilt frame.

After spending thirty-odd years in a dark cubbyhole, we can now once more appreciate Pat's artistic genius as a teenage girl. I choose to regard it as a Valentine gift from one who may be gone, but not forgotten.

When Melanie was visiting me on June 17, 2016, I gave the painting to her to give Kelly. I decided she was the only member of the family who was an active Christian and might appreciate it on another level as a gift from her Grandmother.

Once she left the Institute, Pat never painted another canvas. From the very beginning of our marriage she expressed a desire to resume her painting, but once she started to have children she did not feel she had time to do it properly. Instead, she mastered a variety of crafts to the degree of making them art forms. In a like manner, she never played the piano. I will discuss that aspect of her life later.

Coming back to the chronology of Pat's life, during her high school years Pat's best friend was Mary Clampett.

GRADUATION — JUNE 1950

The event was celebrated with a family graduation party.

Although Pat was an only child, there was another young woman in the household, her cousin Marie. I was never sure of the details, but from what Pat told me, Marie was taken in by Cleo as an orphan under the agreement that she would earn her keep as a housekeeper and barmaid. Under Maryland law, a member of the family could work in family-owned bar at 18.

In fact, Pat was viewed as her replacement when she became of age. A pretty blonde behind the bar would be a boost for business. Her mother and grandparents were not in sympathy with Pat's college aspirations. It was only because the nuns at the Institute nomonated her for scholarships that the idea was considered.

Marie was an understandably unhappy person, considering her circumstances. Cleo reminded her constantly of how generous they had been to her. Pat found in Marie a much needed confidant during her teenage years. In Pat's senior year Marie married one of the bar patrons, Leonard Doenges (at her own expense since Cleo felt no obligation to help). Her new husband did not want her to work at the bar any longer, so she pretty much disappeared from Pat's life until we got married. Our relatioinship with her was casual. Her daughter, Nancy, age 9, was a flower girl at our wedding.

Pat was the Maid of Honor at the Doenges's wedding.

As soon as Pat turned 18, they tried her out behind the bar. She told me that she intentionally spilled drinks, (often in the customers' laps), and conspicuously gave too much change from large denomination bills.

Cleo was in charge of her training. One of her guiding philosophies was the definition of *A good sailor* ... "Good sailor puts humdred dollar bill on bar — does not leave until all used up." (No wonder Helen thought I was a cheap bastard when I did not buy drinks when I first called for Pat).

1952

Pat totally commited herself to life on campus, starting with joining a soririty — Sigma Kappa.

When she could get away from home, she managed to join friends from U of M at Ocean City.

Here Pat is in drag *for a costume party.*

1952 — OCEAN CITY

Weekends that Pat did not come home were often spent with friends at Ocean City, where they rented an apartment and crowded in to sleep on the floor. At that time you were allowed to have bonfires on the beach and all-night parties. It all changed by 1960 due to commercial Boardwalk interests.

Pat enjoyed a freedom like she never before had in her life. Her boyfriend had a motor scooter that she rode with him everywhere. Her mother knew nothing of it. One weekend when her mother drove down to the college for a surprise visit, Pat passed her car while she was on the back of the scooter. She turned away from the car and tried not to look like herself. They did manage to get to the sorority house before Helen, where Pat pretended to be surprised.

1954

UNIVERSITY OF MARYLAND MAY QUEEN SITS ON THRONE, SURROUNDED BY ATTENDANTS REPRESENTING VARIOUS ORGANIZATIONS
runette beauty, Mary Jo Turner, twenty-one, of Virginia Beach, won the top beauty crown, and also was tapped for Mortar Board, the university's highest honor for women

In this picture of the girls in the May Queen Contest, Pat is in the first figure in the back line.

Attending U of M graduation were Uncle Gene, Helen, Pat and Aunt Mayble. Pat graduated from the University of Maryland in June 1954. Having worked at USF&G Insurance Company, the previous summer, she was hired full- time in the Personnel Department.

I regret that I do not remember the first name of Pat's favorite Fells Point childhood friend, especially since she was our Matron of Honor (Mrs. Joseph Katona). Her (also Polish) family owned another bar and fast food joint about a block down Thames Street. The major difference was that they had several kids and lived a normal family life. They were very influential in Pat's decision to have a large family of her own. Pat frequently went there after school and stayed through dinner, until it was time to go home to bed.

Going home was not something Pat looked forward to. Jake and Cleo had usually gone to their house on Shannon Drive for the night and Helen was running the bar by herself. Occasionally, Marie was working as well.

Maid of Honor in a girlfriend's wedding, 1955

Helen's attention was on patrons, so Pat generally put herself to bed in the room above the bar. She shared a big bed with her mother. She told me about a dream she had frequently as she fell asleep. In the dream she flew out the second floor window and up to the sky. She described it as more of an out-of-the-body experience than a dream.

The house had been built in the late 19th Century as a boarding hotel for seafarers. Jake Bochenski bought it in 1917 to open a bar on the first floor, with a family living space above. The third floor was for short-time rentals for sailors. However, the place was (in a word) *Spooky*.

Every night Pat lay in the dark room listening to the noises from the barroom beneath her. In the gloom, she perceived two Siamese cats curled on a chair. Thirty years later, this would not cause a ripple, since she raised Siamese cats for a hobby in the early years of our marriage. However, at the time in question they had no cats of any description. The cats were not threatening, they were just *there*.

What really frightened Pat were the noises she was sure she heard on the top floor. Her imagination went to work and she convinced herself that there was a gorilla on the third floor. When she peeked out from under her covers she was sure an ape face peered around the corner for the stairway to the third floor.

Thoroughly spooked, she would get out of bed and scamper downstairs. When she appeared in the bar, Helen told her to go upstairs and get back to bed. However, she only hid in the stairwell. Usually, she only got up to the fourth step, sat down and fell asleep sitting there. When Helen closed the bar at 1 a.m., she found Pat and took her up to bed.

It set a pattern, and every time she was scared she went down and sat on the steps until Helen closed and took her upstairs. Pat blamed this frequent occurrence for the odd sleep patterns she experienced throughout her adult life. She could never really get to sleep before one o'clock in the morning.

After she told me about the gorilla when we first started dating, I have to admit that *even I* got the creeps whenever I walked past the stairs to the third floor.

A year or so prior to Pat's passing, we collaborated on a short story for a Halloween contest that stuck close to her childhood memories. We spoke with some of our kids to give the story a little more depth. The following story is the result:

THE THIRD FLOOR

"Well, I'll be God-damned!" I said out loud without realizing it. I repositioned the newspaper against the sugar bowl, and took a long sip of coffee in preparation for re-reading the story.

The second reading did not diminish the "A-ha" experience of the first. Again, I spoke aloud. This time it was a slow accentuated, "Son of a bitch." My dog, Bozo, looked up from the floor apparently thinking I was addressing him. I chuckled to myself, and wished someone else would wake up and come down to the kitchen so I could share my discovery.

My wish was granted in the form of my daughter, Rose, who was getting ready to go to work. She barely entered the room, when I thrust the Baltimore Sun at her. "You gotta see this," I said excitedly. "Read it over and tell me what comes to mind."

Still a little bleary-eyed from the early hour, she took the paper and read the story. When she finished she looked up, more awake now, and said, "The third floor at Grandma's?"

"Exactly," I agreed. "Makes you wonder, doesn't it."

"It sure does ... the gorilla on the third floor." For a minute she was no longer 35 years old, but a 9-year old who believed in things that go bump in the night.

"What do you remember about the third floor?" I asked. "What's your earliest recollection of anything strange?"

After a moment's reflection she said, "I think it was when we came for a visit when we lived in Arizona. Remember, we spread out our sleeping bags on the living room floor. Us kids were all spread out. Richard claimed the couch. Chris slept in the big chair. I think he was only 5 or so he could curl up on it. You came in at one point and told us to stop horsing around and go to sleep. The noise from the bar downstairs was loud, and it kept us awake.

"Then what happened?"

"You turned out the living room lights and one by one we drifted off. I was almost asleep, when I heard somebody upstairs on the third floor walking around. I thought it was Captain Bill, but then I heard him laughing downstairs. He was tending bar, and joking with the customers. The sounds came from his room and the hallway up there.

"Then I thought it might be Granny, but it didn't sound right. It was more like shuffling and hopping than footsteps. I got scared and slipped down deeper into the sleeping bag. Mom came in to check on us before she went to sleep, but I didn't tell her anything at that time."

"What did you think it was?" I asked.

"I had no idea. I thought it might be Grandpop's ghost, but I didn't say anything to Mom until the next morning. She told me it was a very old house ... maybe 150 years old, even 200. She told me that old houses make noises because their foundations are still settling and the wind makes funny noises on the tiles on the roof.

"So I asked her. 'Did you used to hear noises when you were living here?'" Rose stopped in her recitations, and poured some milk on her cereal. "Actually, it would have been better if she lied to me and said no, she hadn't." Grimacing in mock exasperation, she said, "Instead she told me that she used to believe that there was a gorilla who lived on the third floor. She tried to tell it like it was a ridiculous notion, sort of a fairy story, but I could tell she was really scared. You could hear it in her voice.

"Well anyway, that night I didn't sleep very well, and I was sure I heard the gorilla coming down the stairs to get us. In later years, I always tried to sleep in the back room. I moved my sleeping bag into your room and pretended that I couldn't stand the fooling around by the younger kids."

"Yes, I remember that," I said. I waited to see if she would add to her story, but she appeared to be finished, so I picked up the conversation from there. "Fells Point was such an odd place, especially during W.W.II with all the sailors coming through from all kinds of ships from all over the world. Your mother was bound to have seen just about anything. Some of them must have had pet monkeys they picked up in their travels. I understand Grandpa Jake even wound up with an anteater in payment of a bar bill. But I'll be damned if I can figure out what the hell they fed it."

She laughed. "Well there were enough cockroaches around if they weren't too picky."

"Correction! They were water bugs. Granny insisted that there were no roaches. They were water bugs because they were right down by the harbor."

As she finished her breakfast and prepared to leave, Rose said, "In any event, I never went up to the third floor until I was 18 or 19 years old."

RICHARD

My oldest son, Richard, works in the neighborhood at a gas station, so he generally comes to the house for lunch. Without showing him the newspaper I said, "What do you think of if I say, 'The third floor?'"

"Grandma's. That's where the gorilla lived." He said without hesitation.

"Who told you there was a gorilla on the third floor?"

"Rosie. I think Mom even said she saw it once. I never saw it. But I was sure there was one up there. Us kids used to think and talk about it. As I look back I think there was a good explanation for it. You know those little rooms Grandma had on the third floor used to be a sort of flophouse. They weren't much more than closets, but they had mattresses in them and I think she used to rent them out to the merchant seamen so they could sleep it off when they passed out downstairs in the bar.

"What Mom heard and what us kids heard was really a bunch of drunks crawling around, wondering where they were."

I gave him the paper, and he grinned when he read it. "Wow, talk about weird."

ROBYN

I called my daughter Robyn, on the phone and simply said, "Tell me about the third floor at Granny's"

"Well ... Rosie told me that there was a gorilla on the third floor when we were still pretty young," she said.

"What did you think of that?'

"I didn't know if I should believe her. So I crept up the stairs once to find out for myself. I'm not as easily scared as Rosie, so I looked around the corner in Captain Bill's room, and there was one of those old coconuts carved in the shape of a monkey head hanging in front of the mirror. I assumed that was the gorilla and continued snooping around until I heard Grandma screaming for me downstairs. I used to hear noises up there at night when we slept over, but it was Rosie who used to get hysterical about the idea that there was a gorilla upstairs. When we played hide and seek in the house, I was the only one who wasn't afraid to hide on the third floor."

CHRIS

On Tuesday evenings, I usually meet my youngest son, Chris, for hot wings at a favorite restaurant of ours. We met the day of the news article, so I asked him to share his recollections on the subject.

He looked very serious, and said, "The only time I went up on the third floor was after Grandma died and we were moving things out of there."

"What was your first memory of anything about the third floor?"

"I was little. I think I was with the other kids one afternoon in the second floor living room. We all heard something moving around on the third. Like I said, I was still pretty little ... maybe I was in the Kindergarten. That's when Rosie and Robyn told me about the Gorilla on the third floor. When I was in Middle school, Grandma brought the gorilla head down from upstairs — you know that coconut thing. That was Captain Bill's. He had just died. She hung it on the mirror in her bedroom. At first I thought it was neat, but as I looked at it, it looked evil. In fact it scared the Be-Jesus out of me. I hated going down there to visit."

"The place really got to you, then," I suggested.

"I'm not alone. I have friends who work for the new owners of the bar downstairs. You know, the guys that bought it from Granny. None of my friends will go up to the third floor. The manager is the only one who has been up there. They hear noises upstairs all the time on the second floor. I think it is Grandma fighting with the gorilla over their territories." He laughed, "Frankly my money is on Grandma."

I had to laugh with him. "You mean they're actually afraid to go up there? Did you spook them up?"

"I never told them a thing. The manager can't store anything on the third floor because no one will go up there for it. Now it's empty. Some of the employees won't even go up to the second floor alone. They always take someone along."

Chris fell silent. "Is that it?" I prodded.

"I really don't want to talk about any more about Fells Point. I hated it there," he said.

"Didn't we all," I agreed. "But I am interested to hear what you remember."

"Really, Dad, I don't want to talk about it," he answered brusquely. "Like I said, I wouldn't go up there until we had to move the junk out of the upstairs bedrooms after Granny died. All that stuff she left me ... I gave it away." He stopped again. "No. Let me be honest. I didn't give it away — I threw it away. The damn stuff was spooky."

He saw me frown.

"Yeah, remember those old wall hanging pictures of Great Grenma and Grandpa Jake?" he said, fright showing in his eyes.

I nodded.

"They used to argue with each other at night."

My eyes widened. "They did?" I asked like a kid listening to a campfire ghost story.

"When it was quiet you could hear these two people yelling at each other off in the distance. I know it was coming from those damn pictures."

"What were they arguing about," I asked, my interest really piqued.

"Please, Dad, I said I'd rather not talk about the whole thing.'

"I'm curious about what you understood them saying."

"It was some foreign language, or really bad English. Let's drop it." That was his final word on the matter. He owns nothing that came from the old house.

MYSELF

While I was driving home, I thought about the things my kids had told me. The time I went to my mother-in-law's house to pick my wife up for our first date, the old woman was at the bar talking to a couple customers. I told her who I was and asked where I could find Joan. I was directed upstairs to the second floor where Joan met me at the top of the stairs.

The first floor was an ancient saloon, with a mahogany bar and foggy glass mirrors behind it. The light was bad, and you could only dimly make out your reflection in the glass. The poetic phrase, "as through a glass darkly" fit it perfectly. The doorstep was marked with her grandfather's name in mosaic tiles along with the year 1917 in red on a white background.

That wasn't the year the building was built, but the year that Joan's Grandfather opened the saloon. The building itself was supposed to be a couple hundred years old. It was at the very foot of Broadway in Fells Point, in Baltimore, and as I understand it, there was a pier that ended there many years ago. Since then the strand of beach had been filled in and extended. Now it was a block from the water's edge.

Joan took me to the room that was positioned directly over the noisy bar below, and looked down on Thames Street. At the moment it was quiet, but it was early in the evening yet. Later, it would be vibrating with noise.

As we passed a semi-spiral staircase that led to an upper floor, I felt a chill. There was no light above and the stairs themselves were dark. If ever there was a corner that felt forbidding or evil, it was that stairway. However, I was led past it into the old fashioned parlor that extended into a bedroom that Joan and her mother shared. Perhaps there had been sliding doors there in years past, but now it was just a wide-open space with no barrier between the two rooms.

We talked for a while and decided that we had better leave if we were going to have dinner and get to the movies on time. As we walked out once more past the staircase, I asked, "Where does that go?"

Very flippantly Joan said, "Oh, that's where the gorilla lives." She laughed at her own joke and I wondered about the humor. We were married for a couple years before she ever told me about her childhood fears of the gorilla on the third floor.

Personally, I seldom went up to the top floor unless I had a specific errand to do for my mother-in-law. The place gave me the creeps.

JOAN

Now here we were, some thirty-odd years later and the topic needed further discussion. Knowing Joan's moods I would have to ask at the right time to get her to talk about it. I withheld the news story that had started my research program without being sure why. The house held myriad bad and unhappy memories, and we had a tacit agreement not to talk about her mother or the house unless she initiated the conversation.

Fortunately, I found her in a good mood, and she sat knitting in her workroom. I broached the subject. "Hon, the kids and I have been talking about something that needs your input."

"Oh," she said suspiciously. "What has somebody done now that they don't want me to know about?"

"It's nothing like that," I said, "This involves your childhood."

"You know I can't remember dates, and events at will. If something happens to pop into my head, fine, but I can't usually recall it at will ..."

I interrupted her. "This is about the gorilla on the third floor."

Joan put down her knitting on her lap, and said, "Now there's something I've never forgotten. How did this come up? Are you hearing gorillas in our attic?"

"No, but the kids and I have been talking about it all day. I'll tell you how it came up after I hear your account of the famous gorilla on the third floor."

"So what do you want to know? What do you think you know already?"

I sat down on a chair facing hers, and she muted the television. "I remember that I had the greatest fear of gorillas after seeing King Kong, when I was around 8 years old. They were reviving the old horror pictures for the Saturday matinees. You know, Dracula, and the whole bunch. I particularly remember "Nabonga" which was a Grade Z movie. Nabonga was supposed to be Swahili for Gorilla and this critter terrorized the jungle villages. I was afraid to walk through the park next to my house when it got dark since I was sure Nabonga lived in the sycamores next to the path. Did you see it?"

"Not that I can recall," she said. "I never even saw King Kong until it came to TV sometime in the '50s."

"Well, there goes that theory?" I said.

"What do you mean? What theory?"

"I thought that you had developed a fear of Gorillas, like the kids in my neighborhood after you saw King Kong. But if you didn't see the movie you wouldn't have imagined him upstairs on the third floor."

I took another tack. I knew that she was a gifted child and could read earlier than most. "I know you were an Edgar Allen Poe Fan from the get-go. When did you read The Murders in the Rue Morgue?"

She thought for a minute, "I must have been around eight or so. I know the Nuns at the school did not want me to read Poe. They took one of my books away from me when I brought it to school."

"So it's possible that you read about this orangutang coming into the locked room, and built a fantasy on the strength of that."

"The word is orangutan — there's no "g" on the end of it. But the answer is yes and no. It made me believe more in the gorilla on the third floor, but didn't cause it," she said with a note of self-satisfaction.

"And why not," I retorted.

"Because I first became aware of the gorilla when I was only 4 or 5. That was well before I could read, and I didn't go to the movies until I was 7."

Joan stopped to gather her thoughts, then began a reconstruction of her life as a kid. "I used to sleep with my mother in the front room — The one over the bar.

"I used to fall asleep watching the two Siamese cats who used to sit on the chair in front of the window. I like them. They were nice. I liked cats."

"I never knew you had any cats. I thought the ones we got were the first ones you had."

"Well these weren't real cats. I could only see them on the chair when I was dozing off. I guess they were spirit cats." Without further explanation, she continued her story. "I knew that the third floor was used for storage of seamen's trunks and personal effects. We weren't renting out rooms then. That didn't happen until W.W.II. There was nobody up there in the 1930s. Even Captain Bill lived somewhere else back then."

"Oh," I said, for lack of a better analysis.

"However, I laid in bed and could hear footsteps in the room directly above mine. They were heavy and plodding. They would make the ceiling shake. Everyone was downstairs boozing. They would have thought a gorilla was just another customer. I never told my mother about the noises. She wouldn't have believed me. I used to lay in the bed with the light on in the living room. That way I could see the door to the hallway reflected in the mirror. After a while I would hear him coming down the stairs and I'd peek out from the covers. I'd see the door to the hall start to open when he came looking for me. This would panic me. I knew the gorilla had come to get me. I burrowed under the covers and shook and shivered in terror. I would finally retreat to sleep under the covers and travel to see my father in my dreams."

I felt goose bumps from her description. Seriously, I asked, "Did you ever actually see him?"

Joan's face suddenly took on the look of someone who anticipates a response when she tells her alien abduction story to the Six O'clock News Anchor. She let her knitting fall to the floor, and said nothing for a full minute. Finally she said. "Yes, I did! I swear I saw him one night. He came into the next room and was poking around at things. I worked up enough courage to scream, and he scrambled out the door and ran upstairs again.

"A few minutes later, my mother and Captain Bill came upstairs to find out what I was shrieking about. I told them, and they laughed. They told me I was only dreaming and to go back to bed. They made shooing noises up the stairs and yelled, 'You better get out of this house, you crazy ape!'"

Her shivers subsided, and she collapsed into her chair. I picked up her knitting, but she put it aside. "I know, I saw him, Hon," she insisted. "There were no two ways about it."

"Did you ever see him again?" I asked.

"No. Once I went to bed I wouldn't come out from under the blankets. Even on hot summer nights I would have a sheet to pull over my head. But I still heard him. When I got older I would get out of bed and sit on the steps leading down to the bar. I'd fall asleep until my mother came up to go to bed. She'd pick me up and carry me to our room. Then I would be able to sleep if she was there."

"You mean to say that this went on for your entire childhood?" I said.

"When I was old enough to go to High School I moved out to Grenma's house on Shannon Drive. I insisted that it was closer to the Institute where they sent me, but I was really still afraid of the gorilla on the third floor.

"When I read The Murders in the Rue Morgue later, I knew my fears were well grounded. I was terrified by the story. I don't remember telling Rose about the gorilla unless she had said something about her own fears. I certainly would never have told that story to her just to scare her."

She looked at me quizzically. I didn't realize it, but I was sitting in a sort of stunned silence shaking my head in disbelief.

"What brought on all this concern about the gorilla, anyway." She asked. "How the hell did you get started on that track?"

I reached into my shirt pocket and took out the clipping of news story that had been in the Baltimore Sun that morning. I said, "Let me read you a story that was in the paper this morning: "The fire department has a mystery on its hands. After a fire in one of the old row houses on Alice Ann Street in Fells Point, they found a skeleton and partly mummified body of what appeared to be a small, deformed child. It was discovered after the fire, when they pulled away part of a wall that concealed a long unused fireplace. It had been sealed off during a remodeling of the house decades ago.

"On the smoke shelf the body was found, totally dehydrated and in a state of partial decomposition. Homicide detectives were called and the body was removed and sent to the city morgue for an autopsy. To everyone's relief, but surprise, the body turned out to belong to a chimpanzee. Forensic specialists at the morgue estimate that the body was at more than 50 years old. Police theorize that the chimpanzee was probably the pet of some sailor who lost it while he was on shore leave. They believe the unfortunate beast probably hopped from roof to roof in Fells Point until it accidentally fell down a chimney from which it could not escape.

"The skeleton is being donated to the Baltimore Zoo for one of its primate exhibits."

Joan gave me one of her you-made-that-up looks, and grinned warily at me. I handed her the clipping so she could verify that it was from the newspaper. She read it again to herself, and said, "I'll be God damned!"

The newspaper article was actually printed in the *Baltimore Sun*, without follow-up.

MARCH 1960

Since we got engaged in March 1960, and married the first week in July, that did not leave too much time for a courtship and dating. We took a couple weekend trips to New Jersey. There was nothing exciting about the period; we went on simple dates to the movies, dinner, or car drives on the weekends. We found an opportunity, however, to get our pictures taken on an automatic photo machine.

JULY 3, 1960

The wedding dinner was an expensive affair to which mostly Helen's friends and family were invited.

Rich Herink was my Best Man and Rich Thoma was an usher. My parents, Elsie and Nick were also invited. My college buddy Bob Wells also came with his girlfriend, but I lost track of him afterwards forever.

As Helen was paying for the event, she chose the venue, a expensive caterer's hall, The Madison Club. However, the weather on that day was a typical Baltimore summer day. It was steamy ... and the air conditoining at the hall failed.

As a wedding present Elsie and Nick gave us a special package. It was a beautiful set of 3-D color slides and a viewer. It disappeared for many years, until Margaret uncovered it in our small bedroom.

The color wedding pictures appearing here are fom that set. Unfortunately, we look waxen in the pictures because we were covered with sweat.

Helen wanted a traditional Polish wedding during which we were subjected to what amounted to humiliation. I was serenaded by cousin Marie with a Polish wedding song, and a straw fedora was placed on my head with pink and blue ribbon of inch-long, plastic baby dolls circling the brim. It was supposed to be a fcrtility charm … and since we had six children it apparently worked.

What I didn't expect, and was embarrassed for my friends about, was the Bride's Dance. After Pat had the first dance with me, her mother led her around the hall with the flower girl holding the dress's train. Guests were expected to throw $5, $10, and $20 bills (not singles) into a pile on the train as she passed them. It was a leftover from the days when the newlyweds were usually broke, and guests gave them money instead of the wedding presents (which we had already received). None of my friends were in a position to be that generous. (This caused Helen to categorically charge them with being a bunch of cheap bastards … one of her favorite expressions.)

Helen noted that the priest who married us failed to show up at the rception. I think I figured it out the next day ... I found the envelope with a $20 bill in it in my suit jacket. I forgot to give it to Herink, who as my Best Man was supposed to pay the priest.

I spent it on breakfast on July 4, assuming he wouldn't really care since he had taken a vow of PURITY, CHASTITY and POVERTY. I was only helping him keep his oaths. I teased Pat over the years that we were not really married because I never paid the priest. (Yes, Helen, I really am a cheap bastard.)

A wedding custom superstition was that whoever caught the bride's garter would be the next guy to get married. We disproved that by the fact that Pat's gay Uncle Gene (also known as Uncle Fruitcake in later years) caught it, and naturally did not get married. From left the men are Richie Thoma, Bob Wells, unknown, Harry Smith, and Uncle Gene.

We were photographed outside the church.

And then through the back window of the limousine.

Then later we took off from the reception.

JULY 4, 1960

On the 4th of July Pat and I drove up to Brewster, Mass. We made the trip in Pat's convertible .

The charm bracelet on her right wrist was Pat's signature piece of jewelry for her entire adult life. We added to it on gift occasions.

We stayed at Mrs. Lund's Bed and Breakfast in Brewster, Mass., where I had vacationed on a cou-

ple of occasions (1953 and 1958).

Daily we toured Cape Cod, with stops at such places as the sandwich Glass Museum.

But we focused mostly on the beach. An unforeseen complication was that I did not know how sensitive Pat's skin was to the sun. The third day we were there she had to cover herself with calamine lotion. She had bought a bunch of sexy silk nightgowns, but she couldn't wear them. Instead, she wore my t-shirts to bed.

However I loved taking pictures of her before she had the breakouts.

Pat seriously thought she was trying to catch a turtle that buried itself in the sand. It turned out to be a crab.

We spent our time sightseeing, going to yard sales, and summer-stock plays. We just enjoyed being together.

On the evening of the third day, when we returned to the Bed and Breakfast, Mrs. Lund told us that Helen had called and urgently wanted Pat to call home. We were concerned that one of her grandparents had died, only to find out that Shultzie, her dog was sick. Helen wanted Pat cut her honeymoon short to attend to her pet Schnauzer.

Pat slammed down the telephone receiver and broke into tears. She was crushed that her mother could be so jealous of her happiness. It took most of the next day for her to get over it.

When we returned to Baltimore, Pat officially moved into our apartment in Catonsville's Uplands development.

Our apartment was of the sunken living room style. The lawn was barely a foot below our windowsill level. Naively, we were unaware of how vulnerable it made us to intruders or voyeurs. We were lucky that the closest we came to trouble was once while Pat was ironing clothes in the  living room. Someone outside the window gave a birdcall, and she thought it was me teasing her. I showed up an hour later, she realized what she heard was a *peeping tom*. We began making plans to move. Years later, Uplands became the scene of serious racial integration riots.

FISHING TRIP AT THOMA'S, SUMMER 1960

Shortly after we were married, Pat and I drove up to Richie Thoma's house in Dingman's Ferry, PA. His little pond had been my favorite fishing hole for years. However, all I ever caught were catfish. In fact, I was convinced that it was the only kind of fish there.

The only fishing Pat had ever done was off the wharf at Fells Point. But Pat lived up to her reputation of excelling at anything she did. I couldn't believe that in a matter of minutes she caught a pickerel.

What made it worse was that I had never caught a game fish anywhere like it in all my years of trying. Then after I took it off the hook she laid the rod down in the grass and caught a bullfrog.

This was followed by seven catfish. While I was filleting them, an old German guy, who was also visiting, told me I had it all wrong. "In my day," he said, "the men caught the fish and the women fried them."

COOKING

Pat had never learned to cook. When she lived at Fells Point, Helen and Cleo never let her in the kitchen. I, on the other hand, had learned the basics, and absorbed the preparation of my favorite home-cooked meals from my mother by a sort of osmosis. Even today, one of the main reasons I cook is that it is the only way to get the German items I like, such as *rouladen*.

However, one of the wedding gifts was a book titled, *The Joy of Cooking*. Pat decided that cooking amounted to being able to read and follow directions. Nevertheless, we struggled through undercooked fish and spaghetti noodles that went down the sink disposal the first time we tried to drain them. Vellegia's carryout was a quick substitute. Jimmy Wu's Chinese provided a frequent back-up. The greatest emergency occurred when Pat tried to make Cleo's pound cake in a GE electric oven. It ended in the butter-rich cake overflowing the pan, enveloping the newfangled device in bubbling blue flames destroying the new appliance.

The food budget was easily strained, so we discovered SPAM & noodles and hamburger/mushroom soup casserole. Both of which are still frequent items on my personal menu. Pat caught on quickly, and graduated to shrimp and curried rice.

Before there was KFC, there was *Pat's Real Southern Fried Chicken*, served with vanilla muffins. Our neighbors were envious in South Carolina and argued they were more like cupcakes (but no one could duplicate them). Margaret has the recipe but has it squirreled away from the eyes of Infidels.

Pat never really enjoyed cooking, and as the years progressed, I cooked as many dinners as she. It is interesting that all three of Pat's sons are excellent cooks. ... Howard is even a professional chef. That is not to say that I like everything they make (I can't eat some of their spicier concoctions). All three make versions of Nana's *Sauerbraten*.

1961

Fearing for Pat's safety at Uplands, we accepted Helen's offer to help us buy our first home. Baltimore was at the beginning of integration problems, with a practice known as "blockbusting" just beginning. However, we learned shortly after we moved into the new house that it was in a targeted neighborhood. The seller just wanted to get out before the fireworks started. True to our naiveté in such matters, we bought a great "end of group home" at a bargain price ... $10,000.

First house on Coleherne Road in Baltimore, 1961.

Along with the new house came the beginning of a sometimes hobby for me — having a garden in the yard. The previous owner had thirteen beautiful rosebushes … each a different variety. Most outstanding was a huge Peace Rose, which provided us with a marvelous blossom for the centerpiece of the Thanksgiving table in 1961. After that year the local climate took a decline in temperature from which it has not recovered. Summers got shorter. Whenever we moved after that, I tried to cultivate something of note.

TECHNICAL TRAINING CONSULTANTS

In 1961 I was working for the Westinghouse Defense Center next to BWI Airport. We were making certain components for the new Gemini Aerospace programs.

One of the features of the manufacturing program was *zero defects*. In those days, there was no way they anticipated being able to make repairs in space; they were still trying to get the stuff of the face of the Earth.

Westinghouse engineers worked out a technique of manufacturing the needed components by training workers to produce product that was 100% reliable. Because it was part of the Space Program, all new technology was to be shared by all contractors.

It could not be patented.

Steve Mahon, the Defense Center Training Manager, met me for lunch one day in 1961 and told me his plan. He had developed a training program for employees that stressed "How to solder with 100% reliability." Actually, the technical aspects were created by two electrical engineers. The work was done by a team under the management of a woman named Sunny.

I think the real secret to success was that you did not acknowledge the absolute reliability of a solder joint until it had passed all the DOD tests. Only then did you enter the component as a production item. The costs of all boards that failed were treated as employee training and swallowed by Westinghouse to qualify them for future contracts.

All the original technical training literature was in the Public Domain.

We then incorporated Technical Training Consultants, Inc. Steve had obtained the membership list for the American Association of Industrial Engineers, complete with mailing addresses. His plan was to offer a series of seminars at key locations (Atlanta, Indianapolis, and Washington, DC) for engineers to attend and learn the secrets of "Zero Defects." He wanted me to write a letter and develop other materials to attract electrical engineers working on (or hoping to get) Department of Defense contracts.

Our seminars would be run over three days, conducted by the men who invented the technique, and demonstrated in a hands-on class run by Sunny The Solderer. The price was $400 per student with a limit of ten students, lunch provided. The price was high for 1961 standards, but the average engineer was only paid $10K a year. We paid our teachers $200 each, and we got hotel meeting rooms free for guaranteeing occupancy of ten bedrooms and buying lunch for the group.

I agreed to my part and we sold out the first three seminars in two weeks. I remember placing one of the seminars in a motel with a view of The Pentagon (as if it were significant). It was the most popular site requested.

Steve had the Public Domain materials printed and we made up binders and training materials (from potential future suppliers). However, when we finished the first three sessions we ran into difficulties. The two engineers decided that they would operate their own seminars. They said they would no longer work for us.

In addition, Steve and I both worked for a long-time Westinghouse personnel manager. Someone told him what we were doing and his orders were to cease and desist. We sold our remaining training materials to the two engineers, but they soon found out they had no idea how to get customers for their seminars.

We dissolved the company and split the profits.

In 1961 Harry Smith and I both became fathers. He and Connie got married shortly after Pat and I did (they had to). I thought our wives would get along well because they were both from Polish families in Baltimore.

It turned out they were as different as I was from Harry. Pat was extremely well educated (as I have explained), and Connie was the product of Baltimore's public school system. That's when Pat told me that her family did not associate socially with "round faced" Pollacks. Connie, on the other hand, regarded Pat as "snooty" since she went to The Institute of Notre Dame (high priced and private).

After a few drinks one night, she recited the taunt she and her friends chanted back in high school:

> *"Rooty toot toot. Rooty toot toot.*
> *We are the girls from the Institute.*
> *We don't smoke and we don't chew,*
> *And we don't go with boys who do!"*
> *Our class won the Bible!!!"*

We only went to their apartment once. They never came to ours.

We only went to the beach with them on one occasion, which I captured on film. Nevertheless, Harry remained my role model, which paid off later in life.

JUNE 9, 1961
MARGARET ROSE IS BORN IN BALTIMORE

Margaret Rose was born on June 9, 1961. Pat and I were guests on a friend's motorboat on the Severn River the Sunday afternoon preceding the event. Pat was just over six months pregnant.

In spite of our protests, the boat owner insisted on demonstrating his boat's speed and performance. The constant thumping of the waves on the bottom of the boat set up vibrations that caused a premature separation in Pat's uterus.

We ended up in the emergency room of old Mercy Hospital that night, and I called Helen to let her know. Then I spent the whole night in the maternity waiting room with Helen berating me for what I had done to her daughter. She repeatedly wailed that both Pat and the baby were going to die. It was all I could do not to belt her by the time the baby was born.

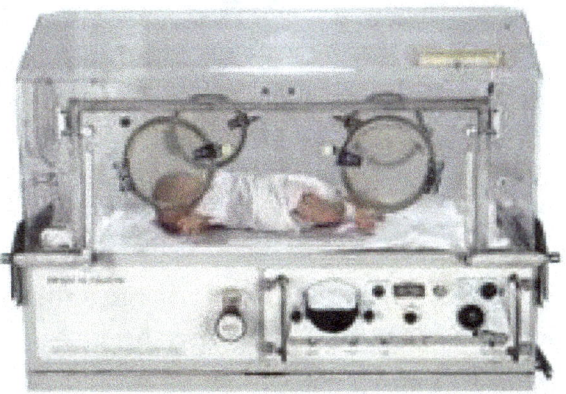

Luckily the baby had just passed the dividing line where the fetus could sustain herself out of the womb. But she was less than five pounds (2 pounds 14 ounces) and required the support of an isolette incubator.

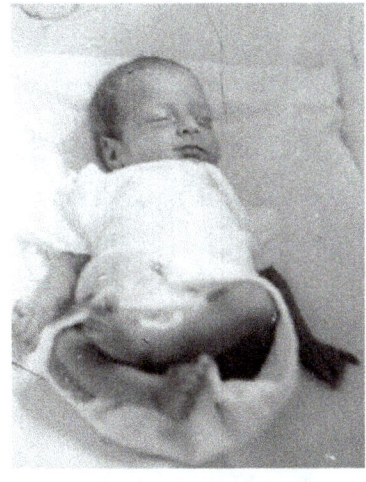

When we got the news that both Pat and her baby had survived the ordeal, Helen suggested the child be named Mary after her mother. I overruled her and told the nurse the baby's name was Margaret Rose after my father's mother.

Pat was released from the hospital, but the baby stayed for close to two months. Hospital rules required the infant to reach five pounds before she could go home. As a result Pat and I went to see her almost every night after supper. We had to reassure ourselves that she was still alive.

Pat's Aunts held a baby shower at Mayble's house in anticipation of Margaret's coming home.

Finally, when the doctor was certain the baby could survive at home at less than five pounds, he released her.

Pat took copious notes on how to handle the fragile life that had been entrusted to her.

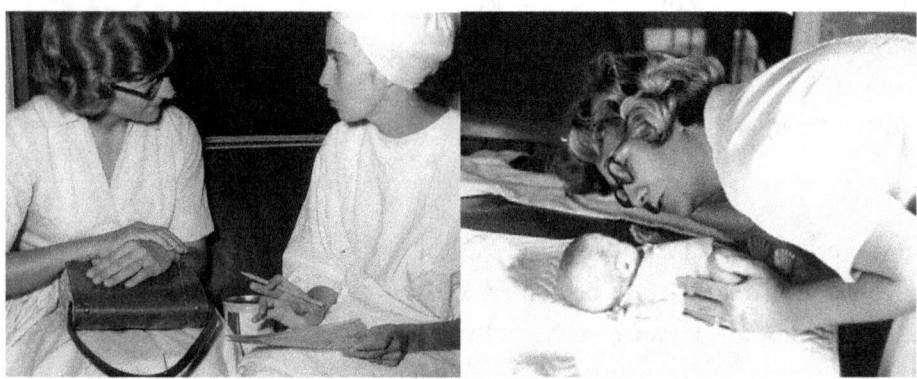

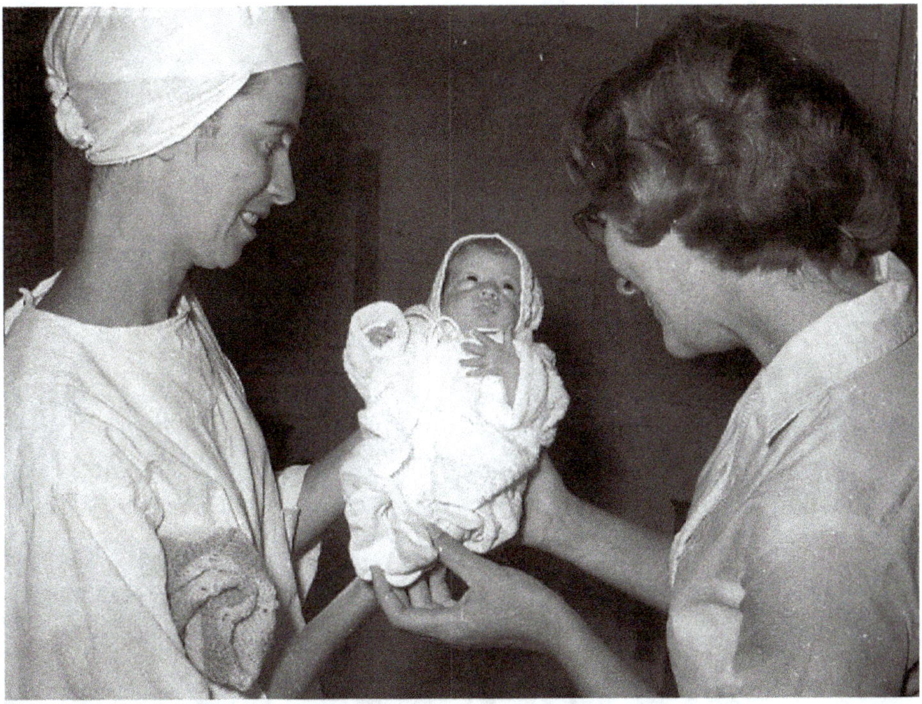

The magic moment arrived. We were finally real-live parents. Pat quit her job.

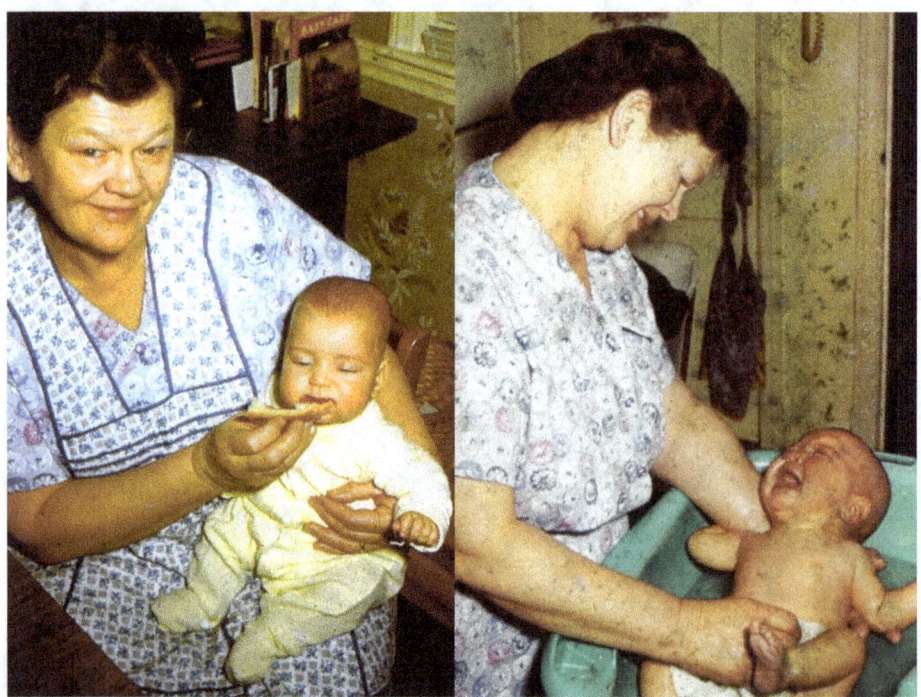

Nana, my mother, came down from New Jersey to help Pat adjust to the new order of things. She was essentially a Professional Grandma since Elsie had provided her with several grandchildren to practice on.

Helen was jealous of my mother's contribution, but was unable to offer any helpful assistance.

Sunday afternoons became a period of time that we dreaded.

About 3 p.m., Helen would arrive with Jake and Cleo in tow. We all sat in the living room, using kitchen chairs to support the backs of the old people. Cleo would sit with her purse on her lap and Jake nodded off, catching himself occasionally in time to keep from falling.

We had nothing to talk about. Our conversation centered about Helen telling Pat about people and inane events taking place in Fells Point.

After several weeks of this, even Cleo became bored. Cleo presented Pat with a beagle puppy, which was the last thing we needed. (Fortunately, we found it another home).

One thing we did not anticipate was the feeding schedule that accompanied a preemie baby. Margaret's stomach was so small that she needed to have a fresh bottle of Enfamil every two (2) hours — 24 hours a day. This was a normal situation in the hospital pediatric ward. At home, it was a full-time occupation. The kitchen became a formula factory with a single customer — Margaret.

We had 12 baby bottles. They needed to be sterilized between uses. Four bottles were in play at any given moment. Enfamil was prepared in batches … one for immediate use and three in the refrigerator. Pat worked out a 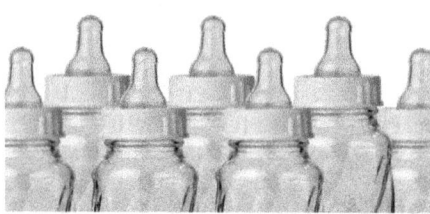 manageable system involving me. I did the eight o'clock feeding and again before I went to bed at 10PM. She fed Margaret at midnight and went to bed. The alarm woke me at 2:00AM. I heated up a bottle from fridge; fed Margaret (it took about a half hour) and went back to bed. I set the alarm for Pat to get up at 4:00AM. I got up at 6:00AM and fed Margaret, got dressed and went to work. The alarms were not really necessary because Margaret had one built-in.

Both Pat and I began to hallucinate from sleep deprivation. Sometimes the only way you could be sure if you did your task was to count the unused bottles.

The daytime schedule was more casual, and Pat's problem. I got home from work around 6 p.m. and performed the 8 p.m. bottle procedure just to give Pat a break. We were delighted that she moved to a four-hour interval after the first couple months.

As expected, Helen had no idea what to do with an infant. She announced one day that we were going to a van Gogh exhibit at the Baltimore Museum of Art the following Sunday. The inappropriateness and problems with the idea fell on deaf ears. Pat gave in and we were all embarrassed. Strollers were forbidden at the museum, so we had to take turns carrying the baby.

The embarrassment came from Helen pushing to the head of a

long line, announcing loudly, "We have a baby here! We have a baby here!" as though it fully excused the rudeness of crashing the line… I couldn't look anyone in the eye in the line behind us.

Fortunately, Margaret had the good sense to start crying inconsolably after the first 15 minutes, giving me the needed excuse for ushering us out of there. We proceeded on to next best thing to taking an infant to a museum … We went to Jimmy Wu's Chinese restaurant.

I am happy to recall that Margaret's first year provided us with many more compensatory events. The introduction of the first Momo into our lives. He was joined by a massive collection that continues to today.

HER FIRST CHRISTMAS

THE FIRST SNOWMAN

Although Pat and I had six children, they couldn't be more different from each other. What they share is a tendency to follow their own interests, which I like to think they learned from their parents. Their interests and behaviors overlap to a degree (reading, art, cooking, water activities, motorcycles, cars, and travel), but each approaches the subject in an individual manner.

The following discussions should not be construed as a preference for any individual, but a reflection of easy access to material. I will discuss significant events of their later lives as they appear on the scene, rather than trying to interlace them in the fabric of family time.

Margaret showed a distinct interest in graphic arts from an early age, and was encouraged by Pat.

Starting as a pre-teen, she turned her cake decorating interest into an art form. Her abilities extended into adulthood and the present.

In junior high school she became interested in the theater. The first play I remember her in was while we still lived in Ellicott City — *Guys and Dolls*— the same show in which I made my theatrical debut years later. Margaret's friends in high school exposed her to plays and musicals of all stripes.

She became so engrossed in it that she majored in theater arts at Towson. She used her skills to make costumes and scenery for a number of productions. Later, she did a professional stint as a stage management intern at Baltimore's Center Stage Theater.

Several years later she realized that her true interests were still

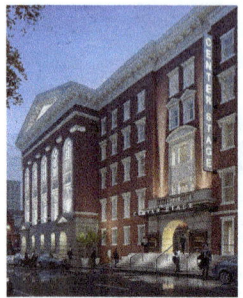
in art. She wanted to do something along the lines that she did not get in high school or college and marriage. In 2004 she signed up for three weeks at Cobalt, an art school in the Catskill Mountains of New York. She took a course in scene painting and set her mind for a later career move.

Expert Hands at Work for SCCC Gala

Democrat Photos by John Price

COBALT STUDIOS OF White Lake offered its considerable talents to the Sullivan County Community College (SCCC) Foundation for its upcoming scholarship fundraising gala and silent auction to be held at Cablevision Center in Ferndale this Friday at 7 p.m. ($100 tickets can be obtained by calling 434-5750, ext. 4249). Above, Rachel Keebler (right), the owner of the studio which does backdrops for Broadway shows, goes over a '50s diner backdrop for the gala with intern Connie Rosenfeldt of Ohio. At right, Lori Koeller (left) of Wisconsin and Margaret Schroder of Maryland mix colors using a blow-dryer and other tools.

The following year, AT&T layoffs started. At that point she decided to go to school full-time, using her severance package and cashing out her pension plan for a three-year professional study plan.

For a summer job, Margaret went to work at the Creation Museum in Kentucky, while she lived in Cincinnati. While she had an intellectual distaste for the basic beliefs of the organization, an extended job would have a great résumé value. Key working projects that they promised never materialized.

As an example of what I like to consider Schroeder innate flexibility, Margaret spent several weeks in California, in 2007 helping her brother Howard fulfill a DARPA (Defense Advanced Research Projects Agency) contract. He was providing computer network support for a driverless-car program.

Afterward, she landed a job in Daytona Beach, Florida, painting sets for a production of *White Christmas.*

She returned to Cobalt later in 2007 to complete her program. As a result, eight months later she was hired to work on the restoration of the Franklin D. Roosevelt family home, Marwood House, in Potomac, MD.

At $20 million, Marwood enjoys the honor of being the most expensive home ever sold in Montgomery County (December 2010). The three-story beauxarts chateau was built in 1926, and once was owned by the Gore family, rented by Joseph Kennedy and frequented by Franklin Delano Roosevelt and members of the Joseph Pulitzer clan. When the project was finished, the Recession ruled out continuing in that work due to lack of funding. The only job available was with a compounding pharmacy, Professional Arts, in Baltimore.

Margaret's artistic specialty was interior faux finishing — painting wood surfaces to look like stone.

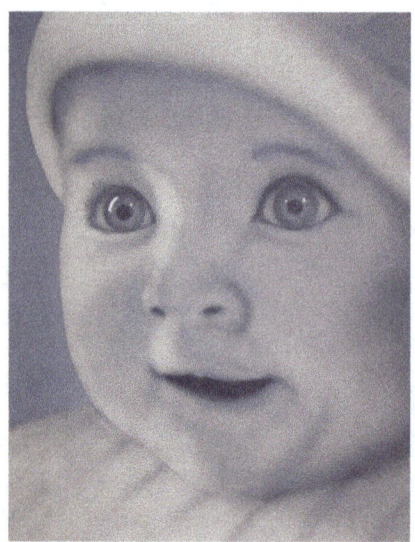

I believe her artistic talents are equal to Pat's, and may have exceeded them, My reservation is that Pat was never exposed to the diversity encompassed by Margaret's advanced education and training.

At her Cobalt Studios graduation, Pat bought her rendition of Johnny Depp as Jack Sparrow.

My favorite painting by Margaret is a three-by-five-foot rendition of a Lincoln Greyhound hood ornament. I can't imagine how one would even know where to start in producing such an outstanding work of art.

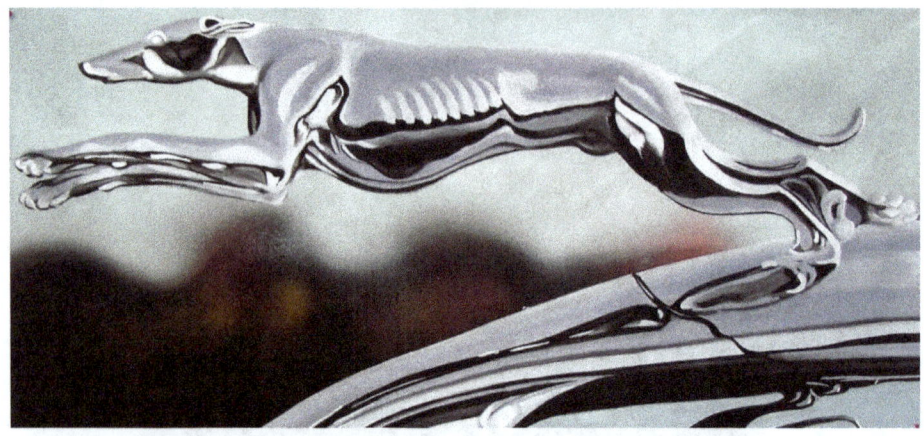

Compare it with a photograph of the real thing, below.

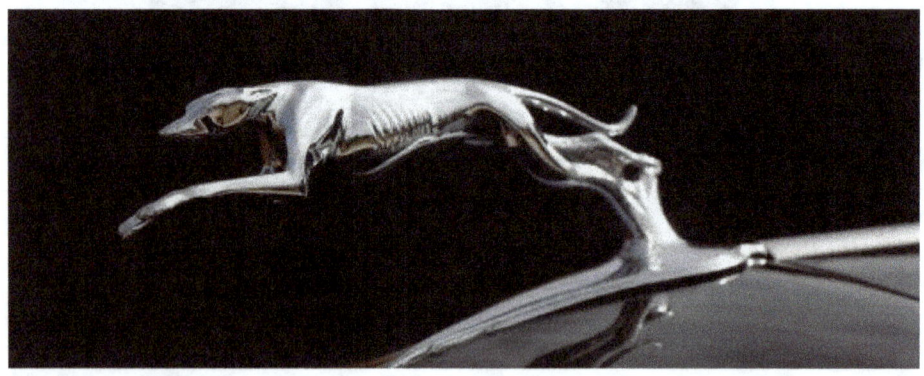

By the way, since they were training her to paint theater sets these were done with paintbrushes with a 3-foot handle.

DECEMBER 1961
PIPPIN'S OLD BOOK STORE

Before I get into family growth and our *Odyssey* that toured America, let me attempt to deal with some of my published books as a unit, rather than a one-at-a-time chronologically. I will expand on Margaret's life development presently.

My personal life went into gear in a big way in 1961.

I wanted to write as book as far back as I can remember, but really had no hard and fast rule as to what it would be about. For a while, after I got out of the Army I entertained the idea of writing about my life in the service. However, I never got much past the title, *Alex in Blunder-land*. In 1954 I wrote a short, short story for the Rutgers NCAS literary magazine, the *Gallery*. It was based on a case I worked on in Korea. I had a head full such stories which are now included in Part One of this memoir,

At this writing I have not been able to locate the diary I kept for the better part of 1953 and 1954. For the most part the entries were very short and sketchy, believing at the time I would remember everything with small trigger sentences. Wrong!

I also have found the letters I wrote to my mother while in the Army. The most they contribute are dates of events. My main objective with them was to keep Mom from unnecessary worry. Fortunately, my memory is quite intact once I start thinking about a given time.

The true beginning of my professional writing career began in 1961.

Just before Christmas 1961, I was driving down Eutaw Street in Baltimore when I spotted a sign on the sidewalk outside Pippin's Old Book Store announcing that the entire place was being auctioned off. I parked the car and went into the shop. The auction was over and the winners had a couple days to get their books out.

The shelves were divided up into numbered sections marked by duct tape. Bidders made their bids on each unit from, ceiling to floor, with no regard for subjects or grouping.

Old Man Pippin died without a will, and his heirs sold the building by court order and simply auctioned off the contents. To someone who had the knowledge and the money, the whole lot would have been a steal. My knowledge was truly minimal and my cash was zero.

Mr. Pippin's daughter told me I was too late for the auction, but there was a Washington book dealer in the basement who only wanted certain things, and was planning to abandon the rest. I went down to the basement and found the guy. All he wanted were bound editions of magazines like *Harpers* Civil War dates. He had no opposition for his bid on the entire basement for five dollars. The reason was clear — every shelf had about a quarter inch of black soot on it. The furnace had a leaky flue. When it was converted from coal to oil it was a sloppy job. Smoke poured out of it constantly, leaving an oily residue on all the books.

The guy confirmed he had no interest in the mess, but would let me have it all for five dollars cash so he could break even. I took the deal. I bought "many a quaint and curious volume of forgotten lore" (about 10,000) for an unchallenged bid of $5. No one else wanted them.

But out of all these books, one of them almost literally jumped out at me. An accidentally knocked-over bookshelf spilled about a hundred books at my feet. The first one I picked up and looked through was titled *Two Hard Cases*, by W.W. Godding, the Superintendent of Washington, DC's St. Elizabeth's insane asylum. One of his hard cases was Charles Julius Guiteau, the not-yet convicted assassin of our 20th President, James Abram Garfield.

The Westinghouse News *did a photo feature in its national edition.*

Godding's account of the case and the trial was a grabber. Who would have thought trying to find out more about Guiteau would wind up becoming a 40-year obsession? I knew who Guiteau was from a book titled *The History of America in Pictures* that my mother bought from an itinerant book salesman in 1946.

It also turned out that there was a false-fronted bookshelf on the third floor. No one knew about it at the time of the auction. Behind the façade were about 30 bound editions of Scribner's/Century magazines starting in the 1870s in excellent shape. Mrs. Pippin gave them to me for hauling them away. I still read them from time to time, trying in vain to find a couple stories I came across but had not indexed.

I rented a U-Haul truck and got my friend, Don Poland, to help empty the basement as much as we could on one Saturday. I took my outboard PennYan boat out of its garage and filled the structure up with books. Sorting the books out was a hopeless task. I had a yard sale a few weeks later and know some of my best books were stolen during it. Don and I were covered with soot, looking like we were in a Minstrel Show.

Pat, my lovely wife of one year, thought I went Christmas shopping and got all excited when I began to unload vast quantities of cartons into the basement through the back yard. I filled five vacuum cleaner bags with black dust trying to reclaim some of the best books. During our move from Baltimore to Detroit, the moving company lost several cartons of books that included the collectible *Penny Cyclopedia* from 1832 to 1840.

When Pat passed away in 2008 I still had not heard the end to that misunderstanding. Many of the boxes were still in the basement waiting to be sorted in 2015. I have several cartons in the living room full of books from the 1700s, including the first English novel, *Clarissa* (1735). But they are in poor condition reducing their value severely.

1961 BEGAN "THE INNOCENT ASSASSIN"

Many years later (1975), a prolonged period of unemployment drove me to hide often in the National Archives when no jobs seemed imminent. Armed with a tape recorder, in six weeks of reading I dictated more than 50 cassettes with information about the *United States vs. Charles Julius Guiteau* trial.

Almost out of the blue, a Xerox copy turned up of the diary the Reverend William W. Hicks kept during his three weeks as the Death Row Spiritual Advisor to Guiteau. It was a whole new point of view, contrasting with contemporary newspaper reports of the time.

Work on the book ceased for long periods of time, but something would always draw me back into it. I consciously put the whole project aside for four years, and wrote two other books on completely different subjects — an American missionary in the Solomon Islands (*John Frum, he come!*); and a discussion of World War II American propaganda (*In der Fuehrer's Face*). The break was just what was needed. I came back to what I named "*The Removal* project" in 2002 with the whole thing completely structured in my mind. The name *Removal* came from Guiteau's insistence that his act was inspired by God to *Remove the President.*

There are so many twists and turns in the story, that it became clear early in my researching that a straight historical recounting of the events would not hold together. For example, there are no other popular accounts of the numerous attempts to kill Guiteau before he reached the gallows. In addition, the humiliation and medical brutality Garfield experienced during the 79 days between the shooting and merciful death could not be glossed over. I stuck as close to the recorded facts and dates as possible, but had to project many probable personal transactions and conversations.

Those who are not happy with the reporting of the minutia of the case are reminded that this book is a *novel,* not a history text. In the Appendix, I have identified many people, places and events that were real, and deserved to be recognized as such. *The Innocent Assassin*, (ISBN: 978160414509) is available from Amazon Books.

After I read *Two Hard Cases*, I began to seriously pursue other sources of information about the Garfield assassination. By some circuitous route I ended up at the Historical Society of Washington, D.C. It was housed in a magnificent four-story mansion near DuPont Circle, and was formerly owned by Christian Heurich, a prominent Washington brewer. After his widow's death, the family donated it to the Society as their Headquarters.

Two events stick in my mind in connection with it. First, they had the bullet that was removed from Garfield's body at the autopsy. A hole had been drilled through it to accommodate a wire to a tag identifying it as an exhibit at Guiteau's trial. I have to admit I was somewhat thrilled to actually hold the bullet Charley fired into Garfield. It was kept in a little drawer of the type used in libraries to hold index card files. I do not know if it survived the relocation of the HQ to the historic Carnegie Library on Mt. Vernon Square. I did not see it when I visited there in 2007.

The other event took place the last time I went there (1963). They escorted me to a reading room on the third floor. I pored over newspaper accounts covering the whole Garfield affair for hours. When I noticed that the sun had gone down, I decided to leave.

However, after descending the huge staircase, I found that I was alone. They had forgotten about me and went home. I called out in search of a security guard ... there was none.

Instead, there was only a single light across from the bottom of the staircase. It cast grotesque shadows

of objects in the lobby — especially the suit of armor guarding the room. I was suddenly eight years old again, and found myself on a stereotypical, scary Hollywood set of a 1940s horror flick. All I wanted to do was get out of there as soon as possible.

I let myself out through the front door, but stopped in the vestibule to make sure the door behind me was locked. The next morning, I made an anonymous phone call to the Society's management, informing them that their museum had no security at night. I never had occasion to go back to that building, so I do not know if they acted on my tip.

The most important result of my contact with the DC Historical Society was truly one of the *most synchronistic events* of my life.

When I told Robert Truax, the Historical Librarian/Curator what I was researching, his face lit up. "I have exactly what you are looking for," he said and went straight to a shelf full of leather-bound volumes. The experience was very similar to one I had thirty-odd years later at the Library of Congress.

"To my knowledge, no one has ever cited this source and I've been here for more than twenty years," he said. He took down a book marked "Minutes, 1919." He opened the book and turned to a page just inside the back cover. "It was the last meeting of the year, and there weren't many men in attendance … Too close to Christmas, I guess."

I was getting anxious to see what he had. It was almost like he had been waiting for me to show up to justify his enthusiasm. Fortunately, the file contained an original and a carbon copy (which he handed me). The heading read *Minutes of the Columbia Historical Society*, December 16, 1919. It was an address given by Dr. William Tindall.

Mr. Truax said, "It was Dr. Tindall's account of his involvement with trying to help General Garfield, after he was shot. He was, in fact, the first medical doctor on the scene, but Dr. D. Willard Bliss was credited by the newspapers."

I told him that's what I had read.

"Actually, Bliss was well known in the District. The first reporters on the scene made the mistake and everyone else just built on it. Dr. Tindall had given up practicing medicine to pursue a political career. I think Garfield would have lived if Bliss had not taken charge.

"Read his speech," the old man said. "I have no reason to doubt him. He was a history buff, and wanted to set the record straight. ... But no one ever read his speech or even put him at the scene."

I studied the minutes of the meeting and made my decision at that time to write, *The Innocent Assassin*.

At one point, I was so interested In Charlie Guiteau that I decided to visit what was left of him at what used to be the Army's Walter Reed Hospital, now the United States Medical Museum in Washington, D.C.

His last residence was Drawer 19 for his skeleton and a Mason Jar for his dissected brain. His skull was stolen in 1909. Details can be found in the Appendix of my book *The Innocent Assassin*.

My ultimate decision as a writer was that I no longer cared if it was too long to be sold to a major publisher. Through the miracle of electronic publishing, the book is now available as an eBook to anyone who has enough intellectual curiosity to follow the whole story to its unbelievable conclusion. I had it printed as a paperback at a later date.

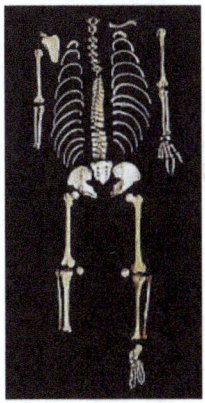

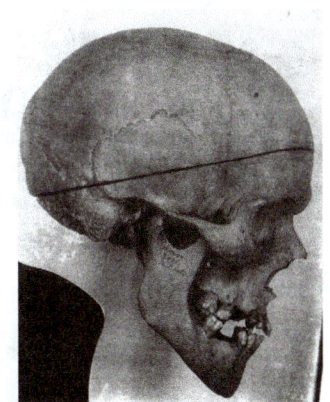

As an example of my obsession with synchronicity, this all came about because of my anger with a foot doctor. He was treating an injury to my right big toe for weeks, and led me to believe he was purposely prolonging the treatment for his personal gain. I sought out a new foot doctor and wound up with Dr. John Douglas Butler. During one of my treatments we talked about publishing books. He had an eBook in print on the argument for and against abortion. It was successfully self-published as a textbook for several European Universities by Fideli Publishing. He put me in touch with Robin Surface, the owner, and we began our relationship to include a total of seven books.

"We now return you to the originally scheduled broadcast at this time," as they used to say on the radio after an interruption.

MAY 31, 1963
WILLIAM RICHARD, JR. IS BORN IN BALTIMORE

Although the doctors agreed that Pat would not be able to birth any more babies after Margaret, she had her own plans (Six kids … remember?) After she accommodated their predictions with a miscarriage, William R. Schroeder, Jr. survived a difficult delivery on May 31, 1963.

I have not been able to locate many pictures of Will until we arrived in Detroit, in August. He grew rapidly, and hasn't stopped since.

The earliest photo was when Margaret held him for the camera. When we moved, Pat said he was in a baby seat under the kitchen table and was almost packed in a box by the movers.

They both became frequent subjects of family photography.

Will learned to walk early and loved running about the yard with as little clothes as possible.

From early childhood, Will and I shared an interest in "all things nature." For example, he learned all he could about the Arizona desert flora and fauna just by wandering beyond our backyard fence in Scottsdale. When he became interested in geology, we bought exploration maps and booklets, sometimes unwittingly risking or lives and safety in search of samples.

My recollection of the most strenuous activity was dragging massive rocks containing Fool's Gold from a Ghost Town near Bisbee. But we loved it.

I was roped into taking over the job of Webelos Leader in 1972 from Pat and spent the next ten years with Will in Scouting.

When we moved to Maryland, he was sent to Boy Scout camp reluctantly, but excelled as a camp counselor for younger boys in spite of himself. He spent summer of 1979 as a Campcraft and Wilderness Survival Teacher. In 1978 and 1979 we went to summer camp together. I spent two vacations as the adult leader.

We often enoyed ourselves in hiking and nature study. Will's notable achievement had to do with his discovery of 14 Black Ratsnake eggs in a lakeside nest while looking for an abondoned copper mine at Liberty Reservoir.

Oddly enough the nest was located at the filled-in entrance to the mine, where the tailings had been pushed back to cover the opening, yet sunk in enough to leave a recognizable depression.

A companion started stomping on the eggs as he was afraid of snakes. Will stopped his uneducated hillbilly aquaintance from killing most of the reptiles and took them home and hatchd them. For a while, they seemed to be everwhere (like inside sneakers).

Pat had no fear of snakes. In fact she did an amazing thing at the Mall when a kid dropped a box from the pet store that contained a Rosy Boa. While everyone was shreiking and carrrying on, she picked it up and handed it back to the owner who was afraid to touch it.

On a competitive canoe trip, Will and I reached the riverside campground first, but got no recognition. Instead, a big fuss was made over the Troop's favorite idiot capsizing his canoe by standing up, falling overboard, and not drowning.

We both enjoyed outdoor activities, but we found that the Troop suffered from "clique-ishness." Carroll County did not welcome outsiders at that time. The other leaders and the boys were all from the area and had known each other from Kindergarten on. The Order of the Arrow (OA) is the National Honor Society of the BSA. Its uses *American Indian* imagery for ceremonies bestowing recognition on Scouts selected by their peers as best exemplifying the ideals of Scouting. The goal was to establish these as lifelong guidelines, and to encourage continued participation in Scouting and camping.

While Will met all the requirements for the Order of the Arrow and Eagle Scout rank, he lost the nomination to another kid who had grown up with the rest. It turned out to be a popularity contest. Afterward, I modified the nomination procedure to include a third party to serve as an advocate for the nominee.

When he graduated from Westminster High, he decided to join the Air Force. In recognition of his excellent mechanical abilities and high scores (98 with the highest possible score being 99) on the Armed Services Vocational Aptitude Battery (ASVAB), he was sent to Jet Engine Mechanic School in Chanute, Illinois.

Will's love of two-wheeled vehicles began at age 5, when he learned to ride Margaret's bike.

Thinking he had a future in jet engines, he was assigned to Dover Air Force Base. But there was no shooting war in progress at the time, so in typical military tradition, he was assigned to painting woodwork and janitorial tasks. Complaining about his wasted talents got him transferred to the Strategic Air Command, doing more of the same.

His enlistment was shortened and he returned to pursuing his automotive and sailing interests.

He started on motorcycles while was stationed with the Air Force in Dover, Delaware. His first and favorite bike was his 1962 Panhead FLH 1200 which he bought in 1990.

After many rebuilds and a final ground-up restoration, he aquired a matching year 1962 Harley-Davidson Sidecar in 2015. Both are awaiting a repaint so the colors will match when they are bolted together and parked in the living room for the rest of eternity. The reason … kick starting this beast with a bum knee is going to be a holiday occasion only.

The culmination of that vein of interest came with building his own completely custom bike in 2009.

The new bike has a high performance aftermarket handbuilt Panhead motor like his 1962, but all custom parts, electric starter, six speed transmission, softail frame and disc brakes. It is capable of exceeding the prior bike's whopping land speed record of 65 MPH.

Consistent with the Schroeder Family philosophy of not being a one-trick pony, Will developed a theatrical resume starting with being president of the Westminster High School Shakespeare Society. Over the years he has appeared as Jerry Reed in *The Mice Have Been Drinking Again*; Petruccio in *The Taming of The Shrew*;

Aesop in *The Fabulous Fable Factory*, and Humpty Dumpty in *Alice and Wonderland*. We appeared on stage together in *The King and I* and *My Three Angels*.

Just for the fun of it, he played a dog during one of Margaret's Towson summer programs. He was so good at acting that he was invited to attend a summer theater workshop at Towson State University in his junior year of high school.

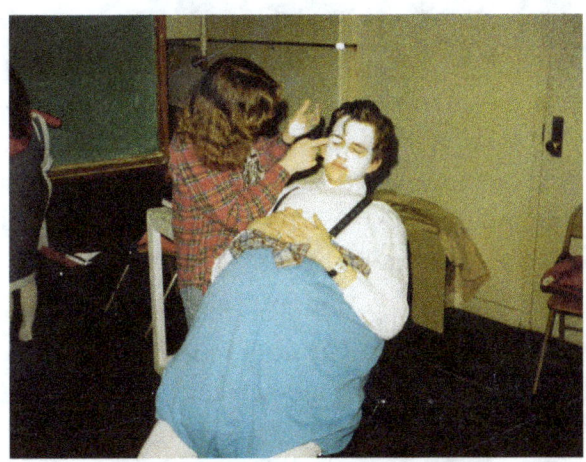

Historical re-enactment can be considered a form of theater or it can stand on its own. In any event, Will enjoyed it thoroughly.

Even when he was a teenager, Will expressed a desire to own a junkyard. His first real job was at Shiflit's Junkyard in Westminster. This ambition has since been realized on numerous occasions, up to the point that it extends to many rooms in our house. I do not expect it to change before I die (at which point it will no longer concern me).

One of the more significant milestones in that story took place with the purchase if a huge used car lot in Hanover, PA.

But Will's energies were diverted to a completely different art project of fantastic proportions — *The Fey Sol!*

He bought the hull of an Aleutka sailboat and allowed it to take over his life. The *Fey Sol* is a 26-foot bilge keel double-ender with a 2'9" draft. It is described as great for gunk-holing in the Chesapeake.

Gunkholing is a boating term referring to a type of cruising in shallow or shoal water, meandering from place to place, spending the nights in coves. The term refers to the gunk, or mud, typical of the creeks, coves, marshes, and rivers that are referred to as gunkholes. While not necessary, gunkholers typically seek out the serenity of isolated anchorages over the crowds of marinas and popular bays. A minimal draft is preferred, since gunkholers tend to go as far up and into the gunkholes as possible, seeking ever more inaccessible destinations.

But the Aleutka is also a durable enough pocket cruiser to cross oceans. It was designed by Dr. Jonathan Letcher in 1970, and was featured in his book, *"Self Steering for Sailing Craft"* She was also in Ferenc Mate's book, *"Best Boats to Build or Buy."* This boat has two keels set amidships. At low tides, it can sit upright on the bottom. It appealed to Will's long-range fantasy of sailing the ocean solo with no particular destination.

He towed the boat to his used-car lot and attracted a lot of attention with his preparations.

When he had to sell the car lot, he took the boat down to Finksburg where he meticulously fitted strips of exotic wood into the deck and cabin. Will dealt with the restoration as a fine art project. I was amazed at the engineering and problem-solving that went I into transporting it to a trailer without the help of anyone else.

Months of micro-managing went into creating the finished product. When it was ready, I went with him to Middle River for a launching and naming ceremony.

Shortly afterward, he navigated it solo down to the Bay Bridge, where it almost lost the ruder in rough water. Through survivalist seamanship and the help of another boater he got it back to shore for repairs.

When he finished the season, it was transported back to Finksburg where it has found a semi-permanent berth in my driveway. I believe it had served its purpose of proving his genius in that field and became a "been there, done that" chapter in his life.

He subsequently experienced an heroic adventure when he helped a friend attempt to relocate her sailboat to a new marina. As he sailed beneath BG&E high-tension power lines, several thousand volts arced from the wires to the boat's mast. Gasoline from boat's auxiliary engine ignited, blowing the deck and wheel skyward.

Black smoke billowed into the cabin, disabling the boat's owner. One other man on the deck of the boat escaped unharmed. The boat's owner was knocked over and was almost overcome by the smoke.

Will picked her up and jumped overboard. Her self-inflating life jacket was not activated, so Will carried her to the shore since the water was well over her head. The posted clearance beneath the wires was not accurate, but in the lawsuit that followed, BG&E's high-priced lawyers kept Will from getting a fair settlement. He still suffers from a cough caused by the smoke irritating to his lungs.

Will owned another sailboat, which he gave to the owner of the destroyed boat. That one has since been bequeathed to Will's friend, Jen Hegner.

At this writing, he has a larger steel-hulled boat awaiting his attention in Florida.

AUGUST 1963–MAY 1966
CHRYSLER, DETROIT, MI

By the time Willy was born, both Pat and I were sick and tired of the Bochenski/Christopher family interference with our daily lives. At the same time, I was growing bored with my job at Westinghouse. As much as I liked Don Poland, my boss, I saw him as a block to personal progress. He showed no signs of going anywhere, either with Westinghouse or anywhere else. I fell back to my old habit of reading *The Wall Street Journal* Help Wanted ads.

In 1963 Clarence (Mickey) Dover sold Chrysler Corporation on an employee communication program in an effort to reach union employees before critical labor contract negotiations in 1965. It was a wholesale copy of the General Electric program credited with fighting unions in their plants across the country.

Dover ran ads in the *WSJ* and hired more than a dozen industrial communicators across the country. The main requirement was familiarity with the GE communication program. I qualified due to my employment by Westinghouse, whose employee communication program was a carbon copy of GE's. This was a fact I did not know until I was well into the job. I was personally involved in all aspects without knowing it. Dover was so impressed with my experience that he made me the communication manger of the Highland Park Machining Plant, located next to the Chrysler Corporation Headquarters. I was convenient to Dover when he needed a live example of the program for showing to executives and visitors.

It was the first plant Walter Chrysler bought when he created the company. It was also the site of the old Maxwell Automobile Plant that produced Jack Benny's famous Maxwell.

I was given *carte blanche* responsibility to create a full-blown instant program. I honestly had no idea how rare that was, but ignorance was bliss. I found I was also responsible for the Safety and Suggestion programs. I had no idea what that meant other than they were favorite propaganda subjects at Westinghouse.

I had never been in an automobile plant before. My personal contact with a manufacturing plant was the Metuchen, NJ, Westinghouse TV & Radio Division, which was an electronics assembly factory. My new plant was full of screw-making machines, transmission assemblies, electric gearshifters, power steering boxes, massive body and fender stamping presses, and torque converters.

I was given a guided tour of the manufacturing process by Bob Gallandt, the foreman in charge of the torque converter line. From him I learned the secrets of the manufacturing culture. For example, he had a daily production quota of six converters an hour. He was responsible for producing no less every day — with no excuses like the production line was shut down for any reason (fire, missing employees, accidents, and breakdowns). Therefore, he operated the line to produce six and a half units per hour. Anything over six went into his reserve storage. That way when anything happened he could fill in the quota from his bank of extras. Management did not want excuses, just product.

He was my link with the real automotive world. I hired him to run the Safety and Suggestion programs. We became good friends and he built on this promotion to leave Chrysler years later to become the Personnel Manager for an archery manufacturer.

John Vacek, Bill Schroeder, and Bob Gallandt

I served as a buffer between him and the plant department managers whose autocratic rule he rightfully learned to fear. When I spoke to the Manager of Manufacturing, I didn't ask for his cooperation, I told him that the new safety and suggestion program was a Corporate edict from President Lynn Townsend.

He initially disagreed about the need for any employee safety program. He said, "To produce one million cars, we accept that it will cost three lives, seven arms, three legs and countless fingers." He said he would cooperate only if the Plant Manager, Tony Maloney, told him to.

The Feudal System was alive and well in Michigan. When I went to the office of the Lord of the Manor, Anthony Maloney, he had already received a call from Mickey Dover, who had the *true word* from King Townsend. Tony acknowledged his reluctant fealty based on impending labor contract negotiations with the UAW.

One of the rewards of the suggestion program was the award of a brand-new Plymouth Barracuda to any employee whose idea saved the company more than $5,000. Much to Maloney's dismay, it wasn't long before one of his employees made such a suggestion and was a winner.

A huge galvanizing tank ran 24-hours a day treating air filters for all Chrysler-built cars. The operation of the process consumed ten bags of chemicals per shift, whereas a year ago it only needed two bags per shift.

The miraculous suggestion was quite simple: *Plug the leak in the corroded bottom of the tank that allowed the chemical bath to drip down into the sewer drain.* To do so would shut down the galvanizing line for at least two days, preventing the foreman (not to mention the factory) from meeting the production quota.

When I broke the news to Maloney I thought the top of his head was going to blow off. His face turned a bright red. He screamed to his secretary to get the foreman of the galvanizing line on the phone. He saw the personal consequences of the news immediately. He was the first plant manager to have someone win a car by virtue of plain incompetence. He would have to pose for pictures awarding the employee a free car (at the plant's expense). Not only would it be in the company newspaper … it would appear in The *Detroit Free Press.* (Exactly what Dover had promised Townsend.)

The secretary reported that the shift had changed and the lead foreman had gone home for the day. Instead, she had the second-shift foreman on the line. Tony Maloney grabbed the phone and barraged the poor man at the other end of the line with invectives and foul language I had never heard before — even in the Army.

When he finished, he glared at me and told me to get the hell out of his sight. The next day I found out that by sheer coincidence (or synchronicity) the foreman Tony wanted to yell at died of a heart attack in his car on the way home. It happened exactly at the time Maloney was delivering his tirade. Had he still been at work, he would have died while Maloney was firing him. He fired the second and third shift foremen, but could not touch the employee in question due to the UAW (and Dover).

However, it was not the end of the story. Mickey Dover was delighted that his communication program had yielded such a high profile event so soon. It would be contrary to what the United Auto Workers said constantly (that Chrysler treated its employees badly).

Still fighting the curse of 1957's sales calamity, Chrysler Corporation also launched the world's first five-year, 50,000-mile power train warranty.

Valiant and Barracuda

One of the items covered by the warranty was the power steering pump made in the Highland Park plant. When it failed in the field due to leakage problems, it cost about $400 to repair it at a dealership. The cost was ultimately charged back to the factory that made it.

The Engineering Department could not locate the source of the multiple failures. However, one of the line employees found the reason. The tool (essentially an icepick) used to remove the temporary fluid fill-cap made a very fine scratch on the finely machined connection surface. In use, the power steering fluid leaked out, leading to pressure failure. Once more an employee suggestion qualified for a Barracuda.

For some reason employee suggestions were bottled up in the plant Manager's office. He repeatedly postponed and delayed signing any of them, insisting on more comprehensive investigations.

Maloney's final straw had nothing to do with one of my programs. Chrysler Engineering Division was located on the grounds of the Highland Park Plant. They were in the final stages of developing the famous Hemi-head engine. However, one morning they discovered the 600+ pound prototype engine had disappeared from the laboratory.

There were no signs of forcible entry or exit. It just plain disappeared. No one had any theories on how it happened. The FBI was called in on the basis of Industrial Espionage. Unfortunately, it took place on property under the charge of poor Tony Maloney.

After an intensive investigation, the engine was found in a pile of scrap metal alongside the railroad tracks at the edge of the factory grounds. The FBI figured it out. On the night before the disappearance was discovered, a forklift operator entered the Engineering building, went to the lab, lifted the machine off its test-bench and took it down on the freight elevator into the adjacent yard. He even waved to the security guard at the gate as he passed, giving the impression of "business as usual."

He placed the engine next to the tracks and covered it with large sheets of scrap metal. He exchanged waves to the guard again as he parked his lift for the night.

FBI agents watched the scrap pile. Two days later a Diesel locomotive and two empty gondola cars rolled in past the railroad gate. One of the cars was equipped with a huge electro-magnet crane. It went directly to the hidden Hemi-head and lifted it to a bare spot in the corner of one of the cars. Then the crane positioned a protective sheet of stamped metal to protect it. At that point the FBI arrested the train crew.

Obviously Maloney had nothing to do with the theft, but since the scrap pile was his, he took the hit from corporate. The plant manager was eventfully persuaded to take an early retirement. But in the meantime, he kept postponing approving any suggestions awaiting his signature.

Chrysler was a big target for crime schemes. One of my favorites had to do with the theft of huge, already mounted tires. The Imperial car production facility had a big mystery. Every week as many as a dozen mounted tires disappeared from inventory. Every vehicle that passed through the gates of the plant was thoroughly inspected. There was no way you could hide a huge mounted tire.

As luck would have it, a third shift foreman was fishing on the Detroit River on which the Imperial factory bordered. The water had eroded the soil at the building foundation creating an interior flooding problem which had not been taken care of.

While he was casting his line he glanced up at the Imperial Assembly Plant. To his amazement the window on the fourth floor was open and he saw a tire fall from it into the Detroit River, followed in quick succession by three more. A guy in a rowboat then proceeded to herd them all together, and push them to a nearby landing where he had a waiting pickup truck. He fished them out and put them in the back of the truck.

Since the observer worked at the plant and knew about the disappearing-tire problem, he got back to shore and raced to the plant manager's office. The solution was quite simple. Guys working in the tire mounting department waited until lunch hour when nobody was there. They simply pushed the mounted tires out the window. Since they were inflated, they floated. Their man waited down below and claimed the day's haul.

Not long after that that I was promoted to Editor of the Management Magazine at Headquarters next door. I was put on what was known as "the Executive Rolls" which qualified me for a company car (a Barracuda) and I ate lunch in the Executive Dining Room. They knew how to reward team members.

Initially, I hired an editor to put out the local plant newspaper ... Bill Haga. But unknown to me, he had a personal agenda. He learned enough about the details of Dover's program to copy it, and sell the idea to a steel fabrication company in Ohio. Dover sued him unsuccessfully and I lost track of him.

He did provide one synchronicity-related event that made a significant impact on my later life. He and his wife went to dinner and a movie one night with me and Pat. The movie was *Mondo Cane*, a 1962 "shock-umentary" that concluded with a section on a tribe in the Solomon Islands. It made me aware for the first time of Cargo Cults. My interest in the subject grew such that I went on to write *John Frum, He Come* twenty years later in 1985.

The most noteworthy news event that took place while I was at Highland Park was the Kennedy Assassination on November 22, 1963 in Dallas, TX. Bill Haga went out to eat lunch in his car and listen to the radio. Company policy forbade listening to a radio at work. In fact, radios were forbidden on company property. He came running into my office, quite excited.

He said that shortly after noon, President John F. Kennedy was assassinated as he rode in a motorcade through Dealey Plaza in downtown Dallas, Texas. We both left the building and went to listen to the car radio. Once it was confirmed, I went back into the office to tell the Personnel Manager.

Then I went to the Employment desk in an adjacent room, where three women employees were working. I said, "Have you heard ... Kennedy has been shot!" They looked blankly at me and one asked, "OK, what's the punch line?" They didn't believe me.

At the end of the shift at 4:00PM the production lines shut down and didn't resume for two days. Office people left work early and I went home to see what the TV had to tell. Pat had seen the news and was quite agitated.

THE HAUNTED HOUSE

When I was hired by Chrysler in 1963, Pat stayed back in Baltimore. Will was only a few months old and Margaret about two years. I needed to find a house where they could be moved into ASAP. I let a real estate agent find me a house to rent, which turned out to be a mistake.

This was 5533 Courville Street in Detroit, Michigan.

Never having looked for a house on my own, I did not have a list of *musts*. What I failed to notice was that it did not have a stove in the kitchen. I stayed there by myself, sleeping on an Army cot an office friend loaned me. The absence of a stove became noticeable the first time I went to make a pot of coffee.

I have to say I found the place creepy from the beginning, but I attributed that to the absence of furniture.

Pat handled all the details of moving the family very successfully, the first of many such episodes in the years to follow.

I found a used stove in the classifieds, and Pat arrived. It was clearly an old house and not to Pat's satisfaction. Almost immediately we looked for a new home built to her specifications. Meanwhile, we had to make the best of the old house in Detroit.

Pat was uncomfortable in the house on day one. She said the first thing she noticed was that when she put the cover on a cake holder squarely, it would move off center when she was out of the kitchen. I suggested that the vibrations from the refrigerator caused it to move. After intentionally setting the cover on several occasions, it definitely moved.

Did we have as poltergeist?

This began a series of eerie and disconcerting events. I am not sure of the sequence but here are ones I remember.

When she was putting Will in for his afternoon nap in the front room over the downstairs entrance, he would start crying after about ten minutes. She noted that when she left his bedroom door open, it would be closed when she went to him. If she left it closed, it was open.

The stairway to the attic had a heavy door in the corner of his room. We left it closed as a matter of course. She frequently found it open when she checked on Will. Wasps nesting in the attic came into is room from there. She feared they were the reason he cried from being stung. But she never found any sting marks on him. When the door persisted on opening on its own, even when slammed shut. I put a bent nail in the frame to secure it. It worked.

The other curious thing about the attic was that it often sounded like somebody was walking in it. The problem with that was, of course, nobody else was in the house. To complicate matters, there was no floor in the attic, only two 12 x 2 planks running the length of the structure.

Margaret stopped taking afternoon naps for a different reason. Both Pat and I witnessed the phenomenon of the room sounding like there was someone in it with a deep, labored breathing problem (as though they were seriously ill). It seemed to be coming from the ceiling of the far left corner facing the street. I went into the attic with a flashlight, climbing on the wooden joists to shine the light down between the roof and the wall to see if there was a hole in the structure that was activated by the wind. I found nothing, but the breathing noises stopped. However, Margaret still gave up naps.

As time progressed, Pat got more creeped-out. One day she told me that as she was changing the bed-linens in our room she left the room to go downstairs with the kids for lunch. When she came back upstairs she found piles of dirty laundry were folded on the bed, and she knew she didn't fold dirty laundry. Thoroughly spooked, she went into the hall and believed she saw a pre-teen girl on the stairway landing who obviously had the symptoms of Downs Syndrome smiling at her.

Another item that we both noticed was that the downstairs foyer closet facing the entrance had a full-length mirror in which little light was reflecting. It was probably a bad silvering job, but it always seemed forbidding. We seldom intentionally looked into it.

Pat confided that she was afraid to go into the basement to do the laundry. It had a dirt floor and we half-jokingly theorized that there was a body buried there.

On November 22, 1963, I came home a little early from work because of Kennedy's assassination. As I came in the front door, Pat was just coming down the stairs and was on the landing near the top. As I was coming up to greet her, Margaret came running out of the bathroom, excitedly crying, "People in toilet! People in toilet!"

In her excitement she jumped from the top step into Pat's arms, clinging to her and actually biting her between the neck and left shoulder. Pat pried her loose and calmed her down. We thought she meant she dropped one of the Fisher-Price little toy people into the bowl. I checked and found nothing. Margaret repeated, "People in toilet!"

Apparently she had seen something that really frightened her.

The TV was agog with the news of the Kennedy shooting and almost in sympathy with the nation's frantic state, the weather turned really stormy. That night the wind repeatedly lifted the roof from under the eaves a few inches and dropped it back on the top of the walls with a loud thump, giving both of us chills. People everywhere had trouble sleeping that night.

The next day when Pat was comparing notes with the next-door neighbor, she told Pat that no one had ever rented the house for more than six months. We decided to move as soon as possible into the new house, even before it was finished.

Oddly enough the old woman who owned the house was named Degrendel. The name of the malevolent being of Anglo-Saxon mythology, Grendel, is one of three in the epic poem Beowulf (AD 700–1000).

Ralph Olsen, the Employment Manager of the Highland Park factory, invited us to Southfield, a growing suburb off Nine Mile Road. He had an older house there with a small farmette. He practically adopted us.

We looked at a development on Plumbrooke Drive and found what we wanted. Pat could pick out the details with the builder.

Again, being new to the game, I did not notice that I would have to do the back-breaking job of laying the sod lawn myself. I didn't realize how much the back yard sloped until I got a price estimate for a low chain-link fence. Rolled up sod and a pile of dirt were dumped in the driveway. This became my new garden. Margaret and Will went through the motions of helping. Pat was pregnant with Melissa, and was cautious about possible strains.

As luck (and Synchronicity) would have it, a tree in front of the Highland Park Machining plant was being removed. It was fed into a huge wood-chipper. When I asked the foreman where they dumped the truckload of wood-chips he said, "Anywhere you want them." I gave him my home address and when I got home that night my backyard had a one-story stack of ground poplar tree.

I filled the sloping space, but I didn't find out the dark side of this until the following spring. I managed to fill he incline to level the backyard even with the front, but never dreamed that the chips would ferment. After I had covered them with sod, there began to be little puddles of green goop developing. My friend Ralph warned me not to strike any matches near them because they were little wells of methanol being generated by the decomposing wood. I could not let the kids play back there until the following year.

When Bill Haga left in May 1964, I hired John Vacek as the editor. I interviewed him on a Friday, telling him that he would start on Monday. However, I spent the whole weekend worrying about the fact that I forgot to ask him if he could type. Fortunately, he could. We began a lifelong friendship and I worked with him again at Butte Knit years later.

As a tangential item, let me mention my acquisition of a very inusual item, which will re-enter the story shortly. Before I left for Detroit, I made a brief visit to my parents in New Jersey.

In 1952 we had moved to this house across the street from Pop's gas station. We lived on the top floor, and my room was marked by the two windows just to the left of the Dodge sign. I can honestly say that the neon lights that illuminated my room, and the traffic noises from the  Boulevard, never caused me to miss any sleep. I simply accepted it as a normal part of city life.

The storefront on the first floor was supposedly a shipping transfer office. We never saw anyone go in or out. Pop said it was a bookie joint that consisted of two guys who took bets over the phone. What went on there was none of our business.

The second floor apartment was occupied by WNY Police Sgt. Harry Harper. He became a Lieutenant when my father loaned him $500 to ensure his promotion. In return, he gifted me with a gold-inlaid pistol.

The circumstances, as I recall them, were that Harper's teenage son was a drug addict. He was stealing guns from his father's large collection and selling them for drugs. When Harry found out, he gave his son a beating. That same night he had a heart attack. As he 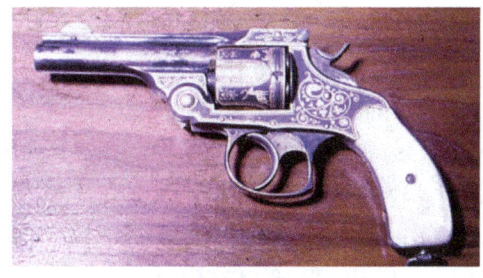 lay dying in the hospital, his greatest fear was that his son would sell the remaining guns after he was dead.

When he was released a few days later he gave all his guns to another cop, with the exception of this one. He wanted Pop to give it to me.

The folklore that surrounds it was that it had been a piece of evidence in a murder trial of a prohibition bootlegger. Allegedly, the bootlegger bought it from a Prohibition rum-runner sailor who smuggled it into the USA in one of his ship's air vents. He, in turn, had taken it off the body of a

Central American Banana Republic revolutionary, whose name is engraved on the handle, along with the information that it was made in Eibar, Spain. Supposedly it is a Smith and Wesson copy. Google shows that there were more than this one made. The basic .35 caliber revolver is worth at least $350. When the bootlegger was convicted, the gun went into the New York City Police evidence locker, scheduled for destruction.

A NYC Police Captain named Black was responsible for dumping such things into the New York Harbor. However, when he came across this gun, he recognized it as a piece of artwork. He pocketed it and later sold it to Harper. Harry asked Pop for it back when he recovered his health, offering a .45 caliber 1911A1 Army automatic in its place. However, I had already moved to Detroit and the gun with me.

At lunch one day I discussed my haunted house with Bart Huthwaite, a work friend at Chrysler. He told me his father used a Spiritualist medium to get leads on business opportunities. They were often good money makers.

He connected me with Kay Cation, who became good friends with Pat and me. She predicted that we would be friends for years and we both would move to South Carolina in the future. I had no idea how I would get there.

She moved to Spartanburg, SC to live with her son when her husband, Cliff, died in 1967. In 1970 I went there to work for Butte Knit and we renewed our friendship.

When we moved from Courville to Southfield we apparently brought a restless spirit with us to the new house. At 5 a.m. one morning, Pat and I were awakened by a loud crash from inside our walk-in closet. I jumped up and opened the closet door. A coffee can full of buttons had left the shelf and spewed buttons all over the floor. We had no explanation.

We started attending Cation's séances held in a dark, light-proof room in her house's basement. Pat got the image of someone standing next to a white hospital room divider holding a coffeepot, shaking his head *no*. She took it to mean she was drinking too much coffee. A few days later I got an emergency phone call from Pat that Margaret had climbed up onto a kitchen counter and got tangled in an electric coffeepot wire, spilling it on herself. She was scalded on her behind and her right leg with 2nd degree burns. I rushed home and we took her to the hospital where they dressed the burn.

Margaret's recollection of the event as an adult was that the coffee pot moved toward her. It would have been physically unlikely (if not impossible), for her to climb up to the countertop because her small size.

At the time she complained that it was too painful to walk since the burn extended down to her foot. The prescribed medical treatment at that time was frequent application of Vaseline over the entire burn and to cover it with a clean white diaper. We carried her from one room to the other until she went to bed.

That night, as I was leaving to go to the store for some milk, we had another strange occurrence. As Pat closed the front door behind me and we both heard a loud noise from the kitchen.

I went back inside with Pat. We found the plastic Dixie cup dispenser, which had been fastened to the wall over the sink, lay shattered in the middle of the kitchen floor. We had no idea how that happened.

Afterward we decided it was time for an *exorcism or something*.

I called Kay the next day and invited her to dinner that night to examine the problem. That evening, after we finished eating, we put Margaret to bed. I gave Kay a test I was sure she could not fudge. It consisted of a large kraft paper envelope, containing the pistol I had received from Harry Harper in New Jersey. I wrapped it in newspaper to conceal its shape.

Kay claimed a healing ability and an ESP talent known as *Psychometry* (from the Greek meaning "spirit measure"), also known as *object reading*, or *psychoscopy*. It is a form of extrasensory perception (ESP) characterized by the reader's ability to make relevant associations from an object of unknown history by making physical contact with the item. Supporters assert that an object may have an energy field that transfers knowledge regarding that object's history. While the concept has been widely criticized, it is far more interesting and fun to believe than to deny.

I thought it would be a good test if I offered an object she could not possibly know about. I started by asking her what she got from the unopened package. However, she immediately identified the contents as a gun just by holding the package.

She said she got the image of someone in a jail cell, saying, "I was framed." Then she saw what she described as a "Black Forest." She was close enough for me. The gun was taken from a bootlegger, charged with murder.

And it was stolen by a Captain *Black* of the NYC Police Department from the Evidence Room.

From there, I asked her to see if she could shed any light on our poltergeist. She said, "He was a very sick and confused young man when he died in the house on Courville Street. But he did not really know he was dead. His family was very unpleasant. He followed you to the new house because he was attracted by the love you radiated. He meant no harm but craved attention." (Pat immediately recalled our fears that someone was buried in the basement's dirt floor).

Kay told him that he had died and now should let himself move to the Light. After a few more minutes of silence, she said he had crossed over. At that time our attention was drawn to the steps. Margaret was coming down from the upper split-level. She stood there in her nightgown and began walking by herself down the stairs. I ran over to get her and she spent the next fifteen minutes on Kay's lap. She said her burn did not hurt any more, and the redness disappeared in a couple days with no scars. We had no further unexplained disturbances.

It sounds like a TV episode, but I was there.

Kay was a card reader, and laid the foundations for my future involvement with Tarot cards 20 years later. We did, in fact, renew our friendship with Kay as predicted when I was hired by Butte Knit in 1969.

OCTOBER 16, 1965
MELISSA ROBIN IS BORN IN DETROIT

Number Three of Pat's six-child family plan was realized on October 16, 1965 in Detroit with the birth of Melissa Robin. I can still recall the look on her face in the isolette as she was rolled out for view. Her bright blue eyes were open earlier than most babies. I'll swear she had a mischievous grin on her face that said, "I'm here! Watch out!"

We quickly learned that to get her attention, the name Melissa was to be half-shouted with a note of exasperation. I learned years later in Arizona, when she was given to wandering about the neighborhood feeding lonely horses, that Pat and I were known locally not as Mr. and Mrs. Schroeder, but as "Melissa's parents." I have not been able to find any baby pictures of her in Detroit, but we made up for it later.

I do not know how Pat came to select her name. This was the name of a nymph that cared for young Zeus in Greek mythology. But when time came for her Christening, the local Catholic priest could not make any Christian associations. There has never been a Saint Melissa. He made up his own (incorrect) justification that the name is a variation of Saint Elizabeth.

Melissa means honeybee in Greek and if you must have a Biblical connection, further investigation reveals the Hebrew equivalent is Deborah. As an English given name, Melissa has been used since the 18th century. In Persian, Melissa means Red Rose.

In defining Melissa as a person, it seems logical to me to take the obvious path of word association. The question being, where do I start? The answer: anywhere! Any one idea blossoms in a dozen directions — horses, dogs, farming, drawing, painting, writing, farm animals and children.

She has always been a bright spot, even when everyone else might be gloomy. In adult life, Melissa sublimated both her artistic and writing talent in favor of helping her children become successful.

She was never one for girlie clothes and fashion statements, but she lent herself to exhibiting Pat's sewing talents when we lived in Spartanburg, SC. All four of Pat's kids appeared in a local television broadcast.

I think the next time she really got dressed up was for her prom.

The other souvenir of Spartanburg was a life-sized fiberglass bear that now lives in her yard in Littlestown, PA.

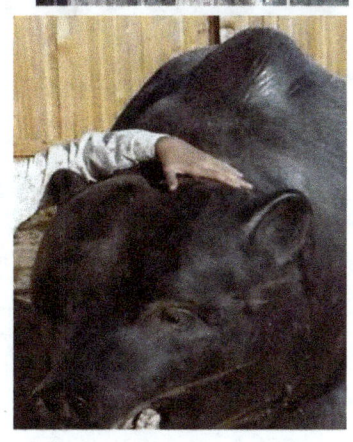

As far back as I recall, Melissa loved to express herself in picture form. When she learned to print, she added commentary.

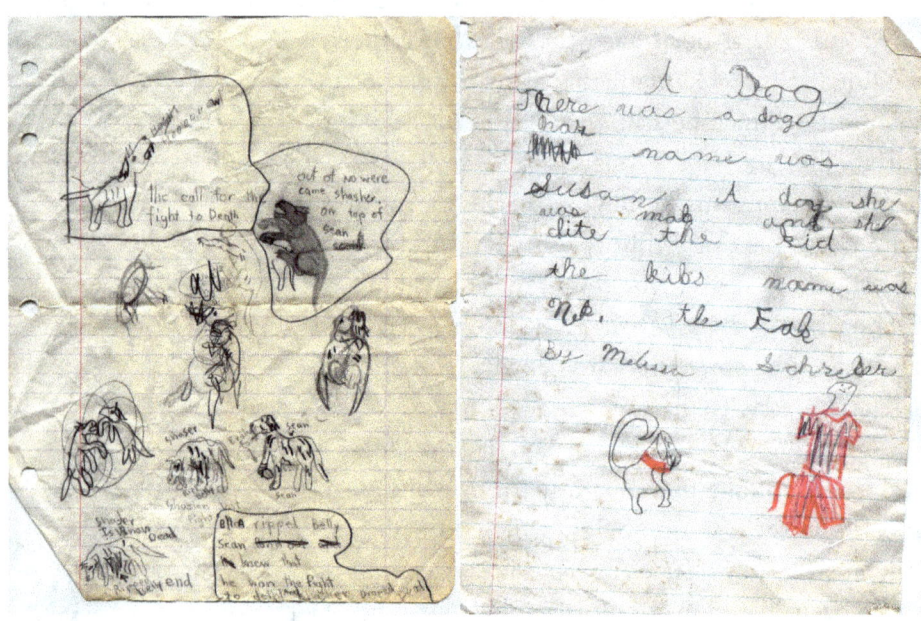

Although I cannot locate an example, one of Melissa's favorite topics was a long shot view of racehorses frolicking in a field. I regard it as prescient — sort of an early view of a future memory.

They were drawn in the style illustrated by this picture.

It was not until we moved to Finksburg I saw the actual scene take shape. Every morning I drove past Sagamore Farms fields in Glyndon that looked remarkably like the pictures Melissa created years before we ever lived near the region.

If I had to pick one photo that captures the true Melissa, it would be this one.

When it came to dogs, there was not a time she did not have at least one. Lingo was one she shared with me. Because of Pennsylvania State wildlife laws she could no longer keep it. Lingo was 1/2 husky, 1/4 German shepherd & 1/4 wolf.

Unfortunately, she influenced the behavior of her kennel-mate Banner. They got into serious trouble with the local dog-catcher because they had reverted to their hunting instincts. We chose not to fight the county about keeping her, which we all regret.

On the other hand, Lingo protected me from possible harm when she accompanied me one Christmas.

I had to deliver children's presents to a welfare location in Anne Arundel County. It was well known that the neighborhood was a dangerous place for white people. When I got there my planned escort had not arrived and I sat in my van, obviously packed with gifts. Lingo sat in the passenger seat while I waited. It did not take long for two tough-looking teens to approach.

I got out with Lingo on a short chain.

"What'cha got? "one kid asked.

"Christmas party stuff," I answered and tightened up on Lingo's collar. She growled and pulled on the leash.

The other kid said, "Why that dog got one blue eye and one brown?"

"She's half wolf," I answered.

"Is that an attack dog?" one said.

I made her growl again, and she lurched at the duo. "Yeah, but I don't know how to control her."

Both of them turned and briskly returned to the yard they had come from.

Before Melissa established her own household, I would say her favorite pooch was PupDog.

Melissa's art painting talents are as good as Pat's in some respects. However, she has not been able to take the time necessary to develop her talents. Instead she has chosen to devote her time to the development of her children's success.

In 1983 Melissa was chosen to attend a Gifted and Talented program session at Goucher College. What sticks out in my memory of that occasion was a demonstration of our family's propensity for getting around the rules. The country was going through one of its food fads. This time it was avoidance of sugar and unhealthy snacks (*as defined by God knew who*).

The theory was that students would perform better on a controlled diet. Hence, no one was supposed to eat anything not provided by the program.

No visitors were allowed, lest they sneak unhealthy food to the kids. Over the phone Melissa laid out a clandestine snack drop. At a given time Melissa was to station herself on the circular drive in front of the college.

We packed a goodies bag (re: Pvt. Schroeder and the Fort Dix C-Ration evasion 30 years earlier. *Synchronicity, Part One, Page 175).*

At a specified time, within ten minutes, I drove onto the entrance drive, spotted Melissa, and handed off the drop. If we were observed she was to say it was clean underwear. It worked. Schroeders just don't like other people interfering with their eating habits.

Halloween was her vehicle for outrageous body paint jobs.

Melissa got swept along in the Schroeder Family's fascination with the stage, but her forte was primarily in the stage crew.

Melissa worked closely with Pat in her many art venues, especially ceramics. I have not been able to differentiate between Pat's work and some pieces done by Melissa.

In 1984, Melissa helped me at a Westinghouse employee event with a performing artist who painted a canvas for her she still has.

In the 1980s, when I was deeply into my Tarot readings, I began to design a deck to be called *The Reverse of the Tarot*. The idea was to project the images on the cards as if the same scene were viewed from 180 degrees opposite of the scene. Accordingly, the reading of the cards was the obverse of the generally accepted one.

Melissa drew me prototypes of three cards as starters … The Magician, The Tower, and the three of Wands. Due to my own procrastinations I waited too long to try to market the idea. Someone else did so successfully, as the *New Vision Tarot*.

Rider-Waite   *Melissa*   *New Vision*

Synchronicity 2 • 151

Rider-Waite *Melissa* *New Vision*

Rider-Waite *Melissa* *New Vision*

1991

In 1991 Melissa made a move I never could have predicted. She committed to becoming a farm-person by marrying Steve Steele.

Actually, she was married twice in one day. Marcia George officiated over both ceremonies, but as she was not licensed to perform weddings in Pennsylvania, a brief wedding ceremony was done earlier at the Westminster Pond Park in Westminster.

Her botanical commitment had been to raising African Violets, and had over two-dozen plants at one time. She made some basic adjustments to her botanical interests, so she focused upon on gardening, while Steve was the farmer. Her garden produced cabbages for her homemade sauerkraut that rivals Pennsylvania Dutch versions.

She feels she found her calling in caring for her children and her animals, which were sometimes one in the same. Nevertheless, Melissa undertook the basic nitty-gritty tasks of feeding the animals and assisting in the birthing of livestock. Caity and Cutter pursued whole-hearted competitive involvement in raising prize-winning steers. It was a rare occasion when we saw Melissa without her kids.

Melissa is the only one of my children who followed the writing road. However, she chooses to write for her own enjoyment. While I re-created specific historical events and time periods in my books, she went on to create a new world in a science-fiction trilogy. I've read some of her stuff. Melissa has artistry when it comes to creating images with words.

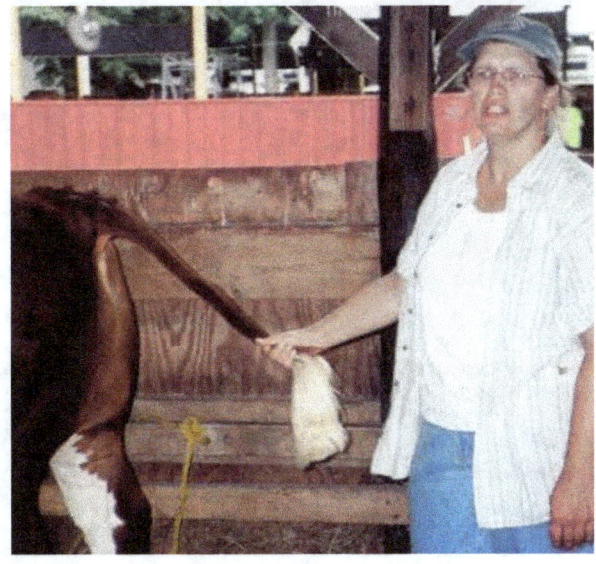

Caity's passion is law, but she and Cutter are able writers. Melissa and

Caity joined me at a writing seminar in case Caity might choose to pursue that avenue of expression in the future.

On December 4, 2011 Fideli published the illustrated edition of *In der Fuehrer's Face*. I included Melissa as a co-author with the hope that she would use the credit toward getting her own work published. It didn't happen.

One achievement I envy is that she got a Jaguar that was better than mine.

1964

One of the people casually introduced into my life was Al Knight, my supervisor at Chrysler Headquarters. The synchronicity that evolved about him was his introducing me to the communication consultants who were directly responsible for one of my most important professional achievements — the Best Annual Report Award of 1967 at Lipton. Without that link, I doubt if I would have won it.

This was Pat with Elsie and Al Knight on a Chrysler-sponsored Management family outing at Belle Isle Park, adjacent to Detroit. It was the first amusement park Margaret and Will had been to. They talked about it for months, constantly asking when we would go again.

Meanwhile, back at Chrysler, after the United Auto Workers contract negotiations with Chrysler were successfully completed, it became painfully obvious to everyone that the communication program was over. Very cost-conscious auto plant managers felt no need for the continued services of the communication mavens until the next negotiation cycle, some years in the future.

As soon as the first two communicators got their lay-off notices we all hit the panic button. My button was, as usual, *The Wall Street Journal* want ads. It wasn't until after I announced my leaving that I found that I was on the list of those who would have stayed employed by Chrysler.

Before I left Chrysler, I decided to fulfill a long-standing dream … I wanted to buy a car right off the assembly line. I would be the first person to drive it. It would have been built just for me. I bought a 1964 Plymouth station wagon at production cost price ($1,900) to replace my company-provided Barracuda. I was very excited about the whole thing.

With three kids we needed our first wagon.

However, after I had it for a month and had left the company, I found that the dark tales were true … when UAW workers were alerted that a car was for a company manager, they subtly sabotaged it.

Sometimes, they would do things like put a marble in one of the doors so it made a mysterious noise every time you stopped and the marble rolled forward. Sometimes a cheese sandwich from somebody's lunch was left under the rear seat to rot and stink up the car.

In my case, they installed a rear left wheel bearing without grease that caused a continual thumping noise. But the big thing was putting the wrong carburetor on the engine that made its performance so bad it couldn't get out of its own way.

One of the things no one warned me about was a surprise after I moved from Detroit to Rochester … Dealers did not want to service cars not bought from them, regardless of Chrysler guarantees.

Before I leave the topic of Chrysler-UAW, one more story:

FARGO trucks were sold around the world. They were made on the Dodge truck line and were identical to those sold in the USA. During a severe labor conflict period, UAW men who put the logos on the truck had a diabolical idea for sabotage. They combined the letters for FARGO and  DODGE to spell FORD. It is believed that at least ten of them found their way to Canadian dealers.

1966 — XEROX

The success of the Chrysler communication program was well-known among the Dow-Jones 500 corporations. In less than a month (June 1966), I got an offer from one of the hottest of the bunch … Xerox. They had been cherry-picking managers from all the other big names. Ted Bonus, a former Kodak career man was lured away with an offer he couldn't resist. He hired me to create a Management Communication Department in the Mickey Dover style.

The relocation package from Detroit to Rochester, NY, was so generous; it almost paid for our new house in Pittsford, NY. It was the most luxurious home I have ever owned. When my parents came to visit us there, my father had only one description: "It looks like a Doctor lives here!"

Working for Xerox matured my professional thinking. The first week I was there, an incident took place that brought things into focus.

One morning I met Ted Bonus outside the Xerox Building, and we entered the elevator together. We were joined by C. Peter McColough, the CEO of Xerox and I was perfunctorily introduced as the new Manger of Management Communication. He acknowledged my existence and Ted and I got off at our floor.

An hour later Bonus came into my office and said, "The President of Rank-Xerox in England died of a heart attack last night. The boss wants you to write a message of condolence to the employees of the English company for his signature right away." So I immediately set about writing a message of McColough's heartfelt grief over the loss to the employees of such a forward-thinking leader. I had only exchanged ten words with the man, not to mention the fact that I had barely heard of Rank-Xerox up until now. I did what I was told and the only thing I heard about the event was that he signed the piece and we modified it for distribution to the American employees.

In later years I wrote many "personal" messages and speeches for Vice Presidents and other top executives. As a result, I doubt if any public figures and politicians have any knowledge or emotions beyond those they are provided with by speechwriters like me.

FOR THE FIRST TIME I KNEW WHAT COPYWRITERS REALLY DO

Life for the Schroeders in Pittsford, NY, met all the expectations we had for my corporate climb to he top.

JUNE 19, 1967
MELANIE RUTH IS BORN IN ROCHESTER, NY

Things appeared to be going well for me at Xerox. Pat's Baby Number Four, Melanie Ruth, was born in Rochester on June 19, 1967.

She lives where I would probably be if I stayed on my original trajectory. Sammy Davis, Jr. said, "When you leave New York, Man, you don't go anywhere." As I grew up in New Jersey I can testify that NJ natives feel the same about their turf. She's had opportunities to go elsewhere, but declined. When she turned down a transfer to Atlanta, I could only assume that she would rather be unemployed in New Jersey than an executive in Georgia. Consider the educational impact on the kids alone.

Melanie is my "Jersey Girl."

Melanie's complaint of her teenage years still rings true today; "I can do *anything* ... but I don't know what it is!"

Ironically she helps other people find out what they can do. In her beginning years her jobs centered on training and education for welfare women up to "At Risk" boys. Later she helped managers become executives. Her employers' names read like a Who's Who directory of internationally known companies — Mercedes-Benz, Mars Chocolate, Simon and Schuster.

Throughout her life she has sought the development of a variety of skills. In high school she undertook voice lessons with no definable objective I can recall. However, when one of her friends died tragically, she performed at her memorial service at Westminster High, doing a solo rendition of Jim Croce's *Time in a Bottle*.

If I could save time in a bottle
The first thing that I'd like to do
Is to save every day
'Til eternity passes away
Just to spend them with you.

It was the only time I recall her singing solo in public.

That is not to say she did not perform in another capacity. She was an excellent actress and played the ingénue role in the Carroll County Arts Councils' 1982 production of "*My Three Angels.*"

It was the only time she, Will and I performed together. In 1984 she played the lead in a play where she memorized virtually everybody's lines in the play, amazing Nana who was visiting at the time. I was equally impressed.

At the Maryland Renaissance Festival she teamed up with Chris Murphy — presenting Shakespeare vignette scenes such as *The Taming of the Shrew.*

When she was a child, she couldn't wait to be an adult. As an adult she does her best to keep herself in a state of physical fitness and attractiveness of a much younger woman. She was a devout sun-worshiper. She gives herself over totally to watching her diet and natural exercises such as running.

Melanie excelled in jobs and activities that drew on her intellect and abilities to get along with others. After laying the groundwork with courses at the community college, she received a full scholarship at Towson University for a Bachelor's degree. Her Grade Point Average of 3.6 allowed her to graduate *cum laude* (with distinction).

Next to me, she is the member of the family whose life was so extensively influenced by contact with Allen Hicks. Through one of his contracts, Melanie met and married Paul McGill, resulting in two outstanding children, Kelly and Eric.

Developing her skills with electronic video equipment, she and Eric reworked my 1951 silent Frankenstein movie into a YouTube event. Eric posted it on YouTube; search for *The Frankenstein Monster and The Enforcer* by Eric M. Go to **https://www.youtube.com/watch?v=aNgqLTD3SmM**.

When I had my stores in Washingfton's Union Station, Melanie often took over the management of the *Royal Flush* playing cards portion. She also took her turns peddling artifacts in *Schrader Scientific*.

The fact that she was my only kid who livd in New Jersey, made her the obvious candidate as a conection with the Nicolas Family. Here we are on Elsie and Nick's 50th Wedding Aanniversary in 1995.

At one point Melanie helped me fulfill a long time secret desire ... I spent a week-long vacation in the kind of log cabin I wanted to build since I was a teenager. I house-sat a place they rented at Greenwood Lake while she and Paul went skiing.

Life seemed to be on an even keel. However, it was the proverbial calm before the storm. My old friend, CEO McColough, made some public predictions of Xerox stock dividends that he could not deliver on. He lost his position, and Xerox Corporation was forced into massive downsizing in August 1967. It caused thousands of employees to be terminated ... The Manger of Management Communication was a one them.

LIPTON TRANSITION

It was obvious that I was becoming what the *Wall Street Journal* calls a "Corporate Gypsy." Every two years I would get a promotion or a better job that required me to move the family. I started in New Jersey, moved to Baltimore, MD; we lived in Southfield, Michigan; then to Pittsford, NY. (Rochester). Now it was time to go back to New Jersey.

1968

The guiding principle was the same as it was the first time I met Harry Smith at the Westinghouse Defense Center in 1959. The only change was that I was no longer interested in being a *young* executive ... I had a taste of being a senior executive, and I liked it.

I had a vision of myself behind a big wooden desk in my own paneled office. I saw Thomas J. Lipton as a means to that end.

Responding to a WSJ ad was becoming *de rigueur* for me, but this episode had a new wrinkle. My boss would be Aaron Rubin, an industrial psychologist, who introduced a psychological-testing regimen into the hiring equation.

Fortunately, I had been reading Freud and Jung since I was 17 because they  interested me. I also had thoroughly enjoyed a course on Abnormal Psychology at the University of Colorado. It spent a lot of time on psych testing. Therefore, I was familiar with almost all the tests I would be taking. They included the *Thematic Apperception Test* (*TAT*), a projective psychological test. It's a bunch of ambiguous pictures of people and the test subject makes up  narratives about them. The objective is to reveal their underlying motives, concerns, and the way they see the social world. They are very effective. I scaled my answers to project an image I thought they were looking for.

I avoided stuff in the Rorschach Test that might seem extreme.

In the questionnaire portion, I emphasized an interest in creativity. For example, when they

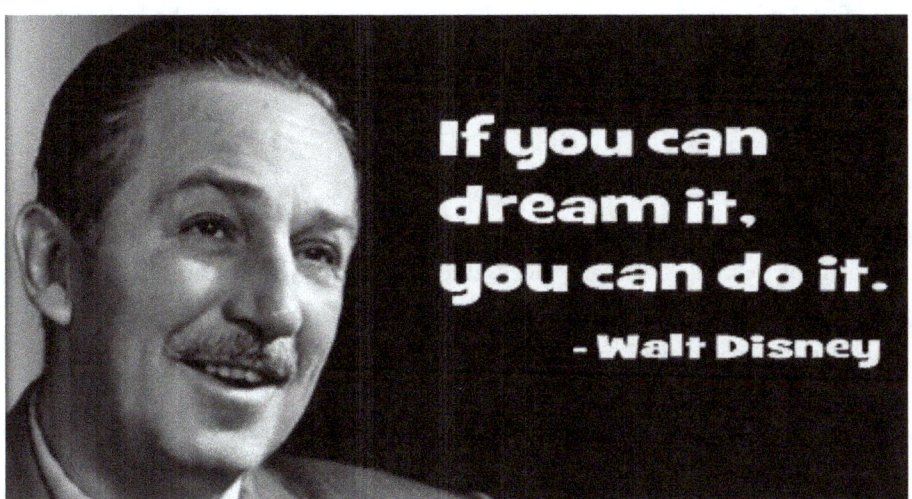

asked "If you could spend a day with anyone living or dead, who would it be and why?" I answered: Walt Disney.

He was the most positive and creative person I thought of.

Apparently I chose the right responses, Aaron Rubin told me I did well. However, a few months later when he got used to me, he said he guessed I knew how to skewer the test results. My answers were too good.

I was offered the job of Communication Manager for the T.J. Lipton Division of Unilever Corporation. It had moved from Hoboken NJ, (where Thomas Lipton would park his Rolls Royce in the freight elevator often) to posh offices at Englewood Cliffs. I matched the upgrade in environment, by introducing an employee magazine that won several awards.

They paid for relocating the Schroeders in Hillsdale, NJ. But, again I proved my inability to make good real estate deals. I contracted for a house I thought would suit our needs, but quickly discovered (too late) that the hot water system did not work, and that the foundation had a crack in the basement wall.

Even worse, it had symptoms of being another haunted house, like the one in Detroit. (No wonder it was so cheap). The history of this house was one of violence. It was being sold on court order because both the man and his wife who lived there were being indicted for attempted murder of each other. (We never followed up to see how it turned out).

Pat, who was psychically sensitive, felt it as soon as she entered the house. When she was alone during the day with the kids, she said she often felt like there was a fierce argument going on in another part of the house. It took the form of hearing muffled voices, like when there is a radio on in another room. You can hear it, but are unable to distinguish what is being said.

Margaret was only 7 or 8 years old, but today nearly 50 years later still remembers the house as a fearsome place. She also experienced the phenomenon of thinking the TV was on downstairs, only to find out when she got up and went downstairs that Pat and I had gone to bed. She gave up her room to share one with Will because of the weird and terrifying dreams she experienced there. When she played in Melissa's room she felt a compulsion to get out of the room after a short period of time

She and Will played in a space off the attic that they called their secret room. Will stopped wearing his cowboy outfit in favor of wearing a skeleton

costume left over from Halloween. He pretended to be invisible when he wore it. Frequently, after going to sleep, they would awake for some reason and sit on the staircase, falling back to sleep until Pat saw them. Reluctantly, they went back in their room.

She also recalled that the small room where we had the TV was the scene of kid fights on many occasions. Pat finally moved the TV out to the living room since it seemed to be the source of antagonisms for no apparent reason.

Margaret feels that the place had some aspects like that of the house in *The Amityville Horror*. There were pictograph writings on the wall bordering the staircase to the basement. In fact, she recalls asking Pat if they were in a Satanic language. Under the white paint in the kitchen was a coat of red-orange. There was a door that looked like a pantry, but when you opened it, there was a short staircase to nowhere that abutted in the ceiling.

We finally prevailed on the real estate agent who sold us the place to find us another house, based on the cracked foundation. We moved to Morningside Avenue in Park Ridge, which fortunately only had normal problems like a flooded septic tank.

FEBRUARY 6, 1969
HOWARD CHRISTOPHER IS BORN IN WESTWOOD, NJ

Baby Number 5, Howard Christopher, was born February 6, 1969, at Pascack Valley Hospital in Westwood, NJ.

The day after he was born, we had a 12-inch snowfall, complete with icy roads. When it came time to bring him home, the roads were too dangerous to drive on. The local Fire Department brought him and Pat home in an ambulance. Tante Ella was already staying with us since my mother couldn't get there. She took over the Granny duties for a couple days until Nana could make it.

INDIVIDUAL ACHIEVEMENTS

Exceptional ability makes itself known in unpredictable ways. Howard's abilities manifested themselves in two diverse fields. In addition to being a master computer geek, he is the Schroeder Family Chef.

One of my earliest recollections of Howard as a child is of him lying on the couch in Arizona. We thought he was suffering from a bad case of sunburn, assuming he was sensitive to our new desert environment. However, the doctor diagnosed him as having scarlet fever.

Scarlet fever develops in some people who have strep throat, and is also known as scarlatina. It features a bright red rash that covers most of the body, and is almost always accompanied by a sore throat and a high fever.

Pat and I panicked, fearing it would spread to the other children. My sister had it when she was ten years old. She was whisked off to quarantined hospital ward for a week. It was once considered a serious, often fatal, childhood illness, but antibiotic treatments have made it less threatening.

Howard ran a temperature close to 104 degrees. At one point, Pat and I spent a 24-hour period changing cool compresses to break the fever. It worked and he made a rapid recovery without any other kids showing symptoms.

My next memorable image is of being called to his school in the First or Second Grade. They were afraid he suffered from a form of attention span deficit since he did not seem to be involved in class activities. We later determined that he was just bored with school. More than one of his siblings observed that school subject matter

was repetitious. "They keep telling me the same thing over and over. I understood it the first time."

Skipping to his high school years, it seems that the problem persisted. Pat and I had to persuade him to finish high school, offering to send him to a technical school as a reward.

In the end, he chose to join the Army, but was rejected the first time he applied because he was too honest — when they asked him if he ever smoked pot, he admitted that he did. At the time it was considered drug addiction. However, it was suggested that he could make another attempt by going to the MD Army National Guard the next day before the information was formalized and spread to all recruiters.

He was accepted and was sent to Machinist's School in Aberdeen, where he excelled as Soldier-of-the-Month and graduated as Honor Graduate at the top of his class.

However, the Army did not meet his expectations, and he managed a transfer/enlistment after a year into the Air Force. Howard's life in the Air Force was dynamic and rewarding. He excelled in the service's cooking school at Lowrey AFB in Denver, CO and achieved Honor Graduate again and unit recognition in the field.

After winning various intra-service competitions, he was assigned to augment Air Force National Guard and Reserve Units to train others in Massachusetts, New York, and Michigan.

As a mess sergeant, Howard was exposed to the AF computer-controlled inventory and activity planning programs. He fell in love with computers.

He remained in the Maryland 175th Air Force Reserve in Maryland. Then in the Bosnian War, their A-10s participated in peacekeeping missions from a base in Italy. Here Howard was put in charge of the Officers' Mess, operating 24-hours a day for the benefit of the A-10 pilots enforcing the "no-fly" zone over Bosnia-Herzegovina as a part of the U.N./NATO task force.

When he returned to USA, Howard continued his pursuit of a cooking career. The Marriott Corporation sent him to Florida to a special cooking school, enlarging his abilities to allow him to become a chef.

However, while he could pursue a career in cooking, his inner desires are focused on the growing computer world.

He joined forces with his friend Cliff Webster and constructed a massive computer system in their apartment, on which they trained themselves in the state-of-the-art computer technology. They prepared themselves to start their own companies and personal careers.

While I was working for the Welfare-to-Work program in Anne Arundel County, one of the teachers of basic computer skills had to leave for health reasons. I was able to recommend Howard to fill the vacancy. From there he ran on his own with the virtual "bit in his teeth."

Subsequent assignments put him in front of a class of Midshipmen at the U.S. Naval Academy in Annapolis. His main problem was to keep them from knowing he was a Sergeant in the Air Force — Naval Officers cannot learn anything from enlisted men.

He has since developed his skills and reputation to the point that he has taught seminars across the U.S., in Europe and Asia, along with on-line classes to audiences in Brazil and the Netherlands (the latter starting at 3:00 AM, EST). At the same time all his professional development was going on, his other interests blossomed and diverged from the Schroeder family norms.

While he was working in Milwaukee, a number of years ago, he took up SCUBA diving in the frigid waters of Lake Michigan. He has since pursued the same pastime in the warmer waters of Central America. Not only there, but in the East China Sea (Japan); Caribbean Sea (Many places in Cozumel, Mexico); Dominican Republic (and others); and the Hawaiian Pacific Ocean. He has also explored many freshwater locations throughout the US and a shark feeding-frenzy dive in Buzzards Bay off Cape Cod.

This led to his buying a home on the Chesapeake Bay, where he docked a power houseboat, which is currently undergoing an overhaul at this writing.

He dabbled in water scooters to the delight of other family members during his super lawn parties prior to a hurricane wipeout.

He is also an accomplished equestrian, but pursued that hobby only while he was dating a long-time girlfriend who owned a horse. Like other members of the Schroeder Clan he enjoyed getting into a costume. His two most notable cases were a 6-foot banana and as a clown for Halloween.

When asked why he did not go to college, his response is "If I had, I would probably be sitting in a cubicle in New York or Washington, doing something somebody else thinks I should do."

Howard has had a long-term romance with cars, going back to his teenage years.

Currently he is farmore interested in motorcycles. Most recently he acquired a sidecar in which he hopes to take his dog (Theodorable) for rides, complete with harness and goggles.

2007 URBAN CHALLENGE

In 2007 Howard participated in The DARPA Grand Challenge competition for American autonomous vehicles. It was funded by the Department of Defense. He won a contract to supply a network of computers to support an extensive driverless-car development program. He hired Margaret to help him set up and maintain it in the California Mojave desert (Victorville).

DARPA's mission was to sponsor revolutionary, high-payoff research into self-driving cars that bridge the gap between fundamental discoveries and military use. The initial DARPA Grand Challenge was created to spur the development of technologies needed to create the first fully autonomous ground vehicles capable of completing a substantial off-road course within a limited time. In this event, the DARPA Urban Challenge extended the Initial Challenge to autonomous operation in a mock urban environment.

After the challenge was over, John and his wife, Nicole, drove Howard's truck back to Maryland from Victorville, loaded with computer hardware. The monitor I am using at this writing was part of that program.

CREDIT WHERE CREDIT'S DUE

At this point I want to give Pat some of the recognition she deserves for making my own personal success possible. It wasn't until years later that I became aware of how difficult it was for the rest of the family. Margaret told me that she had been to thirteen schools during our wanderings.

I honestly did not know how demanding our constant relocations were on Pat. She managed all the moves from state to state, without complaining. I was swept up in the excitement of a new job, filling all my days. But poor Pat had to endure lonely days, taking care of a growing family. I was seldom there to give her a fraction of the support she provided for me. She never complained. If she did, I apparently wasn't listening.

The full impact of how serious things were only recently (January 2017) became apparent to me when I transcribed a letter she wrote me when I had gone on ahead to New Jersey for the Lipton job. I was driving 300 miles on weekends from Englewood Cliffs up to Rochester on Friday night and back again on Sunday night. I was lucky I didn't have a breakdown or accident during that time, but I came close to it once or twice.

Pat's artistic abilities were not lost, they had gone underground, and she created the following cartoon strip. I think there was another one but it has been lost.

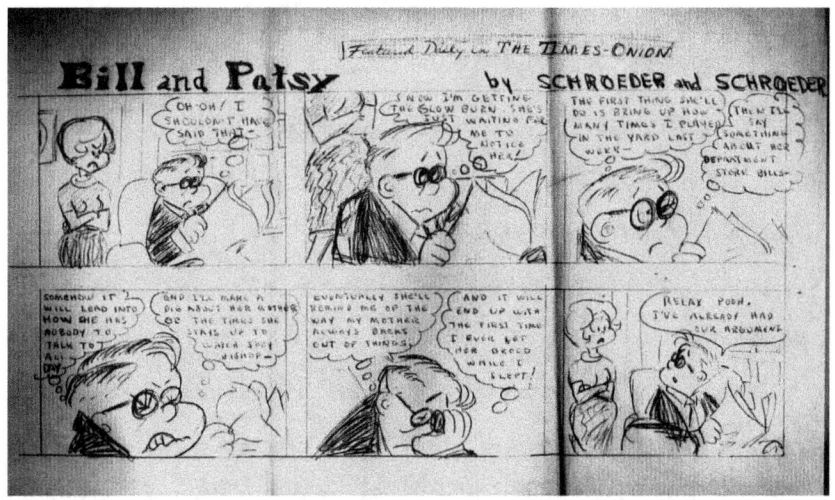

In the letter that follows, note that her writing style is sometimes poetic. Although we were married for nine years, we still used endearing terms (Pooh as Winnie the…) left over from reading to the kids.

October 17, 1967

Dear Pooh,

Sorry 'bout that, but once again I missed the mailman. You're a dear sweet Pooh and I love you, so I decided not to let that old mailman bother me. So what if he suddenly decides to start his rounds at ten o'clock in the morning! Foo on him! He will not discourage my loading him down with letters for you with sneaky tactics like that.

On the contrary, I have made up my mind to write to you whenever I feel so inclined and will do my best to make his burden so much the heavier to bear. My letters to you, as yours to me, sooner or later reach their destination. (The later rather than sooner it seems …) However, I took a vow to love, honor and write you letters when you are away (Now doesn't that sound much better than "obey?") and I always feel obliged to keep you well informed.

Well, I don't know how I'd look in laurels, especially someone else's, but wrap me in compliments, I love it. Some women (darn them anyway) … "walk in beauty like the night" (Lord Byron). I, dear heart, write in beastly hopes of getting an answer right away. Tongue-tied and pen-loose, that's me, Patty Pooh's voice may be good only to read fairy tales over XYZs Children's Hour, but the expression that flows from her pen can be compared to melodious charms from a distant flute, its melodiousness sailing on the soft evening breeze. Sometimes some pretty far out stuff ☐ like why not? Anyway, you can smother me with love, flattery, and otherwise until you get home, (Move over, Irma Bombeck).

I am not upset that you had dinner with John, not at all. Hope you had a miserable time. Margaret keeps asking when you will bring John (Vacek) with you. Said our blushing little Princess, "Won't he be surprised to see how big I've grown?"

We were up quite late last night. It was nine o'clock before I hustled the remaining two terrors up to bed and we said our prayers. Margaret wants to learn some, and then we had to say a special prayer for Daddy. Then we got into a deep discussion of who made what. What was God-made and what was man-made? (No, I didn't tell her everything was made in Japan!!). Anyway, we reached a pretty good definition - God made men, and then He put everything on this earth that we needed. He gave man a mind so that he could think and discover how to use earth's materials to make the things he needed, like steel and bricks and plastic, etc. He used his mind to figure out how things worked like electricity, and how to make machines work, etc., etc.

Then Margaret shyly remarked that she loved Brian. Indirectly at first by asking why a boy didn't like a girl when she liked him. Well, that led to how Mommy and Daddy met. They thoroughly enjoyed it. They thought it was especially funny that I couldn't remember your name the first time you asked me for a date. They were happily anticipating the story of Margaret and Billy when ye olde clock gonged out nine o'clock and the story is to be continued tonight.

I meant to go to bed not long after myself, but got involved in studying the mail order catalogs, so it was almost one when I crawled in. Around 3AM, I thought I was having apparitions again. I opened my eyes to see a light little form standing by my bed, watching me very intently. When I was able to focus my eyes a little, I discovered it was not a ghostly form, but little Melissa Robin patiently waiting for me to roll over and give her room to climb in, which I did.

So then we missed the bus. Yes, it had to happen at least once. The alarm went off and I kept pushing it for ten minutes more, until there were no more ten minutes left. Margaret flew in, followed by a very worried Billy crying that Margaret missed the bus. "So you did," I said, "now let's all go back to sleep." We'd never have made it.

Melissa, dear child, must have been playing with the alarm clock, because upon going downstairs I discovered a difference of one and a half hours. That bus must have been there and gone long ago.

Today... Today is over, thank God. Nothing accomplished. Nothing gained. It was simply an uncontrollable type day. I just rolled with the hours. I finally gave up and decided to write you.

My apologies for not making this weekend all fun and games. Think you are beginning to see my point about having just a little time together is harder on all of us than being apart. Although I can't wait for you to get here, the emotional strain of knowing you will have to leave again and having to see you drive off, upsets me all over again. And it takes the next couple of days to settle down to your absence.

Honestly, Honey, it might be better for all of us if you skipped a weekend. Anyhow, I'm delighted about your finagling off the past long weekend. Not only did we have you longer but neither of us will have to worry about the long drive.

And I'm saying if I appeared miserable again, I know Saturday was hectic for you. And Sunday morning, there was so much I wanted to talk to you about and the children kept interfering. I just got tired and you allowed their rudeness to go unpunished.

Being polite is not something to save for strangers, and denied to members of your family. I felt the whole bunch were very, very rude to me. So you keep on talking and all that's happening is that you make little ripples in the air and getting lost in the clamor all around you. So I just drew into my shell like the turtle in the stream. Think about it. Imagine yourself standing alone in a group of people chatting among themselves and you keep talking in hopes someone will hear you and turn around.

Melissa is up, Melanie is hungry and the twin terrors will soon be devouring food and drink again.

The weather was up in the 70s, but overcast. Why don't we plan to go somewhere this Sunday?

All our love,
Pat and the Poopsie Four

(If variety is the spice of life and little girls are made of sugar and spice, then big girls (like me), can offer not only a little variety but a lot of sweetness on the side).

182 • *Bill Schroeder*

Pat also illustrated the anxieties of daily life with the kids with cartoons she enclosed in the letters

1967
MEANWHILE, BACK AT LIPTON

At work, one of the highlights of my professional career was publishing the Best Annual Report in 1967 for the Thomas J. Lipton Company. It was the key to opening doors for other jobs in the future.

There was a nationwide annual report competition managed by two senior citizens from Chicago, Bob Newcomb and Marge Sammons. They were communications consultants, well known in the public relations field. I first heard about them from my friend and boss at Chrysler, Al Knight. He was one of their protégés in his youth and was still in active contact with them. They were, in fact, responsible for his being hired by Chrysler.

When I joined Lipton, their Annual Report was in 14th place. The Company President, Gardy Barker, and Secretary-Treasurer Jack Rheim were embarrassed by the standing. I promised I could do better. When I bumped it up to second place in 1968, they were delighted.

So I developed a plan to take first place. I asked Al Knight to introduce me to Newcomb and Sammons. I then got Lipton to pay my way to Chicago to talk with them about how they went about judging Annual Reports. Rheim was all for it. I took detailed notes during our discussions at their apartment and took them out for a prime rib dinner.

When I got back to New Jersey I used the notes as a road map, following them to the letter. When I submitted my entry, they had virtually no reason to do anything but award me First Place. I understand they used it as an example for future inquiries.

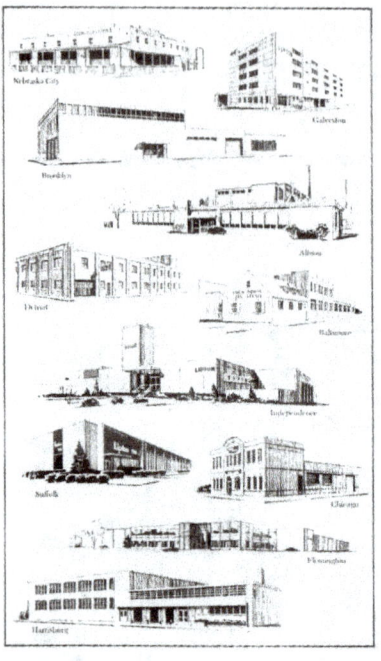

The production of the Annual Report was an adventure in itself. I employed the theory of "Alternate Facts" long before Donald Trump made the idea famous. Confronted with the need to show the Lipton manufacturing facilities, I found that they were all in need of some kind of cosmetic surgery.

They looked ramshackle and broken down. I found the answer in having an artist render them in flattering line drawings, based on the available photos. They became what we called *artist's conceptions*.

Pat and the kids appeared in the pages as a typical family shopping at a supermarket.

I hired an art director, Ed Weinrich, to supervise the complex undertaking. I rented a helicopter and I shot the Englewood Cliffs Headquarters myself from above, a thrill in itself. I decided to make a Centerfold, a *la Playboy*. We created a marvelous color picture of the products of all Lipton Products in place of a nude.

We had to rent a spot on a golf course where we staged a Lipton Fantasy picnic. I found a Jewish Golf Course that was closed for Yon Kippur while the Food Technology Lab supplied a Winnebago mobile kitchen (with food techs) to prepare the meal for the camera. We built a picnic table setup that was painted only on the side that faced the camera.

I hired a fashion photographer, Don Bennett, to shoot everything, including the executives. To get a good outdoor set at the course's lake, the art director had to throw rocks at the ducks to make them fly on cue. We had to airbrush him out of the picture later.

While we were shooting the picnic, the grounds-keeper, who did not like our being there, got into a fight with the photographer when his dog stole the prop roast beef from the table.

The photographer had to chase the dog and would have killed him to get the meat back. He had to shoot the premier shot before the sun went down, and it was fast approaching.

When I got the product prop boxes back, they were all empty. The photographer was broke and he and his family had been eating the contents of the boxes.

1969

After you get a first place award in your field, what do you do for an encore? Chances of repeating it were slim. I had no ideas.

To top it off, Pat did not like New Jersey. She wrote a four-word poem that summed it up:

Me thinketh It stinkith.

As I have said, I had made it a practice to subscribe to *The Wall Street Journal* at any place I worked. The main reason was for the image — it made me look like I was a real management-type businessman. In reality, I didn't understand 90% of its content. The two main things I read were the daily feature story on the front page, middle column, and the help wanted classifieds.

It was there I read the ad for Butte Knitting Mills in Spartanburg, SC.

Andrew Teszler, a Hungarian-born New York entrepreneur had established the Butte Knit Division of Jonathan Logan producing double-knit. It became an extremely profitable coup in the fashion industry. But they had community relations problems.

An ad was placed in *The Wall Street Journal* by a New York headhunting firm; Towers, Perrin, Forster & Crosby, who had General Electric among its clients. That meant the parameters for a Communication Manager fit me, as it had when I interviewed for Chrysler with Mickey Dover. I knew the GE Communications Manager in New York from the Industrial Editors Association, and he vouched for my professional qualifications. They also contacted Newcomb and Sammons to reinforce my Lipton success.

I was invited to TPF&C's New York office for an interview. I went, of course, but not before talking to my GE contact. He told me that the job was virtually mine on paper, but I needed to make a first class personal appearance. He likened the headhunters to Central Casting in Hollywood. You had to look the part to be recommended by them. He laid out some suggested preparations.

TPF&C's office was opposite Grand Central Station. It was a wilting 90-degree summer's day, and I was scheduled for 1 p.m. If I left my home at 8 a.m. in New Jersey I would be a sweaty mess by the time I got there.

So I choreographed my morning. I wore my Rogers Peet (be sure the label is visible when you open the jacket) wrinkle-proof Dacron suit.

I went straight from the Port Authority Bus Terminal to a barbershop on the grand concourse of the train station. I got a trim and a close barber shave at 11 a.m.

Next, I went to a men's store and bought a new starched, button-down shirt (not wash-and-wear). In the men's room I freshened up, put on the crisp shirt, knotted a tie I had brought along in my brief case. I sat in an air-conditioned lounge that bordered on being cold.

Then at 12:45, I crossed the street to the interview office. I arrived looking *fresh as the proverbial daisy*, and passed the "looks right for the job" test. The interview bordered on perfunctory, and I was scheduled to go to Spartanburg in three days.

All the way back home I was humming my favorite tune from my favorite Gilbert and Sullivan's *HMS Pinafore*.

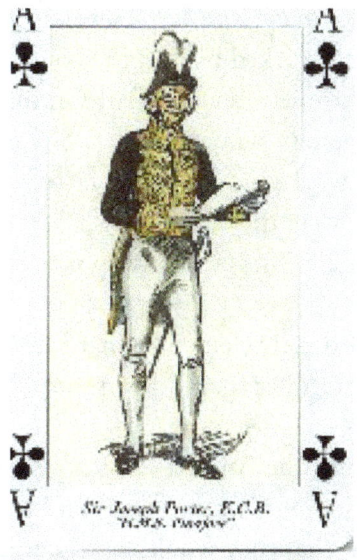

"*In serving writs I made such a name
That an articled clerk I soon became;
I wore clean collars and a brand-new suit
For the pass examination at the Institute.*"

SPARTANBURG SYNCHRONICITY

At this point, let me point out the synchronicity that evolved about Spartanburg and me and West New York.

I had never heard of Spartanburg before Butte. I had no idea where it was even when I was hired. I was plunked into the job without knowing what it involved. I needed someone to help me figure it out. John Vacek had recently been discharged from the Navy and was available. I hired him to help me with the heavy lifting.

One of my recommendations was the development of a TV training program using the new SONY equipment. I liked the idea but needed someone I could trust to make it happen. John and I could learn together, so he joined me. He remained long after I left.

At the same time we arrived in Spartanburg, so did a fellow named Frank Perricone, as manager of Research and Development for Butte. His widow, Ethel (Brokhoff) Perricone, graduated from my high school in 1947, three years before me. It gets *curiouser and curiouser* (Lewis Carroll) when you find out she had, at one point, worked behind the counter at Gimmel's bakery.

To add to the synchronicity factor, Carl Gimmel moved to Lexington, KY, and is married to woman named Shelley. She told me during a visit to Finksburg, that she too worked at the Butte factory in Spartanburg in 1970 when Ethel, John, and I were there. None of us remembers ever meeting the other. Yet here we are in 2017 when I have spoken to all the aforementioned in one day.

The crowning synchronistic element is that Kay Cation told us in Detroit in 1966 that we would meet her again "down south." Four years later she was only six miles away.

Using my success with the Annual Report contest in 1969 at Lipton, I levered myself into the job of Communications Manager at $25,000 a year. Only later did I find out that they would have paid $30,000. But $25K was a good salary at the time, especially in South Carolina.

They were looking for a Public Relations Manager to help solve a community relations problem. Their company lawyer suggested getting a non-Jewish PR man since the problem hinged on two points. Locals did not like the idea of Jewish management and the introduction of a union in the area. (The International Ladies Garment Workers Union, ILGWU… called *Igloo* in the trade*)*.

I played up the fact that my Westinghouse and Chrysler experience had to do with fighting unions. But in reality, all I knew was I wanted to make $25,000 a year. I had no idea how I would deal with the problem. But they hired me anyway.

They virtually took over my life. The hooked me up with a real estate agent to buy a $48,000 five-bedroom house that looked like a girls' school. They bought my dump of a house in New Jersey that had a leaky septic system, and paid all the expenses of moving a family with five kids.

I fell into an undefined competition with next door neighbor, Dave Bennett, in growing things. The first round was raising tomatoes. Dave took

the position that the red clay soil did not support them as they did further north. I planted eight tomato plants but used my own technique. I used a posthole digger, making a hole 12 inches across and 12 inches deep. I filled it with black potting soil, before I placed a tomato seedling in it. They all flourished.

The second plant was box hedges. Again the soil was not expected to support them. I used the same approach as with the tomatoes. I dug a trench alongside the front sidewalk and filled it with a mixture of potting soil and fertilizer. Same result ... they grew.

When it became time for the family to move from New Jersey to South Carolina, Pat took Margaret, Will, Melissa, Melanie

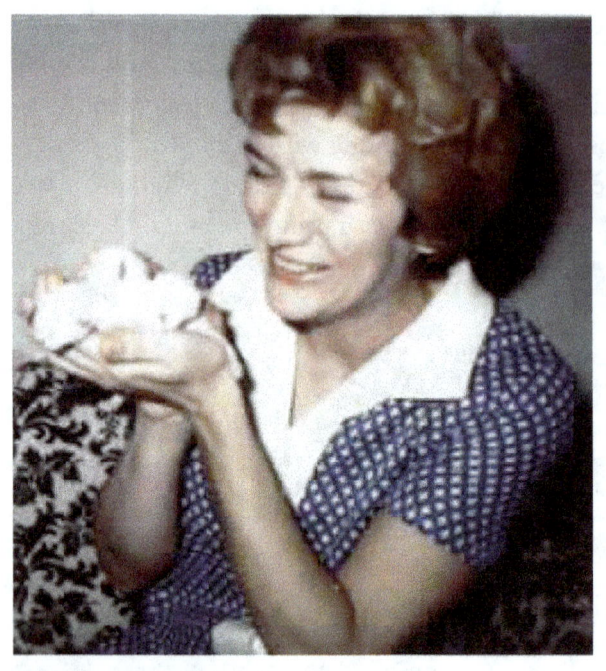

and Howard on a plane. I drove down a day or so earlier with a Siamese cat and a parakeet.

The cat got out of its box and while I tried to catch it while driving, it bit my hand. The parakeet was in a large, brass parrot cage with what seemed like solid bars. When we stopped at a motel overnight in North Carolina, I moved the zoo inside the bedroom while I went to dinner.

When I returned to the room I found the cat on the bed cleaning itself and two parakeet feet, a beak, and some feathers on the bottom of the cage. The bars were forced apart.

At one point, we were overrun with cats. We had two or three cats that had litters at the same time. When we moved later, we only kept the Siamese.

I was happy as a pig in a mud puddle. However, I caused more problems than I solved. The fact that we were nominally Catholic was no better than being Jewish in local eyes.

Much of the problem had to do with our Northeastern Liberal view of blacks. We hired women to hand-press dresses, paying them by piecework. The net result was black women making more money than most local white men.

Where black men were working at minimum wage driving trucks, the ILGWU contract called for paying then premium rates since they delivered dresses to other factories across state lines. Now they were making enough money to buy new houses.

However, I did come up with ideas that helped the company be accepted in the community. Most of our success had to do with finding high-paying jobs at Butte for local Spartanburg politicians and their families. If Butte failed, none of them would find jobs that paid anywhere near their new salaries.

Margaret told me that she recalls seeing a chain gang at the roadside when she was a kid in Spartanburg. Since she remembers them wearing striped uniforms, I said it was probably a state gang since the Spartanburg chain gang wore a different uniform.

The reason I knew that had to do with an episode at Butte Knit. We hired a New York accountant and the first week he was there he resumed his

DETROIT PUBLISHING COMPANY PHOTOGRAPH COLLECTION — LIBRARY OF CONGRESS

old NYC exercise regimen. He got up early to jog for a mile or so before going to work. A few minutes into the run he was stopped and arrested by the Spartanburg Sherriff's Department.

I had to go down to the jail to get him out. He was wearing a blue sweatshirt and blue sweatpants with a white stripe down the leg. That was the official uniform of the Spartanburg County chain gang. They thought he was an escaped convict. He quit his new job the next day and went back to New York.

It turns out that this is all part of the local political culture. If you are found guilty of a crime in Spartanburg County court, the judge makes a pronouncement before sentencing: "If anyone present has any extenuating circumstances, let him come forward now."

Then, if you have paid off the right people, the Sherriff stands up and says, "I claim this prisoner for the Spartanburg County Chain Gang." He takes the prisoner away and after a few days he is "released for good behavior."

When we first went to the pediatrician with the kids, upon finding out Pat was Catholic, he shook hands and said, "I'm Jewish. We need to stick together."

That came more into focus much later when I worked for Olympia Mills. At that time, I realized that the former owners if the building housing my factory were building another like it next door. They would make the same product but on more modern machines. When I reminded them that the agreement said they would not engage in the same business for at least two years, they said. "You have that in writing?"

I said no and remarked that the agreement was done over a handshake, they laughed and said, "A handshake with a New York Jew don't mean shit down here."

Fortunately, I developed a number of community projects that won Teszler's approval, including a coloring book for distribution to local grade schools. It took the reader on a guided tour through the double-knit manufacturing process.

SPARTANBURG SEWING SCHOOL

At the same time, Pat caused ripples in the community on her own. Black women generally could not pass the sewing test for better paying jobs because they had no way to learn the skills. Nobody had access to electric sewing machines.

She told me about the problem and I found out that Butte had four obsolete sewing machines in our warehouse. They worked, but were too slow compared to the industrial models used at the factories.

We made an arrangement at a black church to set up the machines. Pat had a vast number of clothes patterns from her own hobby collection. Butte also had odd-sized rolls of unused fabrics left over from their dress factories that were often just dumped.

I filled up the back of my station wagon with bolts in every color of the rainbow. Pat set up classes and they practically created a factory to turn out clothes for seniors, children and poor women. Teaching four hours a day, four days a week, she took her children to play with the students' kids. While she saw it as a solution to the baby-sitting problem, some of our neighbors did not see it as such.

I was invited for coffee to the home of the Episcopal Minister who lived across the street, only to find several others also there. I thought it was a nice neighborly gesture until the minister spoke for the group. "Bill, we realize that you come from New Jersey and this is the first time you're living in a southern community—"

I laughed a little and said, "That's no secret."

"We understand that *your* job at Butte, calls for you to defer to the Negro community, but that's business. What we're concerned about is that your wife takes your children to play with colored kids while she teaches sewing at the church."

"That's right," I said in a defensive tone, seeing where this conversation was going.

Someone else spoke up, "What Reverend Drake is trying to say is that we have something here called *segregation*, and we intend to keep it. If your wife needs someone to watch the kids, there are few of us here who will help her."

After we sat in silence for a few moments, I stood up and said, "Thank you for your offer. I will tell Pat about it."

Neither of us was ever invited for coffee again in the neighborhood. We became good friends with the Bennetts next door (who were not represented at the event). They were also a Catholic family who had a lot of kids. Pat's response was outrage, but we did something they never would have expected. She went on television with our kids. I used my professional contacts at the local CBS station to set it up.

Pat worked with a Spartanburg fabric shop to make outfits for Margaret, Melissa, Melanie, and Will.

Nobody knew that during her interview she would talk about our sewing school for minority women who wanted skills to get better jobs. *There was*

no better way to reach potential students since this was the only live TV station in our county...

and **Butte paid for the air time.**

The reward we got for our efforts is still with us … a life-sized fiberglass brown bear. It was once part of a float in a parade, and no one wanted it. It was given to the black church for their playground — but the children were all afraid of it.

Since Pat's kids were the only ones who played with it, we received it as a "thank you" gift. It has travelled all over the country with the Schroeder family (Arizona, Virginia and Maryland) and now resides with Melissa in Pennsylvania.

OLYMPIA MILLS

Just when things seemed to be sailing along at their height, Andrew Teszler, the CEO, announced he was leaving and creating a new company named Olympia Mills. It would be located in Spartanburg and did not have a union.

Chaos ensued. He was taking all the management people with him, including me. He called me into his office and said, "We don't need a Public Relations Manager. Did you ever manage a factory?"

I said, "No."

"Well, you start Monday!" he retorted, in a tone that was appropriate for just having hired me to run a hot dog stand.

I went over to the address I was given on Friday afternoon and found an antiquated brick building containing about 125 small knitting machines. These were sock machines. They were set up to produce continuous sleeves of cotton tubes, much like sweat socks. The product was to be cut into strips to encase balls of yarn during the dyeing process.

The guy who was overseeing the operations was the brother of the Butte Manufacturing Manager. He was from Union City, NJ, and typical of the sports jocks of that area. I was accused later by his brother of having insulted him, but have no recollection of such an event (unless my contempt was transparent). My first thought was, *If this guy can run the place it can't be very hard.*

I asked him to show me the place. When I asked how the machines worked and he said, "I don't know. If you have any questions ask one of the older operators … or call my brother… but he gets pissed off if you do that."

"What do I have to do?" I asked.

"They all know what they have to do. Just make sure that nobody sits down or goofs off. Keep track of their hours and you turn in their time sheets at the end of the week."

The place ran three shifts seven days a week. There were four people walking up and down the aisles between the machines making adjustments as needed. They were not only old, but archeological in nature. Only half the machines were in running condition. The whole thing was run by a series of overhead wheels and pulleys and belts. I guessed that the machines were made in the 1920s.

There was one old guy who had worked there 20 years who knew how anything and everything worked. I offered to make him the foreman and he actually recoiled at the suggestion. "I ain't gonna be no fuckin' boss," he said indignantly, and walked away insulted.

I showed up Saturday morning and found the plant manager didn't come in on weekends. But the place was humming right along as it had the day before.

I introduced myself to the employees and left my home phone number in case I was needed. Immediately, I called the local newspaper and was in time to run a classified ad for a shop foreman. It ran on Sunday and I only had one response on Monday morning. In those days you went physically to the address given and the hiring decisions were made on the spot.

The sole applicant was named Hank. He had been a weaving loom repairman for a shirt company that moved out of town. To keep his job he would have had to give up four pigs and the family farm of three generations. He declined to relocate and had not worked for about a month. Declining to move with the company after 12 years on the job raised questions of his loyalty in the minds of local businessmen.

I told him I needed somebody to actually repair the dead and dying machines and get them back on line. He wasn't sure he could do it since he only worked on weaving machines, but I insisted that I had no mechanical experience and he could figure it out. When I offered him $3 an hour I thought he was going to cry. He had never made more than $2.25 an hour, even after 12 years with the shirt company.

I put him on the payroll, starting from the time he walked in the door. After that I think he would have killed anybody I pointed to.

My next employee contact was a black kid about 20 years old, named Freddy. He could be described as a factotum … he actually knew how the business ran. He was a Vietnam vet and highly regarded by black and white employees alike. He was the shipping clerk in charge of getting our product over to the warehouse. He got a dollar a week from each employee on payday. In return he checked their time cards against the money in their pay envelopes — he knew how to do arithmetic.

After a month, Hank's understanding of the machines enabled him to repair them. Beyond the needles, there was no such thing as spare parts. He cannibalized the broken machines and boosted the number of those operating from 75 to 93. The resulting number of productive machines heralded a proportionate increase in gross output.

The next big thing was increasing the speed of the machines. Everything ran off one power plant. Even though my college degree was a Bachelor's in English I understood that putting a larger drive wheel on the main belt drive would have a positive effect on the whole place.

Hank found such a wheel in the storeroom and installed it. Afterward you could actually hear the increased decibel level on the shop floor. It sounded like a hive of angry bees.

Joe Grey, the Vice President of Personnel, called me when he heard about the dramatic turnaround in production. "Do you know what we are paying the machine operators in your plant?"

I was embarrassed to say I didn't. No one had ever complained or mentioned it. They were conditioned to be happy to have any kind of job at all. I said, "I assumed it was the minimum wage."

Grey said, "South Carolina doesn't have a minimum wage."

"Those two Crackers we bought the factory from paid them the princely sum of between 93 and 97 cents an hour. That's what we are still paying them. They are not covered by any Igloo (ILGWU) contract. Give them a raise to $1.85 an hour and they'll never let a Union Rep near the door." (The federal minimum was $1.60 an hour.)

I sat in stunned disbelief. No wonder Hank thought he died and went to heaven when I hired him on at $3 an hour.

"What should I do?" I asked.

"Call everybody together at lunch time and tell them, 'Olympia President Andrew Teszler has to decided to pay them New York wages, just like the people at Butte Knit. The hourly wage increase is effective immediately and is retroactive to the date Olympia bought their factory, three months ago.' Let me know what happens."

After a few minutes, I called Hank into my office and told him the news. He sat there and forgot to swallow. Genuinely flustered he choked out "You're kiddin', right?"

I assured him I wasn't, and told him to get all six of the employees into the office now, but don't tell them why.

The employees naturally assumed that there would be some kind of bad news, like a layoff or shutdown. I said, "If I had some more chairs I'd tell you all to sit down. What I have to tell you is good news like you all never heard before."

Pausing for effect, I went on, "Everyone's is now getting $1.85 an hour — New York wages, just like the people at Butte Knit."

Jaws started to drop, lips quivered. One of the black women shouted, "If you wuz colored, I'd kiss you!"

I blushed and said, "My wife don't allow that."

They all began laughing, talking and shouting as if it were a revival meeting. When they quieted down I said, "That's not all! It's retroactive — that means it starts from the day Olympia bought this factory. You will each get a lump sum for correct back wages for about three months!"

Freddy, the wage checker said, "I'd better brush up on my arithmetic!"

Everyone was so excited that production actually fell during that afternoon. When I addressed the second-shift employees, they already knew. In fact, the *Spartanburg Herald* newspaper called to confirm their lead story.

When I called Joe Grey, he said, "Big deal! We're only talking about 25 people at the most. It's a fart in a hurricane. But it would have cost us a fortune to fight Igloo's attempts to unionize them."

We were able to maintain the previous production level by only running six days a week. The employees had never had Sunday off since they began working there.

The phone call that really punctuated the day was the former owner planning a new factory next door. He had only four words for me, *"You lousy Jew Bastard!"*

While Andrew Teszler was a brilliant business genius, he had a fatal shortcoming ... he loved to eat. It left him with an obesity problem that threatened his heart. He spurned medical advice and fell into a dieting fad that consisted of apples, cheese and amphetamines. His chauffer got him "speed" pills from a contact at a local truck stop. He lost 60 pounds in two months, and saw no reason to stop the downward spiral.

His work hours knew no limits. He was in his office or on the manufacturing floor almost 24 hours a day. One night about midnight, while he was dictating a letter, he had a heart attack and suddenly fell out of his chair to the floor. His secretary tried to find medical help, but no one was available (after all, this was the middle of the night in Spartanburg, South Carolina). By the time an ambulance was found he was already dead. An autopsy revealed that his blood sugar level had dropped below a life-sustaining level, causing him to have a heart attack.

All his plans for Olympia died with him because he had not written down how it was all to take place. Competition in the women's pants suit industry was extremely competitive, and he would have lost a possible edge if someone else beat him to market.

He was survived by his father, who spoke only Hungarian, and a brother who taught physics in California. The latter was summoned back east to try to dispose of the assets and save the family fortune.

MAY 1970–JANUARY 1971
COMMUNITY RELATIONS DIRECTOR, ALLEGHENY GENERAL HOSPITAL, PITTSBURGH, PA

In May 1970, my idealism overtook my better judgment. Once more I answered an employment ad in the *Wall Street Journal*. I was totally disillusioned with the corporate business focus on profits. I wanted to do something in the public interest. Allegheny General Hospital in Pittsburgh needed a Community Relations Manager. Again I used my prize-winning Lipton Annual Report to get me the job, and I produced one for them.

I should have been tipped off about my disillusionment at my initial interview with Lad (Ladislaw) F. Grapski, President and Chief Executive Officer. In our first discussion after my hiring he said, "*Non-profit doesn't means unprofitable!*" I have quoted it often since.

Grapski was initially trained as a Registered Nurse, but went on to get a degree in hospital administration. He was despised by the doctors on the medical staff. Their favorite slogan about him was: "There's nothing worse than a Polish nurse."

His main objective was to make Allegheny General Hospital a primary educational teaching hospital. The problem arose when the predominantly black neighborhood community used the hospital Emergency Room as a family doctor's office. I made my major mistake of being sympathetic to the community's needs. If I had done my homework properly, I would have found out that I was the fifth person to hold the job in two years. None of my predecessors got along with Mr. Grapski.

His goal of establishing the hospital as a regional teaching hospital ran into trouble with the national community hospital group. The most immediate problem was that the only American doctors who went to Alleghany could not get in anywhere else. Most trainees were foreigners, irritating Grapski no end.

My office was the most grandiose setting imaginable. In a dramatic scandal at the hospital prior to Grapski, the CEO of the hospital was found to be operating the organization for his own benefit, making millions of dollars. He lived in the penthouse at the top of the building. There were five rooms, in which the living room (complete with fireplace and furniture), was my office.

The reason the place was so beautifully appointed was that Westinghouse had rented the penthouse as a confined space to accommodate former President and CEO Gwylim A. Price *(Harry Smith's Uncle Bill)* when he had a nervous breakdown and behaved very erratically. As far as the public was concerned, he was staying at the hospital as a very ill patient.

The penthouse was accessible only by a private elevator. No one like news reporters could talk to him. The reason was that he was psychotic. However, the secret was out when he evaded his keepers' observation and took the private elevator to the lobby. The problem was that he was stark naked. When he was recognized by people in the crowd in the lobby the game was over, and he was moved to some other remote location.

Although my job description included running the fund raising operation, I was never allowed to see the donators' list. The philanthropic donors were Grapski's personal contacts. He also ran the 14th Floor with a hotel atmosphere. The public elevators did not stop at that floor. It was open only to patients recommended by a donor (such as family members). Wine was available with meals, and staffed with selected Medical Staff.

My ultimate problem came when a very sick child was refused admission at the emergency room. She was the daughter of one of the black community's leaders. The intern on duty was unable to be awakened from an exhausted sleep. He had taken the 12-hour work shifts from two other scheduled doctors for $10 each. He had not slept in 48 hours and could no longer stay awake. The child was sent to the local Children's Hospital in time to save her life.

The newspapers seized the story, and I could not realistically defend the hospital's actions. There was a bomb scare in the lobby, grabbing the headlines. I resigned shortly thereafter and returned to Spartanburg, SC.

I had not been able to sell my house in South Carolina, so we moved back there. In spite of my earlier lack of popularity when we lived there before, now we were the focus of a southern tradition known as *"Pounding."* When a neighborhood family was down on their luck, everyone pitched in, donating them a pound of sugar, a pound of flour, etc. Dave and Barbara Bennett organized it.

I had no job, but I didn't think I could go back to Olympia or Butte. Dave Bennett interceded on my behalf with Olympia and he got me a job as a textile warehouse manager. (Another job for which I had no training) The problem was that it was at a rate $10,000 a year less — $15,000. It was a good job by local standards, but far below the budget we were used to.

When I went to the warehouse I found I had three black employees; two teens and a recent Vietnam vet. The latter had assumed charge. They saw themselves as a rock band waiting to be discovered, but had an obvious shortcoming … they were all drummers and vocalists. The cardboard boxes and barrels were their instruments. The noise level in the building was overwhelming. They banged away constantly and sang as a trio. It seemed to me that there was only one song, consisting of loud an rapid drumming followed by a pause and everybody singing, "I love ya, Baybee (thumpety, thump) but I ain't gonna take no shit!"

Theoretically, the order of work consisted of receiving a stack of fabric orders first thing in the morning. The company truck was supposed to pick the orders up around four o'clock to deliver them to the dress-making factory. My predecessor was another brother of the same manufacturing VP as I encountered at the other facility. He had organized the storage system to an operating level.

The procedure was to give the workers job tickets with bale numbers. They would find them and put them on the loading platform. But it didn't take long for them to find out that I would find them if they couldn't. In a day or two I was locating virtually all the bales to meet the pick-up deadline. I wasn't the gruff New Yorker they had worked for before ... I accepted excuses.

I told Dave Bennett about my problem. He was expecting me to have a problem. "They know you're a soft Yankee. They don't have any respect for you as a boss. What you need is a straw boss — a Negro who will see that the work gets done."

After a few more explanations, Dave said, "I know somebody who is what you're looking for. I'll send him over tomorrow."

The next morning, a very solid-looking black man about five feet six was waiting for me on the loading platform. He introduced himself as "Little Joe" Lewis. "Big Joe spelled his name different. I do some boxing, but can't make the weight class. Everybody calls me "Little Joe."

Pointing to the three warehouse guys, he added, "Your boys all know me ... everybody does." They nodded in unison.

Further discussion revealed that he was dishonorably discharged from the Army for repeated fighting. The new order of work would consist of giving him the day's order tickets and he would assign the boys to find the bales.

We agreed on a salary, and he called the boys together for an orientation. They stood together in a tight knot and adopted an attitude of attentiveness I had not seen before.

"You all know who I am," he said. "Mr. Schroeder has just hired me as your foreman. So when you talk to me, call me Mr. Lewis. Once I figure this shop out, I will tell you how it works. When I give you a ticket to find a bale in the racks, I don't want to hear that you can't find it. If you don't finds it, tell me. If I finds it I'm gonna kick your black ass."

Even I was afraid to challenge him.

"If'n you can't find somethin' twice, I'm gonna kick your ass and fire you for good measure. I know lots of guys who would like to have your jobs."

He turned to me and said, "Anything you want to add, Mr. Schroeder?"

I said no, and confirmed he was the foreman.

He closed with, "By the way, his name is Schroeder, not Stroger, like you been calling him. But that shouldn't matter to you. You don't go botherin' him with your problems. I'm the only one you gotta talk to. Like they usta say in the Army, 'give your soul to God because your ass belongs to me.'"

I proceeded to give him a tour of the warehouse, so he could begin work the next day. It had not been that quiet since I first got there … nobody played their cardboard drums.

We met our delivery deadlines from then on. Having learned the true work culture of the region, I spent most of my time reading the *Wall Street Journal* in my office, looking for the next want ad. For meeting my objectives, I was rewarded with a Volkswagen Beetle.

Mansanto bought Olympia and closed it. All they wanted was the texturing machinery in the factory.

JULY 28, 1971
JOHN PATRICK IS BORN IN SPARTANBURG, SC

The birth of John Patrick marked the achievement of Pat's life-long ambition — *a six-child family*. As the first-born son was named for me, the last child was Pat's patronymic (Joan Patricia). Now we had to concentrate on making this large family operational. Let me add that it was a lot easier while Pat lived. She offered them the kind of counsel I could not. She was the glue that kept us all together.

John is the only member of our family who spent his entire youth in one school system (unlike his oldest sister, Margaret, who tells me she went to 13 different schools). He was born in South Carolina, moved to Arizona and ended up in Finksburg, MD. He started in kindergarten and went on through high school in Carroll County.

He was never a bookish kid. Nevertheless, I remember his telling me that his friends were always impressed with his vocabulary. We never talked down to him, and he grew up with definite opinions on politics and the nature of reality.

I do not remember the year, but I bought a version of the Radio Shack TRS-80 Micro Computer System, a desktop microcomputer. It was later derogatorily known as the Trash-80, but was a big deal at the time. It was one of the earliest mass-produced and mass-marketed retail personal computers.

From the day we got it, John became self-educated in the field and grew exponentially to the level of designing computer programs for managing automobile sales for a major distributor for the East Coast. However, at the climax of his career development, company politics forced him out. I believe it was such a blow that he never again felt the same about corporations and the people who ran them.

His easy grasp of plumbing and mechanical principles then came into to play. He worked his way up in the retail swimming-pool supply industry, only to run into similar philosophical problems with management.

John felt that his solution to the problem was self-employment, but lacked the financial wherewithal to make it happen. He possesses a natural gift for food preparation … from growing it to cooking and baking. He did not foresee the complexity of Health Department nitty-gritty rules that govern food marketing.

John built his own meat-smoking apparatus and hosted Thanksgiving one year featuring a smoked turkey.

After a number of trials in other fields, John has decided to focus on the design and manufacture of tie-dyed team clothing and other sports related items. He and is wife, Nicole, sold most of their worldly possessions and are buying (and living in) a motor home.

Their plans are to travel the United States, following the route of fairs and festivals, selling the merchandise produced on their own equipment. John made me a brightly colored jacket for my latest birthday. It is made of (believe it or not) bamboo fiber, which has the texture of fleece (I love it).

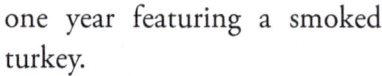

If he maintains this kind of quality in his work, it should have a good chance of success. Items made from spun bamboo fiber include athletic socks.

From an early age Pat and I perceived that John's outlook on things was different from his siblings. John's own self-image is that of a "free spirit." He dislikes labels and he says, "I simply want to be myself ... not trying to live up to someone else's life expectations."

His choice in clothing as a teen was not in fashion, but seemed to harken back to an earlier decade. Even today, he chooses bare feet, even in the city, and tie-dyed shirts. That makes a picture of him in a suit jacket a rarity.

Both Pat and I embraced the concept of reincarnation. (Pat insisted she was on her last trip through the process, and was not coming back again). One of our favorite writers on the subject suggested in her studies of "past lives" that there was an average of 50 or 60 years (as we perceive time) from the death of one life and rebirth into another. The premise being that the soul in question used that period to meditate on the lessons learned in its previous life.

We discussed the subject with a friend who shared the view of that possibility. It

was suggested that based on John's affinity for clothing, hair styles, and behaviors of the 1960s, he could be a soul who perished in the Vietnam War or the public unrest of the period. However, his resentment of the unjustness of his early demise caused him to return at the earliest opportunity. He needed to find an understanding host such as Pat to birth him. He recently told me that he expects to come back again.

Like everyone else in the family, John was a Pupdog worshiper.

Unfortunately, I have been unable to find any photos of John in his Hippie outfits. As has been pointed out to me, the first couple kids in a large family have innumerable pictures. But of you are Number Six, like John, the novelty of photographic records has worn off.

John's creative artistic abilities were best expressed by his annual make-up creations at Halloween. He was always a willing co-conspirator with Melissa. His artistic renderings began with her covering him with body paint one year.

John became a master of the art of make-up. We looked forward to see what he would do every year on Halloween. One of his best jobs was as Dr. Zaius from *Planet of the Apes*. When he showed up at my front door, I did not immediately know who they were ... but Howard's face looking out the face-hole in a six-foot banana gave it away.

To illustrate his skill, compare his Dr. Zaius to the movie version.

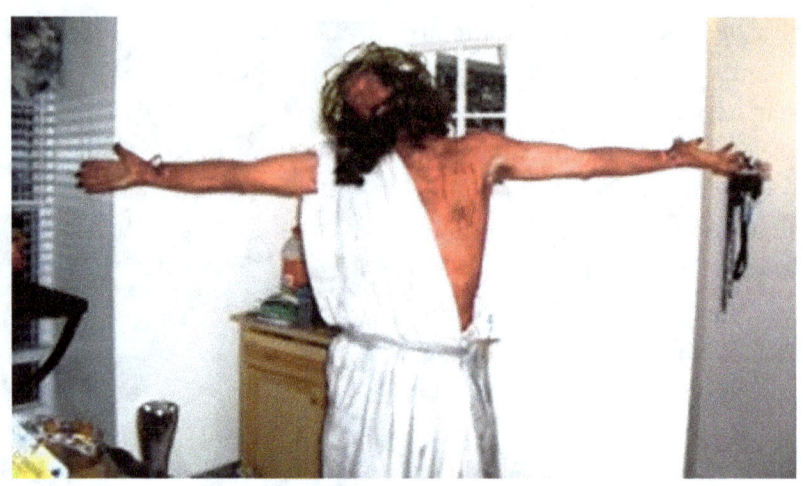

His most controversial portrayal was Jesus Christ.

When I made my 8mm movie of Frankenstein in 1951, we settled for a rubber mask. If you wish to see it, go to You Tube, search for The Frankenstein Monster and The Enforcer, by Eric M.
https://www.youtube.com/watch?v=aNgqLTD3SmM

John was not into acting as much as his siblings, but he participated in our Shakespeare scenes at the Renaissance Festival.

The following sequence shows how elaborate John's preparations were for his version of *Frankenstein* and *Bride of Frankenstein*.

The guise that most impressed me was his portrayal of a very old man. It was so good that when Pat and I met him in the Westminster Mall, we had no idea it was him.

He was even wearing one of my old sports jackets. Security guards made him leave (Halloween or not) under a violation of hiding his identity in a public place. It was absurd.

For a number of years John lived with Howard, until he met Nicole and established an independent family life.

THEATER ROLES 1981–1987

As I recall it, in 1981 I decided to try out for September Song's Guys and Dolls. Because I was constantly driving my kids to play rehearsals of all kinds, I decided I might as well see if I could fit in somewhere myself. Also, I secretly wanted to be "on the stage" since childhood. I was never picked for school plays in grade school, and the closest I ever came to being in one was when I provided off-stage sound effects for the HS senior play.

My friends and I recorded radio dramas for our own amusement from scripts provided by George Wagenhauser from his WOR-NY job. Then, of course, there was our one shot at 8mm movie making in 1951.

When I tried out for Guys and Dolls, I was a natural for New York Police Lieutenant Branigan by virtue of my natural NY accent.

My only mistake was when I exited stage left I walked flat into the wall. Everyone at the audition roared with laughter and I got the part.

While September Song produced musicals, the Carroll Players staged dramas. In 1982, My 3 Angels had three Schroeders in the cast. Melanie played the ingénue lead. I was the rich uncle who gets murdered, and Will played the villain. My greatest private joke about the play was when they needed someone to play a French tune off-stage on the harmonica. Since I didn't know any French tunes, I played the Horst Wessel Nazi recruiting anthem. No one ever suspected.

My proverbial "big break" came in 1983. I was picked to play Mayor Shinn in *The Music Man*. I had a marvelous time.

In 1984, in *The King and I* my role was the Krolahome (Prime Minister).

It was the closest thing to real acting I ever had to do. Not only did I have to memorize and deliver a long speech, I had to project emotion in blaming the *Anna* lead for destroying the King's integrity. I was glad when it was over.

In 1985 I chose not to be in *South Pacific*, when I didn't get the part of a Navy Captain. Only much later did I admit that I really wanted to get the part just to have my picture taken in the costume.

That same year Carroll Players did The *Andersonville Trial*. I played a southern farmer who delivered food to the infamous prisoner of war camp.

Later in the season, I was a Middle Eastern Sultan in Woody Allen's *Don't Drink the Water*. It was my favorite make-up and dress-up role.

"And now for something completely different…" an independent group of friends staged *Murder on a Train*. It was a dinner theater on wheels.

I played couple or three trips (from Westminster to Hagerstown), both as a murderer and a victim. It was very challenging because I had to interact with the passengers/audience. The chore was to make myself no-

ticed by the passengers so they could all participate in the solution of the crime. I portrayed an out-of-work standup comedian whose *shtick* was terrible limericks and deserved killing. One Sunday afternoon, when I was playing the murderer, I made it a point to show a knife display with at least nine examples from my own eBay collection.

My last non-musical was in 1987 — *The Butler Did It*. This comedy parodied every English mystery play ever written. "Miss Maple" hosts a group of detective writers (think Agatha Christie or Erle Stanley Gardner) at eerie Ravenswood Manor on Turkey Island where they are to impersonate their fictional characters. I played the Charlie Chan Chinese detective send-up.

The plot successfully interweaves all the classic elements with an imaginative approach. It's described as a stylish cross between *Ten Little Indians* and *The Cat and The Canary*.

Although I played a minor part in *My Fair Lady* in 1988, I consider my last role with September Song to be Merlin in *Camelot* in 1987. Curiously, I was besieged by cast members to read their Tarot Cards while in my Merlin costume.

My theatrical career ended as abruptly as it had begun. I adopted a philosophy of been there … done that … bought the Tee-shirt. Spinning off from the contacts I made during that period, I did a number non-memorable local TV commercial extra spots for about $50 each.

I even got to do an infomercial on Uri Geller spoon-bending that involved Allen Hicks and members of the Schroeder family.

1984–1990

In 1985, The Maryland Renaissance Festival was held at the Merryweather Post Pavilion in Columbia, Maryland. It was planned to simulate an Elizabethan fair, featuring jousting and wandering troubadours. I read in the papers that they needed someone to put on Shakespearian vignettes.

When I sought the job as the Director of the Shakespeare portion of the Festival, it was offered it on the condition that I would fill at least one other slot. Everyone who worked the Festival wore two hats, and they needed a fortuneteller. So, I was appointed as the 1985 Director of the Shakespeare Festival part of the Maryland Renaissance Festival. My alter ego was the Mad Monk.

Although I really had no idea how to do it, Pat and I were familiar with the procedure from our exposure to Kay Cation's readings back in Detroit 20 years before. *Synchronicity* lit up our world once again; we never could have foreseen how such an anomaly could ever influence our lives so dramatically in the future. Through synchronicity I became the Mad Monk who read Tarot cards.

But getting the job was one thing, *doing it* was another. I had four weeks to learn. Luckily, a Towson "New Age" shop was offering a four-week course in reading the cards. So Pat and I

went for two hours every Wednesday night for the month of September to learn the Secrets of the Tarot. It turned out to be essentially a matrix memory feat.

Each of the 78 cards had a range of meanings determined by numerology (Ace through King) and the suit. These are augmented by 22 Major Arcana or Trump cards. Each Major Arcanum depicts a scene, mostly featuring a person or several people, with many symbolic elements (Death, Tragedy, Love). In many decks, each has a number (usually in Roman numerals) and a name, though not all decks have both, and some have only a picture.

The four suits consisted of Cups (hearts), Wands (clubs), Swords (spades), and Coins (diamonds). Roughly, they dealt with the general fields of emotions, work, thoughts, and money.

The artistry for me was being able to construct an exciting story about each card, drawing from a memorized mental matrix of the elements. Being a writer enhanced my ability to sound convincing. Pat was good at it, but felt her readings were too negative to share.

I needed to set up a stand and have some kind of costume. The site needed to blend into the Medieval Time bracket. The cheapest venue was the Mad Monk, since it only needed a brown hooded robe and our stand was a lean-to made of saplings and branches already at the site.

We cut down the needed pieces in the ambient woods. (Shades of my NJ cabin in 1951.)

"True Believers" among readers like to say that doing a reading draws heavily on their emotional energy. For that reason they can't do more than two or three readings back to back. Not having heard that until I was already successful at the festival, I did them for hours on end.

As soon as I sat at my table in the leafy lean-to, a line of ten to twenty people formed with five-dollar bills clutched in their hot little fists for a 15-minute reading. The only stress I felt was a need to take a pee-break ever hour or so. John worked as my assistant taking the money and selling decks of Tarot cards.

Since I was well into the Westminster theatrical community and had just finished doing *Twelfth Night*, it was easy. I organized a group of folks that would play the parts just for the fun of doing it. We had virtually no budget but scraped together enough for costumes. My key performers were Chris Murphy and Melanie.

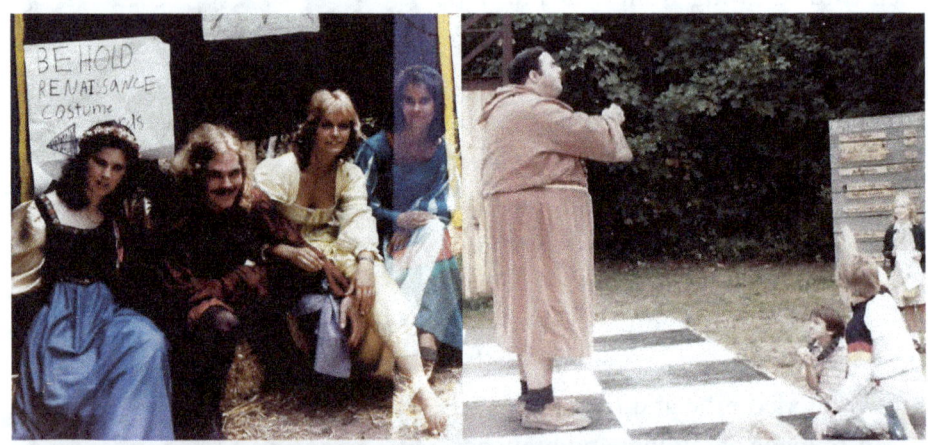

I could never really believe I had any psychic powers beyond years of personal interaction with people. It was a necessary skill if you worked in Public Relations or Personnel. Also, I believed that a reader should never give a client bad or negative readings. They were paying to be entertained, not frightened. However, one morning at the Fair, my first customer was a dismal-looking 60-year old woman who was waiting for me to open my booth.

The first three cards I turned up for her were the top three negative cards in the deck (The Falling Tower, Death, and the Devil). I was unable to think of anything positive to say, so I told her, "I'm sorry, but I can't read for you. No messages are coming through." I gave her five dollars back to her and said, "I think you should go over to the Gypsy Lady in the tent near the entrance."

She did so, but about a half hour later, the Gypsy Lady came storming up to my table. "Did you send that poor old lady in the red dress to see me?" she demanded.

I said, "Yes, I did, I couldn't read for her. Her cards were just too dark."

"You're goddamned right they were. She'll be lucky to get out of the park alive. I never saw a person with such a dark aura around her. Don't send me anymore of your rejects!" With that, she turned on her heels and ran back to her tent.

When the fair was over I launched into doing readings at Tarot Parties for women's groups. I participated in Psychic Fairs, and assorted functions.

I later grew through several iterations to become *Prince Ali Baboon — Knows Nothing Tells Much!*

At a fund raiser for the Hagerstown library, one of the patrons was so impressed with my performance that he hired me to do my readings at his company Christmas parties for next four years. I became the highlight of the evening for many, telling me how accurately I had predicted their futures the year before. I got $250 for an evening from 6 p.m. until 9 p.m.

One day Harry called me into his office and said, "I hear you are telling fortunes at the Renaissance Fair. How can you do that stuff, married to a Catholic?"

I said, "It's easy. I make a hundred dollars a day."

It was a satisfactory answer. "Oh," he said. "As long as you don't believe any of that crap."

I was relieved. I was afraid he had heard of another incident connected with the Fair. A couple paid for a joint reading ($10) and after seeing the diamond on her finger, I told them they would be married and have happy future. Like all the other readings, I assumed this was a done deal and I'd never see them again.

Not so. About a month later I got a phone call from the guy. He had bribed someone from the Renaissance Festival to give him my name and phone number. He wanted to tell me that they had gotten married and wanted me to come to their new house for a private reading.

Never having such an event occur before, I hemmed and hawed. When he offered me $25, I figured, *What the hell?* I went that Friday night after work. When I pulled up near his house I saw the car in the driveway had a Westinghouse parking sticker on the bumper. I was ready to bail when he came out the door. I jumped out before he might notice *my* parking sticker and met him in the driveway.

It was winter so I had an overcoat over my suit. "I need to use your bathroom before we begin," I said. Then I ditched my coat on their couch and made a hasty retreat to the restroom. Once inside, I swiftly shoved my Westinghouse ID badge into my pocket, put my Westinghouse shirt pocket protector into my inside jacket pocket, removed the Westinghouse calendar clip from my wristwatch, and turned my Westinghouse ten-year service belt buckle inside out. I was sure that the last thing this guy wanted to do was pay a guy from the personnel department to read his fortune. I gave the performance of my life.

I quickly determined that he worked in the maintenance department. I knew his foreman, August D'Serio, personally because he was known as a *problem employee* who was scheduled for management training. He was a lousy foreman.

We settled down and I began reading his cards. I told him "I'm getting an image of a large building where you work. It looks like an airplane hangar. You are unhappy with your boss … but he doesn't just harass you, he harasses everybody."

"That's right. Sometimes I want to quit," he responded.

I turned over another card and said, "That's funny ... I'm seeing a kiddie cartoon character. ... My kids watch him on TV ... his name is Augie Doggie."

My client exploded. "That's what everybody calls him behind his back — *Augie Doggie!*"

"Don't quit!" I advised him. "He's going to leave soon. He's not fired, but he decides to take early retirement. You will get a new boss."

After that, my conscious stream of thought was Gospel Truth to him. The news that his boss was leaving was worth the money he paid me. But I never did a home reading again.

Much to my own surprise, I was eminently successful in that identity. I earned several thousand dollars over the years doing so. At another library fundraiser, I set up my table, added a crystal ball and an ossuary for effect, and donned my turban. I had a steady stream of seekers sit down at the table, and I proceeded to do their readings.

About an hour before the event ended, I noticed an old gentleman wearing a tuxedo in keeping with the 1890s theme of the gathering. He sat diagonally from my table, about 10 feet way. He was within earshot and was obviously listening. He made notes on a steno pad, often in response to something he heard me say to a client.

He had the stereotypical look of a Freudian psychologist. I anticipated his game. When my last client had left, I took off my turban and began to pack my gear. He got up from his seat and stood in front of my table.

"Excuse me," he said, smiling a wise smile. "But where do you get this information you give out so readily?" Obviously, he was about to debunk any New Age explanation, after an evening of gathering evidence.

I smiled back at him, and answered, "Can you keep a secret?"

He assured me he could.

I said, "I just make this shit up."

His smile faded and he said simply, "Oh!"

For a moment I saw his lip quiver, and I was afraid he was going to cry. He was planning all evening on an argument that didn't happen. He turned and left without another word.

I taught *Reading the Tarot for Fun and Profit,* in the Carroll County Adult Education Program for four weeks. Since the most students I could handle at one time were 15, I planned to run it again, due to the over-subscription to the program. However, The Born Again Church of the Open Door (but closed minds) assailed the Board of Education for supporting such a Satanic ritual program. We were lucky to finish the one we started. It was pointed out that there was a Carroll County law forbidding fortune telling or even the discussion of it. (So much for the First Amendment.)

I did, however, give an annual Halloween lecture at the Carroll Community College. It was for the Advanced Psychology Class. How it happened was unusual. I had taken a class on *Death and Dying,* and became friendly with the professor. We talked about Spiritualism and ESP and Tarot cards. When I told her I was a reader, she asked me if I would talk about the subject to her Psych Honors class.

At the first meeting I had each student pick four cards from the deck and not let me see them until I called on them later. The teacher also joined in and took four cards. I started with her, and when she told me which cards she had chosen, I said, "You are going to get married." She was not wearing a ring, so it was just a wild-ass guess. She was stunned. "Nobody knows that," she said. "We have not even announced it to our families."

In true showmanship style, I said, "The cards don't lie."

I did the ten students and she asked them at the end, "Did Bill tell you something significant?"

At least six of them raised their hands. As a result I was invited back for the next three years until Pat died on Halloween in 2008. I gave up reading totally after she passed.

Annual Halloween Lecture 2007.

1988

From 1984 on, I worked for Westinghouse in the Management Training Department as a facilitator and instructor. In 1988, word came down that employees could not be sent to our classes unless they had a budget to charge their time to. The result was that we had practically no students. There were four trainers with nobody to train.

However, Bob Dillon, the department manager, knew that we had to look busy anyway. He had us design courses we knew would never be taught.

The year before, I had bought Gene Hochman's modern playing card collection. For income, I began selling playing cards and Tarot cards through the mail and other venues. While waiting for the final word at Westinghouse, I sold cards to fellow employees on the sly. One of them, whose name escapes me, worked in the TV training area took a bunch on approval to give to her lawyer husband for a birthday present. This opened a continued dialog with her on any number of subjects. She said I reminded her of her father, a Johns Hopkins professor. She came to think of me as sort of a Renaissance man.

In that vein, her best friend had an unusual job, working on the Renaissance of Union Railroad Station in Washington, DC.

She was trying, without luck, to find someone to open and manage a unique store in the Mall of Union Station. It would sell what the Smithsonian only displayed. It would be a satellite location of a similar store in Manhattan. Their only candidate for the job was Henry Galiano.

He was a tough neighborhood kid who got a job sweeping-up after the museum types who built dioramas at the NY Museum of Natural History. He learned the names of the specimens, and in spite of a lack of a formal education they loved him. They even took him on a paleontological dig in Utah when he was a teenager. (While there he uncovered a type of saber tooth tiger that bears his Latin name *smilodon gallianus*).

Henry was allowed to keep bones, butterflies and what-have-you, if the scientists threw them way. This filled the rooms of his tenement apartment in short order. With the Museum's approval he did this for years until he got married and his wife complained there was no room for the kids. He got his orders: "Get rid of them!"

In response, rather than trash his private collection of skulls, he and a friend took the subway, loaded with shopping bags full of bones, to the downtown Canal Street sidewalk flea market. They returned that evening with an unbelievable $1,100 in cash. It got to be a weekly habit. He did so well for several weeks in a row, that Henry rented a storefront.

The former museum janitor became an entrepreneur. He was the founder and operator of *Maxilla & Mandible*, "The World's First and Only Osteological Store," in New York at 78 W. 82nd Street. It became the darling of Madison Avenue designers, using his bugs and fossils in a wide variety of ads. He became a successful businessman. Only a city block from my favorite Museum, it was known as "the bone store."

The renovators of Union Station approached him about opening a second store in D.C. He wasn't interested. He was making a small fortune in NYC and had no time for a second store outside New York.

They bugged him incessantly. They saw it as a publicity gem for the opening of the New Union Station. Finally he said, "Find someone who understands what I am doing and I will cooperate. Get me someone who knows enough about natural history to meet my standards and I will stock the store." He thought it was a grandstand gesture until I went to his shop.

In their search they found that scientific types were not interested in retail business, and retail merchants knew little about natural history. My friend's JHU professor father told her about their inquiry to him and she said, "I'll bet they never asked Bill Schroeder."

They called me and made arrangements for me to take Amtrak to New York with their headhunter. When we got to *Maxilla & Mandible*, I looked at the display in their window and realized that all those trips to the Museum with George Wagenhauser were about to pay off.

We hit it off right from the start. Henry Galiano was an unusual combination of a Chinese mother and a Puerto Rican father. He grew up only two blocks from the museum and endeared himself to the staff by cleaning up around the taxidermy shop for a couple bucks. In time, he became an official employee and demonstrated an unusual ability in taxidermy.

My test began immediately. I identified about eighty percent the skulls in his store window. We discussed the insects displayed on the wall to his satis-

faction (Thank you summer of 1945 in Mountainview, NJ. See *Synchronicity, Part One*, pages 114 and 115).

So we took what he called *The Walk of Death*. In an alley next to the store was a line of buckets. Each one had a decomposing skull of an animal swarming with bugs. He asked me what I was looking at and I said, "Carpet beetles stripping the flesh off specimens." The woman who came with me couldn't bear to look at them and ran for the alley gate and gagged.

Henry was pleased. I went for the extra points by telling him what I thought which animals the skulls were from. He stopped walking and yelled to the sick woman, "He's got the job, as far as I'm concerned!"

It took forty-two years for synchronicity to engage, only a block from my old weekend destinations. I was entering the museum curator field through the back door.

When they renovated the Washington DC's Union Station in 1988, I opened *Schrader Scientific.* Our slogan was "We sell what the Smithsonian displays." I sold everything from dinosaur bones to American Indian artifacts and stuffed piranhas.

While I had the pseudo-scientific knowledge needed, the only real retail experience I had was Schroeder's Service Station and selling stuff in the kids clothing department of Sears. They nev-

er really pushed the question of my retail sales qualifications, so I didn't volunteer anything. I had never let lack of experience stand in the way of previous jobs. I took over on an "AS IF" basis — as if I knew what I was doing.

I am reminded of the of the old joke; "Yesterday I couldn't spell entrepreneur — *Now I are one!*"

The LaSalle Partners/Union Station Venture made me an offer I could not refuse. Since I met the Westinghouse requirements for early retirement (55 years old and 15 years with the company) I quit my job and got a $40,000 lump sum settlement.

When I went to Washington and saw where I would be working I was stunned.

My shop would occupy the second blue-paneled alcove on the right.

Our doorman was a human skeleton named Oscar.

I mention this in my book, *The Rub*, but it is worth repeating because of the profound impact it had on the rest of the Schroeder Family's life in numerous ways. Forty years earlier my mother took me on a sightseeing trip to Washington. We had lunch in the same room when it was a big restaurant.

Henry Galiano provided $40,000 worth of bones and other paraphernalia like bugs and stuffed piranhas (with no money down). The Union Station Renovators guaranteed the deal and we embarked on designing a store that was supposed to reflect an explorer/scientist/professor's office. We went to an antique dealer in Frederick, MD, and bought an oak desk, institutional-looking glass-fronted display cabinets, and a chair. (Melanie has since bought them from me.)

On September 28, 1988, LaSalle Partners/Union Station Venture hosted a gala to celebrate the re-opening of the Station and to benefit the National Trust for Historic Preservation — thousands gathered for the grand reopening.

It was a public/private partnership that funded the $160 million restoration of the Station per legislation enacted by Congress in 1981 to preserve Union Station as a national treasure. It was the largest, most complex public/private restoration project ever attempted in the United States.

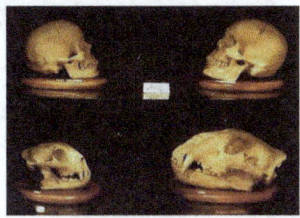
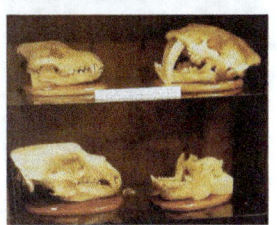

The moveable display cases on wheels could be cleared out for evening meetings and events. I rented one setup opposite the second alcove where *Schrader Scientific* was located. It was called the *Royal Flush* and we sold unusual decks of Playing Cards for an average price of $7 each. They were perfect as last-minute gifts for train travelers to buy for gifts to the folks back home.

I hired Margaret as the manager, and Melissa and Melanie as sales clerks. We dressed in Jungle Jim Safari clothes.

LaSalle Partners' Publicity Department provided a steady flow of newspaper and television crews to highlight our existence.

Merchant Bill Schroeder with some of his African antelope skulls. He also stocks rat fetuses that come in test tubes.

I even took out a few of my own ads in local publications.

When I offered mountain goat and deer pelts, I got flak from anti-fur animal lovers, but sold out anyway.

At the beginning of 1989, my luck ran out. The store outlived its usefulness to Union Station as a Publicity Magnet. They had been overlooking my monthly rent of $1,000-plus, but now I was expected to make the monthly payments. I then discovered that retail stores have to make enough money during the Christmas rush to cover expenses for the rest of the year. When the publicity stopped in January, sales plummeted to barely enough to cover the salaries of the employees.

One night in February, the store was looted. Apparently, during the construction phase of the stores before the September opening, security guards were given keys to all the stores before they were officially opened. They were either never returned or were duplicated. All the thieves had to do was wait until everybody involved forgot about it and the shelves were stocked. Then one night six months later, they let themselves into three different stores and did their shopping for free. None of the store owners were able to collect any insurance on their losses because the police would not confirm that there

were any forcible entries. Personally, I had to pay an archeologist $2,000 for African tribal masks I had persuaded her to leave in my shop on consignment.

The thieves, in my case, clearly did not have any cultural or scientific knowledge of what they were stealing. They stole items with high price tags, not realizing the limited market for them. The fossil mammoth molars had sold for over $100 each, but there was a fat chance of any merchandise fences in DC finding ready buyers.

The items I regretted losing most was a carton of Missouri Indian artifacts. They were believed to be the last relics of that tribe. In the final analysis, to the uninitiated it was just a box of rocks (including a fire-making stone). The box had just been unsealed, and had a $300 price tag on it. I had only bought it the day before the robbery and did not have the chance examine and display the contents.

I had just enough in the bank to pay my March rent when my Mom died. When I went to New Jersey to attend the funeral, I found that I was expected to pay for it. Elsie had supported Mom for years and with my apparent success I was expected to pay the funeral expenses.

I did so, but wiped out my bank account in the process. In short order I was served an eviction notice, along with a DC sales tax assessment, and an impossible business insurance bill. . We shut down, and I sold my inventory to a West Virginia roadside museum at a barely break-even price. We were all unemployed.

SAM SMITH PARK PRATT AND LIGHT STREET

Even before the Washington stores closed we had discussed opening a store in Baltimore. Now it became a necessity. I managed to save the playing card inventory and took it to the Inner Harbor. I talked the Rouse Company into renting me a space on the upper level. We called it the Royal Flush and I furnished it with IKEA drawer furniture. The income from sales barely broke even and I had to close it.

We managed to stay open until August 1989 but vacated the premises "under cover of darkness" telling the security guards we were moving across the street to Rouse's new *Galleria* Building. Otherwise, the Rouse Company would have padlocked the store and I would lose everything, including the furniture. I was now back in the Mail Order business on eBay.

The loss of a third store caused deep psychological anxiety. According to a floppy disk dated Monday, September 18, 1989 things took a turn for the better:

HARBORPLACE MARKET

I have told this story before, but no discussion of synchronicity would be complete without it's retelling. It hinges on some minute timings and situations. It is so unlikely that I have trouble believing it myself, but it is true.

I was so tired I did not sleep well. In response to my aches I got up much earlier than usual. Although confronted with a myriad of things that needed

to be done, I could not resist the impulse to go down to the Inner Harbor to see what could be salvaged from my nearly vacant store. After the usual number of starting delays, I finally got into the car and drove away from the house.

As I entered the commuter parking lot, I saw the train coming into the station. If I hurried, I could park the car and catch that train downtown.

However, just as I went to change from my prescription sunglasses to my regular ones, the left lens popped out and bounced off my lap. It slid between the two front seats and into an unreachable crevice. I stretched my fingers and squirmed them deeper into the space, feeling fruitlessly for the missing lens.

"Damn it," I thought. *"The day's off to a great start."*

Unable to even touch the lens from this angle, I got out of the car and reached under the seat from the rear. I picked up the smoky glass and pressed it back into the empty frame — just in time to hear the train make its "Poot! Poot!" signal announcing its departure.

I watched the departing train glide down the tracks as I walked across the lot. With nothing else to do, I fished out a paperback from my jacket pocket and read until the next train took me to Baltimore.

At the Charles Center Station I emerged from the escalator full of desire for a change of scene. For six months I had always walked the shortest route to the Inner Harbor, but no schedule bound me today.

What the hell, I decided, *for variety's sake I'll walk down Redwood Street instead of the usual route.*

When I reached the corner there was no sidewalk since it was under construction. The heavy traffic meant crossing the street. Intent on getting to my store, I was not looking at the passers-by, and I was startled when one almost jumped out in front of me.

"Hey, Bill, how's it going?" the fellow asked.

I ran the man's face through my mental Rolodex for a name to match. It was Roy Williams, of *Williams, Jackson and Ewing*. He was the man who had made it possible for me to get the $13,000 construction allowance at Union Station the year prior.

"Your name came up in conversation, just the other day," Roy said. "What are you doing down here in Baltimore?"

"I'm sorry to say that I am on my way to Harbor Place to officially close down my store," I answered.

"Oh? I didn't know you had *opened* a store there. What kind? "

I told him that it happened right after closing the Schrader Scientific shop in Washington, then proceeded to explain that a combination of IRS debts, and a $100-a-day loss at both the Baltimore and the Washington stores forced me to pull out.

"Quite honestly, Roy, the only way out is personal bankruptcy. My daughter, Margaret, is getting married in a month and I can't even contribute to the event. My wife, Pat, can't even buy a new dress for the occasion." I was haunted by the fact that the $22 in my wallet was the last of my bank account.

"How much do you owe?" Roy inquired.

"It approaches $100K."

"How much would it take to get you back on line?"

I reflected for a minute and said, "It would take about $5,000 to get my mail order catalog out."

The conversation continued about what kind of work I was looking for. I told Roy I was interested in a writing job or public relations, but I preferred to interact with people.

Roy took one of my business cards. He promised to get back to me on the job business and we parted.

Two days later I received a check in the mail from Roy for $5,000, and nearly passed out in shock. I never saw him again

Had my sunglasses not broken … had I caught the first train … if the sidewalk on Redwood was not torn up, my timing would have been off by seconds. *I would have missed meeting Roy the moment he was exiting the office building, and my entire life would have been different.*

PAT'S LATER WORK

While Pat never did another painting after graduating from Notre Dame, she till bubbled with creativity. Her devotion was to developing her dream of a large family. Nevertheless, she found innumerable outlets for expressions of her inner creative spirit. She chose not to differentiate between arts and crafts ... everything she tried her hand at became art.

While we lived in Detroit she fabricated a silk-lined, yellow knit dress and coat for herself under the tutelage of a master dressmaker from Europe. Unfortunately, due to continual pregnancies she was unable to ever wear it. I did not get any photos of it, but Margaret has it stored safely in a box.

But what she learned was not wasted. She created a sewing school for black women in Spartanburg to help qualify them for previously unattainable jobs at Butte Knit. At the same time she made matching outfits for four of her own kids for a television show sponsored by a local fabric store.

Later, when we first moved back from sunny Arizona, she found her girls didn't have warm jackets, she knitted them matching ponchos.

When she decided to try embroidery, she chose the most difficult pattern available, an Indian chief in full headdress. She undertook a form of sewing that employed micro-stitches — petit point (22 stitches to the inch).

It was so difficult in fact, that she found other designs boring.

Later she switched to making needlepoint embroidery wall-hangings that

were the equivalent of paintings.

She broke into the field of ceramics while we lived in New Jersey, but made her first major piece in Phoenix — a huge German beer stein. It was in ceramics that she made a lasting footprint. On our 1974 cross-country trip from Arizona to Virginia we detoured all over the map to visit mold-makers (many of those purchases are still sitting in the Finksburg basement).

Pat entered her first public display of her work at a Phoenix Honeywell Employee Arts and Craft show. She had the widest display of items.

In 1979 Pat began selling her work at the Carroll County Farmers Market. At the same time we went to Mall Shows across Maryland. I worked at them all. It was not uncommon for people who bought an item elsewhere to comment that they wished they had waited until they saw Pat's fine, superior detail.

She bought a potter's wheel, but never used it. She devoted her efforts to detailed painting, for more than 25 years. Ironically, one of her entries in a competition was disqualified on the grounds that "decals are not permitted." ... She had painted it freehand.

I could fill a 100-page picture book just illustrating

20-plus years of creative work. But I am forced here to limit space to things that I love and illustrate some of the things she made. She never wanted to keep her treasures. We now find ourselves buying back her work when it turns up at the Goodwill Industries store in Westminster.

She loved working on everything she did, and the items were mostly dictated by holiday themes. Christmas nativity sets were her specialties with Halloween running a close second.

In regard to the variety she produced, to quote Shakespeare: *"Age cannot wither her, nor custom stale her infinite variety."*

Pat also did a number of varieties of Chess Sets.

This is the only one remaining in the family's possession.

Pat experienced numerous physical malfunctions, usually of the nervous or cardiac system. In one instance, after being treated by incompetent doctors for allergies, it was determined she had a non-cancerous brain tumor. She had been very proud of her waist-length hair, but had to have her scalp shaved for the operation. The strength she exhibited during the ordeal was truly enviable.

After the surgery, Pat found it increasingly difficult to handle the weighty ceramic molds. In an effort to regain finger dexterity, she reverted to an earlier love … knitting.

And, as usual, she soon developed a reputation for excellence. This time she strove for wider recognition by entering the Maryland State Fair. She was rewarded with a phenominal number of prizes …

Including Best In Show!

At the Carroll County Farmers Market, people who bought her ceramic creations now clamored for her sweaters, hats, scarves and baby ensembles. Personally, I still wear a Hogwarts Slytherin knitted cap to bed on cold nights .

When she found her fingers partly paralyzed, unable to paint details, she reverted to knitting sweaters to establish new neural patterns. Her story was told in the local newspaper:

Local crafter heals from surgery with knitting, ceramics

Pat Schroeder (AKA: the Night Knitter) has done it again. Her sweaters took eight first prizes for Excellence in knitting categories at the 2000 Maryland State Fair. In the past four years, Schroeder has won 35 first prizes from the Maryland State Fair and she's had a long history at the Carroll County Ag Center's Farmers Market. It's strange to think that her success began almost two decades ago due to a brain tumor.

An operation to eliminate the tumor virtually knocked out certain of Schroeder's motor control centers. Seeking to regain them, she used knitting needles and ceramics as therapy. Two other operations followed in subsequent years, but she refused to allow them to become setbacks. (The operations, too, affected her sense of time. She tends to work, uninterrupted, while her family sleeps, in the quiet hours of late night and early morning. This is the source of her nickname: the Night Knitter.)

Fine, detail painting on ceramics forced her not only to restore, but exceed her earlier proficiency.

If asked why she pushed herself to be better than ever, her blunt answer was, "Because I wanted to ... what other reason is there?"

About five years ago, with the arrival of several grandchildren, Schroeder focused her talents on her past hobby: knitting. More than three decades before, she had knitted at least two wool dresses, two jackets, a coat and several children's sweaters, so she had no lack of experience.

"I now have as many as six sweaters in the works at one time," Schoeder said. "When I get tired of one, I move on to another. I can't do all the patterns I like, but I'm trying."

When her production level for knitted items skyrocketed, she tried two years ago to limit her sales at the Ag Center's Farmers Market strictly to sweaters. But after her 22 years of selling prize-winning ceramic creations, there were some unhappy people.

Her long-time followers and collectors of her work wouldn't allow her to abandon her first love. They insisted on leaving orders for Christmas angels, nativity sets, Noah's arks and, of course, Santas. The pressure resulted in a compromise: She now fills two tables at the Christmas Market — one for sweaters and one for ceramics.

Talent and determination are big factors in the Night Knitter's success, but the quality and versatility of yarns now available make a big difference.

"I buy my yarn from local, national and foreign retailers who supply a wide variety of yarns for knitting and weaving," Schroeder said. "Many of them are hand-dyed.

"The countries my wool and patterns come from read like the roster of the Olympic Games: Italy, Norway, Australia, Ireland, Scotland, Greece and Canada (also some 'exotic' places like Pennsylvania, Maryland and New England)."

Many of the yarns are spun from high-grade virgin wool combined with specialty fibers like linen, silk, cotton, alpaca and rayon. She also embroiders her own embellishments to the original designs to make them unique.

The darkest moment for Schroeder's knitting career came last spring. She received a call from the Home Arts Department planning the 2000 Maryland State Fair.

"I was afraid they wanted me to be a judge," she said. "I'm not qualified to judge anything. I want to compete! And to continue trying to do the best I can. It's a continual learning experience for me."

Melissa Steele lives on an herb farm with her husband, two children and numerous animals. She can be reached at The_kiyotee@hotmail.com .

Photo submitted
Pat Schroeder (the Night Knitter) wears one of the sweaters which recently reaped a first prize at the 2000 Maryland State Fair. She also cradles a ceramic Noah's Ark, one of her best-selling works.

As I have said, Pat's life was made up of creative ativity of all sorts, and enjoying the children she looked forward to in her formative years. She said she regretted that we only had four grandchildren.

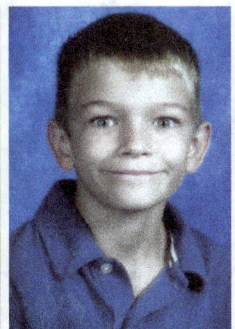
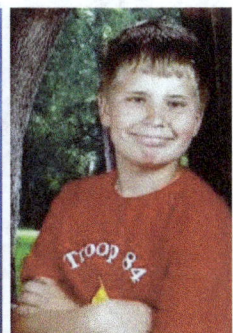

Pat ofen substituted for me when it came to cheering at sports events involving grandkids.

She never cared to go with me and the kids on any extended vacation. The one exception was celebrating our 25th anniversary in 1985 with her friend Analeise Gaun in Arizona.

She did thoroughly enjoy day trips to King's Domnion and Hershey Park, though. Fortunately, I had a job that supplied me with complimentary tickets for the whole family.

Family gatherings of all varieties were satisfying events in her life.

The biggest and most memorable of these was the surprise 40th Wedding Anniversary party staged by the kids in 2000.

No discussion of Pat's life would be complete without mentioning her love of fantasy fiction. On TV it was *Dr. Who*. In the world of print, it was Harry Potter. On more than one occasion we were in the Mall's Waldenbook store at midnight to be among the first to buy a newly released Harry Potter novel. To her he was a real person.

Ranking in third place, behind the Family and Art, were Siberian Huskies. After 1980 she was never without one.

At one point she became a breeder.

Prior to her passing, she made light of her failing health. I worked with her on a mock press release to inform family and friends of the situation:

OFFICIAL PAT SCHROEDER PRESS RELEASE

FINKSBURG, MD — January 3, 2007: When Pat Schroeder passed out one day early for New Years Eve (7:30 p.m. Saturday, December 30) she took a 911 trip to the New Improved and Updated Emergency Room of the Carroll Hospital Center. At 11:30 p.m., despite her attempt to flee the hospital, they transferred her to a regular room to spend the night.

She told them she would be better off at home resting on her brand new mattress, not the flat cot they call a bed. In the morning, finding herself unable to drink their decaffeinated glurg called coffee with 1% milk, or eat the wallpaper paste they claimed was oatmeal, or the rubber pancakes obtained from the Hospital Joke Shop, she demanded to be free.

She negotiated a treaty with her doctor, and after some compromising, like promising not to faint anymore, not to be carted back to the hospital again, and swearing she would see Dr. Nagama today, he grudgingly decided to let her go.

He examined her this afternoon and found that she has now shrunk to the height of 5-ft. 5-inches (which is a mistake), but could not determine anything else extreme. Her blood pressure was higher than normal, but may have been due to consumption of very salty shrimp the night before.

She is scheduled for an Echo EKG at 4 p.m., Wednesday, January 10. The next afternoon she will go to a local facility to be tested for Carotid Artery flow, and an MRI on the site of the previous cranial surgery.

The regular family Doctor, Dr. Mathew, will be consulted about her recent blood work which may have indicated a thyroid imbalance. Another press release will be issued when there is further information available.

Pat suffered an a*ortal aneurism* in the early morning hours of October 31, 2008.

We decided that we would establish a Maryland State Fair Memorial Award for outstanding knitting excellence. A poster proclaiming the award was at the 2009 Maryland State Fair:

STAR ISLAND REMEMBERED

In 1955, when I started at Rutgers Newark College of Arts and Sciences, my faculty advisor was Frederick T. McGill, the head of the English Department.

He immediately became my "go to guy." I honestly did not know anything about college. I saw it as an advanced high school that was free to me under the GI Bill of Rights. My choice of English as my major was primarily governed by the

fact I did not need to take any math-related subjects. All I knew for sure was that you needed a degree in something to get a good job, and English seemed to be the easiest way to accomplish that goal. I had read extensively by choice and I knew how to write declarative sentences as required for US Army Criminal Investigation reports. To me, the next few years amounted to simply reading a lot more books and discussing them with others.

Fred signed me up for virtually all the courses he taught ... American Literature. In 1956 Fred McGill hosted a weekly hour-long television program about American authors. In the final installment he invited three of his students to take an on-air oral exam on the subject matter.

With my usual over-inflated self-confidence, I agreed to appear. I had not really seen any of the TV programs, but I was sure I could bluff my way through. It turned out that I had to do just

that. He gave us no advance information about the questions he would ask and picked me for my weakest topic — Mark Twain. I beat about the bush for a full minute, trying to beat the big red hand on the studio clock. Fred saw I was in trouble and interrupted to thank his viewers for watching the series. He assured them I knew the answer but we were out of time. He told me 20 years later that he knew right away that I didn't know the answer.

He taught his classes with a strong Unitarian bias, laying down a path of understanding I have followed ever since. He provided me with a spiritual foundation for life without having to pretend to be a believer in the Jesus Christ myth.

He grew up Unitarian and put his beliefs to the test when he had to choose between spending a summer getting his PhD or managing The Oceanic Hotel on The Isles of Shoals, seven miles out to sea from Portsmouth, NH.

He said he never regretted his choice. He never got his PhD, and spent

the remaining summers of his life at the Oceanic. He invited me to see him in the summer of 1957. I never enjoyed a summer like it before or since.

Twenty-odd years later I spent five successive summers there again. Fred was still there.

Each week the hotel hosted a different intellectual conference. The first one I attended was "Religion in an Age of Science." I caused a ruckus when I gave a Tarot demonstration in the Blue Room one evening and I drew a larger crowd than the scheduled speaker that day. The chairman of the conference approached me at dinner when he saw my announcement on the bulletin board. He was quite angry and said I was defiling his serious conference. He said, "What makes you think these educated people would want to hear your superstitious nonsense?"

I asked McGill if I should go ahead with my talk. "No one is making them go!" he said. The response was overwhelming. I held a drawing, letting the audience select the three highest cards from the deck to win three readings I would give the following day in the hotel library. The funniest thing was when the chairman's wife asked me secretly to read for her and not tell her husband. I did a dozen readings during the days that followed at $3.00 each.

In the years that followed, I attended the theatrical improv group that met the first week of June each year. Almost all my spare time during these weeks was spent doing readings. In 1987 I had two women for whom I had read the previous year, catch me on the pier to tell me how impossibly accurate I had been.

I had told one, a chemistry professor, she would visit her daughter in California. At the time of the reading her daughter did not live in California. (No explanation).

My roommate was one of the speakers; "The Pope's" Astronomer." He was an American Jesuit priest who worked at The Vatican Observatory (*Specola Vaticana*) an astronomical research and educational institution supported by the Holy See. It was his job to keep the reigning Pontiff updated on the world of science. I read the Tarot for him "for kicks." He was a fascinating guy who offered Holy Communion one morning using orange juice and oatmeal cookies instead of wine and wafers. His point was that the whole thing was symbolic, and he performed his role in the historic Unitarian Chapel on the island to illustrate that where it was performed made no difference.

In 1987, I credit synchronicity involving the Improv Class with keeping me from making a serious mistake regarding my marriage. That was also the year that Melissa and I drove there to attend. She was the only other member of the family to go there. We decorated the end-of-week party dance in an unforgettable style. The following year many of the decorations were still hanging on the walls.

In later years, back problems made traveling there too painful a prospect.

4/89 TO 6/89 TELEPHONE TAROT READING

During the months following the closing of the Inner Harbor Royal Flush Store, I found it virtually impossible to find any kind of job.

However I saw an unlikely classified ad in *The Sun* for Tarot card readers. I went for an interview and demonstrated my Prince Ali Baboon skills. The job was reading Tarot cards over the phone in response to a 900 number promoted on TV. It was a very popular activity at the time, but was stopped a few months later due to fraud charges against the business operators of the scam.

The problem was not the veracity of the readers, but of the complex mechanism that lay beneath the surface. I initially saw my readings as harmless feeding of a gullible public.

Readers were paid a commission of ten cents a minute on any readings that went beyond the first three minutes. We were all given a script of idle chatter to get past the three-minute minimum. We had to get the callers to say they were 18 or older, and were calling from their own phones. The charges were collected by the phone company (pre-cellphone era), and split with the 900 Company.

At the beginning, the customer was charged one dollar a minute, but about the third week of operation it had jumped to three dollars a minute.

The longer you kept the client on the phone, the more was added to the phone bill. Since most callers were low-income people (often welfare recipients), their phone bills soon reached a point where their service was discontinued by the phone company for lack of payment.

The whole system was overturned by the *Baltimore Sun*, not for any compassion for the victims, but by the fact that so many callers were employees of the city. They were running up the office phone bills to unbelievable heights. The telephone company's lawyers totally withdrew its cooperation and claimed they had no knowledge of what was going on.

Fortunately, I got my last paycheck the day before they raided the "boiler room" and arrested the managers. I never went back to see what happened. No one ever called me as a witness.

EBAY, ETC.

I have been asked why I was so successful with eBay. The answer is simple … *I find everything interesting.* It's the same reason I am a writer. The world is an interesting place and I have enjoyed being a part of it, not just to look at it on a TV screen, but to participate in it. Ownership of something is not necessary if you can hold it and learn about it. Then pass it on to someone who wants it more than you do. The net financial proceeds allow you to acquire something else for a while.

Getting into semantics for a moment, Thoreau said, "the cost of a thing is the amount of our time required in exchange for it, either immediately or in the long run." The biggest nugget of truth was, "A man is rich in proportion to the number of things which he can afford to let alone." (I couldn't let anything alone.)

Before eBay, I was fascinated by libraries, museums, nature, auctions, yard sales and flea markets. While I collected a lot of things, I kept relatively few of them (unlike some members of my family who can't bear to part with anything). Books might be a possible exception, as they may contain ideas I want to review at later date.

When this book is finished, I plan to do a lot of browsing of books and poetry. I was remiss in following one piece of advice Thoreau offered: "Read the best books first, or you may not have a chance to read them at all."

I have mixed emotions when it comes to electronic advancements in communication technology. I was stunned when one of my grandkids equated listening to an iPod with reading books. As a writer I was outraged. However, I realized we were talking about the medium of distribution, not the content. I realized that I have been a fan of audio books since they were first invented. In fact I sold scores of tem on eBay.

I look forward to Googgling lots of music and Youtube discussions. Google simplifies my approach to the intellectual life by eliminating the need to physically go anywhere. As I said in one of my books, "Google is an ocean of information, but it's only three feet deep." Fortunately, I am generally satisfied with mental wading.

Toys were among the first items I bought at yard sales, but only to stock my own tables at flea markets. I named my table "Interesting Finds," allowing me to sell anything that caught my fancy.

SCHRADER SCIENTIFIC

Schrader Scientific in Washington was the ultimate extension of that notion. There, I tried to limit my inventory to stuff with a scientific or cultural connection. Here are a few of the items I sold:

ARCHEOLOGICAL AND ANTHROPOLOGICAL

NATURAL HISTORY

ANTIQUE AND HISTORICAL

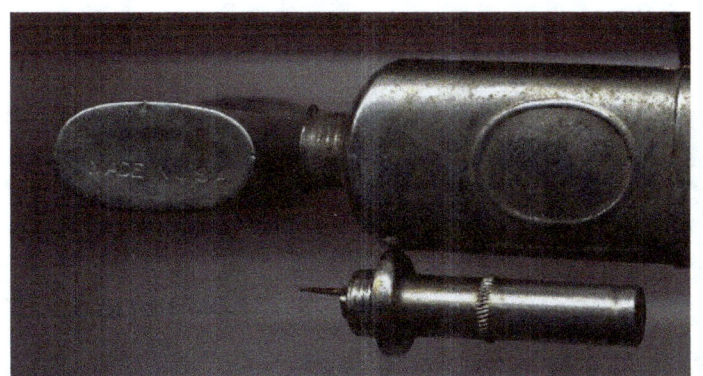
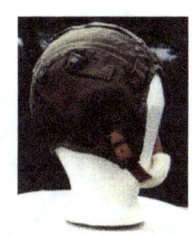
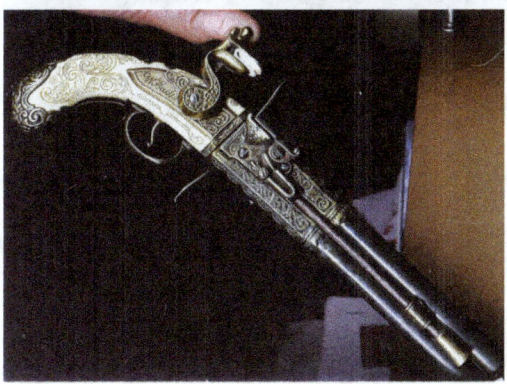

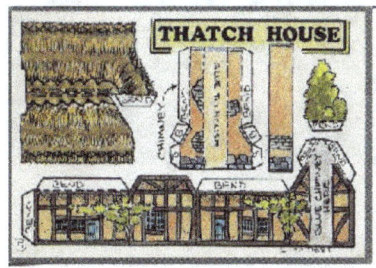

FLEA MARKETS & EBAY

When it came to eBay or flea markets, there were no limitations.

NEW AGE

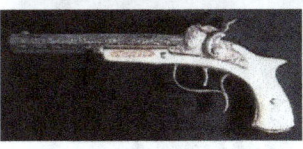

TOMATO HARVEST 1996

Never satisfied with doing one thing at time, I renewed my interest in gardening. In the spring of 1996 I began an adventure that earned me the local title of "The Tomato Man."

I had planted a dozen or so tomato plants I got at Baugher's Farm Market. They were thriving, so I went back to get some more. What I found was a wild tangle of tomato vines Allen B. had not sold. They were in various stages of bearing fruit. No one was buying the plants so late in the season because real farmers knew that the season for starting tomatoes was long past. The entire lot was scheduled for the dumpster to make way for fresh produce coming in from the fields. Not being able to stand by while such gems were being destroyed, I bought the entire mess for ten dollars and crammed as many flats into my station wagon as it would carry.

When I got home, I pulled the car on to the huge lawn adjacent to Timber Lane on the east side of the house. Aside from being the site of a former septic tank field, it was the lowest point in the neighborhood. When it rains, a river runs through it.

I unpacked the flats, putting one plant in the center of a square one-foot-by-one foot. When they took root and flourished they grew into each other with such gusto that it looked like the Amazon Jungle. I counted 93 empty plastic starting-boxes of untold varieties when it was over. It got so thick, a zoning official stopped by to give me a citation for allowing my lawn to be overgrown with weeds. He was stunned when he found out the three-foot high weeds were actually tomatoes.

I provided a habitat for numerous rabbits, groundhogs, and squirrels. My neighbor told me that when he left for work at 6 a.m., there were often a deer with two fawns browsing there. I quickly ran out of people to give tomatoes to. I regularly left shopping bags full at them at the Library and the Post Office. Women waiting outside Food Sunday were regular recipients.

Pat and I were not into canning, and frankly we were tired of eating tomatoes. Howard and John helped me harvest them and I ground the vines to mulch with the riding mower. For years afterward, random, rogue tomato seedlings sprang up amid the blades of grass.

PRISON UNIFORMS 2002

In September 2002, I was in the waiting room of the Carroll Detention Center to deliver a box of playing cards to the Librarian. They were for the use of prisoners to give them something to do, easing up the pressure on the guards.

For a short period of time the Carroll County Detention Center dressed prisoners in stripes, especially on work release details. For some reason someone else was there with a bundle of used, striped uniforms. The ensuing conversation led to my buying the bunch of them for a dollar each.

I sold them on eBay very quickly at $10 and proceeded to buy a quantity of new striped and orange prison uniforms and caps from the manufacturer. I sold a large number of them as Halloween costumes on eBay.

I persuaded John to model a uniform for eBay. The response was fantastic, even after the Halloween costume season. One customer was a defense

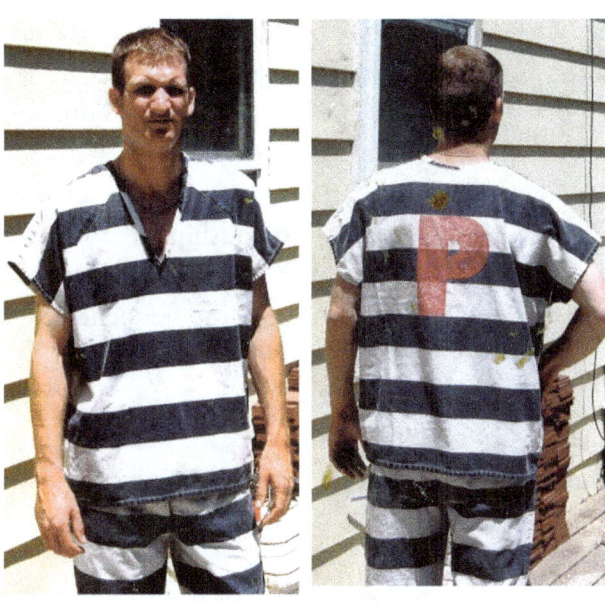 

lawyer who displayed a striped uniform on a manikin in his office to argue with clients that he was keeping them from getting one of their own.

They were made by inmates at a prison industries company in Florida. They actually came in a variety of colors, such as pink stripes for the infamous Sheriff Arpayo's detention center in Maricopa County, Arizona.

PLAYING CARD COLLECTING

There were a number of threads that led to my collecting playing cards. The earliest was a Christmas present from Pat. It was a double deck of unusual playing cards with custom art work. It was a 1961 Neiman Marcus Christmas catalog item. I never actually had the chance to play poker with them since Pat didn't play and I did not have any friends who did. They simply became part of my growing collection of curiosities.

My mother taught me how to play Rummy when I was about seven years old. She was a big card-playing fan and went to many Card-Bunco parties which were popular in the pre-TV 1930s and '40s. Bunco was a Yahtzee sort of a game. We had four over-sized dice used to play it. But, like so many things they got lost over the years.

When I was 14, I went to the Lutheran Catechism Class at St. John's. I made friends with Carl Gimmel, Jack Voth, Warren Burker, and Jimmy Dehling, friendships that lasted through our adult years. We formed a Saturday Night Poker club that went on for years. They honed my skills to enable me to join the frequent poker games in Korea.

In later years, I developed my interest in Tarot Cards. The first few decks I bought to use in my fortune-telling business. In the end, I had more than 150 differently themed decks, which I sold to a fellow collector for over $1,000 in 2009.

I became interested in non-standard playing card decks and eBay at the same time. Like me, Elsie's husband Nick was a great yard sale fan. He picked up a deck of French souvenir playing cards for a dollar and sent them to me as a gift. Since I was only interested in Tarots, I decided to sell them on eBay.

To my astonishment, I sold them for $20 and sent Nick $10. I never dreamed it was the beginning of a new career — Playing Cards and eBay. I went at it with a vengeance. I figured it out one day, years later, that I was making an average of ten thousand dollars a year on eBay for about ten years.

About 1983, *The Wall Street Journal* changed my life once more. Only this time it was not centered on the Employment Classifieds ... it was a front-page feature story. It was about Gene Hochman, a one-time garment industry salesman, who became the successful head of an interesting world-class, off-the-wall business collecting and selling playing cards. He had the largest collection of non-standard decks in the United States. I can honestly say I was never more excited about anything as I was about his story. I wanted to get in on it somehow. It overwhelmed my thinking. I was in a dead end job in the Training Department at Westinghouse, and I knew the company was headed toward disaster.

I had been involved with the making of several training films and thought this might be a way to get an interview with Hochman. I would propose to make a short TV flick about him and his cards. It turned out to be totally unnecessary as he was very approachable, and my personal interest in the cards was evident. We hit it off well and within a few months I had a mail order business selling cards to collectors with his help.

With nothing worthwhile to do at Westinghouse due to budget cuts, I began secretly running the business from my cubicle. I got a P.O. Box at Hunt Valley since I thought a Finksburg address would be too humorous sounding for a serious business. However, my boss, Bob Dillon, caught on and I had to work at home.

Just before the Westinghouse bubble burst, Hochman decided to sell most of his inventory. He wanted $18,000 for it. I wanted it so badly I maxed out my credit cards and made a loan from the Credit Union to raise a total of $16,000. Gene accepted the offer.

Hochman's story was one of his own synchronicity. A few years earlier he had retired from the garment business and had no particular plans. One Saturday he went to a local flea market in New Jersey. He told me, "I looked into the dark back of a big moving truck and all I could see was an orange glowing dot. On the tailgate were four bushel baskets filled with decks of playing cards. Since I am a bridge and poker player, I thought I would buy some.

"The glowing orange dot was the end of cigar connected to a gruff looking old guy. I asked him how much for the cards?"

"Two bucks," he said. "I got the leftovers after I moved somebody who didn't want them."

"I'll take a couple of decks," I said.

"He said, "No. It's two bucks for a bushel basket full. I just want to get rid of them."

Gene bought all four baskets. When he got them home and examined them he found that they were from all over the world and some were obviously old. He devoted himself to the scholarship of researching playing cards in a manner not previously known.

Gradually, he became known among card enthusiasts who were persuaded to begin collecting. He joined a European card collecting club and subsequently went with his wife to visit card manufactures across Europe, buying large numbers of collectible cards which became his inventory.

In 1976 he began serially publishing *The Encyclopedia of American Playing Cards* in six parts. The last book of the series was published in 1981. It was a complete cataloging of American playing card makers as well as details, types,

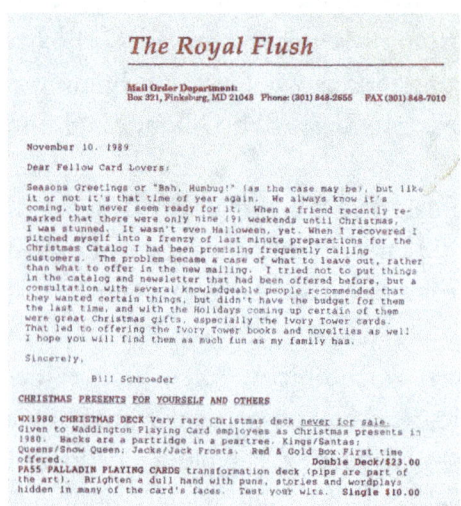

and brands of playing cards from the late 1700s to the early 1930s. They were later combined into a single volume in 2000 by Tom and Judy Dawson.

Gene Hochman joined with some other collectors to form *52 Plus Joker*, the primary American collectors club, which I joined. I bought Gene's inventory of American cards, and began my mail-order card business, The Royal Flush ... 1984–1990.

One of my major development factors was going to their convention Cincinnati in 1991. Allen Hicks loaned me $400 to make the trip and I made $1,700, beginning my new career.

At the time of Pat's passing on Halloween of 2008, I had become recognized nationally as having one of the largest personal collections of decks of playing cards — somewhere about 7-8,000 packs. I was acknowledged as a major collector and authority on the subject. However, Pat's death had a serious effect on my life motivations in general.

In August 2009 my friend Pete Peterson in Colorado asked me if I would be interested in evaluating a collection of playing cards in Philadelphia. A long time collector (1971–2001), Dr. Frederick Minn died the year before without any heirs and left all his worldly goods, including his card collection, to a next-door neighbor, Anna.

She sold a special deck he had left her with instructions as to how to do it, for an auction price of $3,200. Pete had to reassure her that the rest of the cards would hardly be worth anything near that. However, she was independently wealthy and did not need the money. She regarded the card collection as more of an annoyance and an obligation she owed to Dr. Minn. I called her and made a date to view the cards on August 8th.

Margaret drove me there and when we pulled into the driveway, my first comment to Margaret was: "Wow! This is money." It was an estate that had been divided into three residences. Deer families were casually wandering the grounds, nibbling the tomatoes in the gardens without fear of being shot.

We went inside the house and Anna dumped three boxes of Tarot cards on the kitchen floor for me to examine. There were about 100 of them, some expensive but nothing antique. They were all recent or current decks.

It was before my first cataract operation, so my vision was limited. I had to limit myself to four hours of looking. She chose to present the American cards next. They turned out to be the kind of cards generally available from eBay and in catalogs, but there were a lot of them. In fact, some of the sales receipts showed that Dr. Minn had bought a number of cards at my Washington store and from me on eBay.

At the end of four hours I could hardly see straight. I had to call a halt to the activity without looking at the vast overstocked warehouse of European decks. We agreed that Anna would simply count the European cards and give me a total. We then would negotiate a price on the total number as a group.

Two weeks later, we found she had 1,500+ decks. She asked for more than I had expected to spend, but when she threatened to give them to a friend to sell at a Philly Flea Market, I could not resist buying the lot to save them from falling into the hands of the Philistines who would (God forbid) play cards with them.

On September 5, John drove his pickup truck up to Pennsylvania to get the cards. He deposited ten steel shelving boxes on my deck and I began viewing my treasure. To my amazement, the European cards were the opposite of the American cards. They were genuine antiques and collectibles having been purchased during Dr. Minn's numerous travels in Germany, Italy, France, and the UK.

My inventory of the first 100 decks indicated a market value of about $6,000. This confirmed my need to go to the International Card Convention in Toronto, Canada on October 8–11. The cost of getting the cards there became a problem. If it were in the USA, just driving them there would have been no problem. But crossing into Canada meant Customs and the need for the driver to have a passport. Will, Jr. was the only candidate for the job.

I priced about 500-600 decks and boxed them up. The cheapest way for Margaret and me to get to Toronto was to fly to Buffalo, and rent a car from Budget to drive from there to Toronto. Bill borrowed Howard's truck and drove north. Margaret and I arrived at the hotel at 5:00 PM and waited to hear from Will.

No call. Finally we contacted him at 10:00 PM by cell phone. Canadian Immigration refused him entry based on a computer record of single arrest (no conviction) for alleged drug possession twelve years ago. They sent him back to Niagara Falls, which was better than being arrested for attempted illegal entry to the country.

That left me at a very expensive card convention with no cards to sell. The only answer was for Margaret to drive back to Niagara Falls Friday morning to transfer the boxes to our rental car. She did so and returned to Toronto late in the afternoon.

I spent the day sitting at my table with only four decks I brought with me in my suitcase. But I sold two of them for a total of $100. Everybody at the convention knew that the famous Minn card collection had been held up at the Canadian border. All day long people asked me what the status was — where was my daughter now? — What was the latest? I became a living international soap opera.

That evening Margaret and I sorted boxes and set up the entire Tarot Collection on our hotel room table. An interested collector made an appointment to look at the Tarots Saturday morning at 8:15 a.m. He liked them and bought the lot for $1,000. We took the rest of the boxes downstairs and set up the cards on our table.

When the doors to the trading room opened, European collectors descended on my table like a seagull feeding frenzy. In the course of the day I sold over $4,000 worth of cards.

Sunday morning we made a few more sales and then folded our tent and silently stole away back to Niagara Falls to put the card cartons in Will's pickup. He drove them home, while Margaret and I flew back.

I could not have done it without Margaret. We did a role-reversal. She took charge of the whole operation at the convention from setting up to collecting money. At the Airport I became a Toddler in a stroller (wheelchair) and the Nanny handled all the details of security and ticketing. I will never attempt to fly anywhere again without her. More likely, I will never go anywhere on a plane again.

It was so stressful; I spent most of the next few days napping intermittently to recover from the Great Canadian Adventure.

I sold the balance of the Minn collection on eBay for a grand total of $15,000.

LOCAL RECOGNITION 2005

While presenting my work before the Library of Congress' *Meet the Author* program was tremendously ego-boosting, I still had a craving for local recognition and also by my peers in the card collecting world. My ego was boosted in one instance when Richie Herink bought a large number of copies of *The Rub* and mailed them to people whom I knew in high school. The focal point for them was the portion of the book for titled *West New York Stories*. I received phone calls from people all over the country with whom I had not spoken in sixty years.

I wrote a number of feature stories for the *Carroll County Times* senior citizen publication, *The Advocate*. That led to being able to get the editor to do a small feature on *In der Fuehrer's Face* in January 2006.

Another high spot was a publicity grab for the FDR deck. The decks were being sold at the gift shops of the FDR Library, The Smithsonian, The Library of Congress, The Archives (and other lesser spots) for $19.95.

Several years later, in 2010, they did a feature on the FDR deck.

Recognition by other playing card collectors as an authority on the subject was something I also prized highly. I wrote a number of articles for the 52 Plus Joker Magazine *All Hands On Deck*. After successes with the *Fuehrer's Face Deck, The FDR deck,* and my book *Seven Decks You Will Never Play Poker With,* I got to be known as the guy who collected decks that never existed.

I was more than pleased to write a multi-page article for the Chicago Playing Card Collectors' Magazine for Spring 2008. The subject was a definitive discussion of politically-themed playing cards. It resulted in a marked increase in m eBay sales activity.

Following my successful talk at the LOC, I was delighted to essentially give the same presentation at the 52 Plus Joker Convention in Delaware. The biggest local ego boost was being part of the CC Community College Holocaust Memorial Lecture Series.

I have little patience with people who claim they are bored, whether they are 17 or 77. When I go to bed at night, my last thoughts are usually, *I wonder what interesting stuff will happen tomorrow?* Key to that philosophy is to be open to new opportunities, then to act on them.

My last big personal event in that category was a display at Baltimore's Enoch Pratt Free Library that highlights my then five books. I never dreamed of anything like that happening, but in January 2017 Will Jr. drove me down to see it for myself. The lighting was terrible and the only camera we had was Will's cellphone. I was glad to get what we did.

I did not know anything about the Library Display until my friend, Allen Hicks, had already made the arrangements. Allen took over my playing card col-

One of the biggest surprises was being invited to display and discuss my books at Carroll County Farmers' Market Writer's Day, on November 7, 2015.

lection last year and he has thrown himself into it with the zeal of a new religious convert. He engineered the display of the World of Playing Cards including my books: *Seven Decks You Will Never Play Poker With* and *In der Fuehrer's Face*.

As it turned out, The Pratt Library's Art Director became a fan of my writing. He negotiated with the Circulation Department to buy an undetermined number of copies of my five books for the Pratt, including: *The Rub; When John Frum Came;* and *The Innocent Assassin*.

All five books were previously available as Kindle eBooks but now are also paperbacks. They are being sold by Amazon and everywhere else that sells books.

FDR DECK 2010

In 2010, I made the winning bid on what was billed on eBay as "Depression Era Playing Cards." The item turned out to be a unique historical gem — one of a kind — a pack of Franklin Delano Roosevelt *New Deal Deck of 1934* playing cards. All copies of the deck were believed to have been destroyed by the Secret Service under orders from FDR himself.

How they survived undetected for 65 years is a story in itself. Students of American History will recall the struggle Roosevelt had introducing his radical programs for his New Deal to resolve the economic problems of the Great Depression. He created what are known as the "Alphabet Agencies."

The story on the deck's origin turns out to be an "eBay fabrication," most likely to create a false provenance to help sell them. Allegedly, a well-meaning supporter in Dallas, TX, designed and printed a deck of playing cards listing 25 of the new federal agencies on the backs. However, they never got permission from FDR to do so. To compound the problem, the court cards featured FDR on the Kings, Eleanor Roosevelt on the Queens, and Vice President John Nance Garner on the Jacks.

The story goes that the President felt that they played directly into the hands of his enemies. It was about this time that an anti-Roosevelt group (The Royalist Party of America) was laying the foundation for a derogatory campaign whose slogan was "Roosevelt for King." This deck of cards would fuel the fire.

The eBay vendor held the key to the mystery. According to the seller, he bought them at a tax auction. Being sold were the personal effects of an eccentric fellow named Old Jeff (No last name). Old Jeff told him that someone had them printed in 1934 by a novelty company, J.M.A., Inc., that he worked for.

I perpetuated this myth *In Six Decks You'll Never Play Poker With*. However, researching the subject with the help of friends at the Library of Congress Copyright Bureau, we could not find any evidence that the *New Deal Deck of 1934* had ever existed. The LOC concluded that the tag reading, "1934 J.M.A, DALLAS, TEXAS" was only a ruse, and it was not actually copyrighted. Printers often used the technique to discourage others from copying their work without going through the paperwork.

Supposedly, FDR was so furious at his face being on the Kings, and Eleanor on the Queens, he told the Secret Service to "suppress" them.

Two Secret Service agents showed up at the Dallas printing shop and bulldozed the owner into a panic. They told him that he was in danger of being arrested on serious charges, possibly treason. The only way out was the consignment of all the decks into the furnace. Old Jeff was only about 18 at the time and was given the job of burning the cards under the supervision of the government agents.

However, while the agents were distracted Jeff stuffed a deck, plus a handful of loose cards, into his pockets. At the end of the day, everyone but he believed all the cards were gone forever.

Jeff took his stolen cards home and put them in a shoebox. Then, thinking better of his actions, he put the shoebox in the attic and spent the next 65 years expecting G-men to break down the front door and arrest him for "God-knows-what." In 1999, they were sold with the shoebox and everything else for unpaid taxes.

Acting as sort of a playing card detective, I made a number of valid research contacts. The publishers of *The Hochman Encyclopedia of American Playing Cards,* the world's foremost authorities on the subject confirmed that there were no other decks like it.

A while ago, I conferred with historians at the Franklin D. Roosevelt Presidential Library & Museum in Hyde Park, NY and confirmed that no others are known to exist. I copied the original cards and have reprinted them as they were originally designed.

FDR AND THE ALL

I have to admit that the story about FDR's ordering such a Fascist-sounding order to suppress a deck of cards, never quite sat comfortably on my progressive-liberal mind. It was something I'd expect from Trump or Nixon.

But, true to form, Synchronicity came to my rescue. While I was researching something else, Google led me to "An attempted American coup d'etat: 1934." In spite of all the books and articles I read while writing *In der Fuehrer's Face,* I never came across this. My grade school and high school history teachers (avid Roosevelt New Dealers, all) had never mentioned it. Things were a lot raunchier in Washington than I ever suspected. Just making fun of the Democrats was not at the root of "Roosevelt For King." The whole idea would have been laughed off by my father's friends at the gas station.

In my sheep-like mode of public thinking, I believed that Big Business and the Republicans were benignly disenchanted with The New Deal's government reforms. Somewhere in the political gobbledygook was the monetary Gold Standard — Nobody in real-life America had any idea what that was all about.

I never dreamed that a group named The American Liberty League (ALL) hatched a plot that today would be labeled *terrorist*. Known as the Business Plot, the ALL consisted of top executives of corporations like DuPont, Singer Sewing Machines, General Motors, and the Sun Oil Company. They also attracted the support of wealthy individuals like Hal Roach, Hollywood producer, director and financier.

The League's chief Modus Operandi was a propaganda blitz that would have made Nazi Josef Goebbels envious.

The League produced 135 pamphlet titles during its first two years, printed for easy distribution by mail. Half of them originated as speeches or radio addresses delivered by League officers or its most prominent supporters. On the mailing list to receive at least five copies of each were newspapers and government agencies, public and college libraries, all members of Congress, and other political groups. They often generated new stories and reports in other publications. The ALL also produced two-page monthly bulletins, distributed to the same audience as the pamphlets.

A different promotional tactic that downplayed the role of the League itself was the creation of a syndicated news service. Before its discontinuation near the end of 1936, the League reached 1600 newspapers through the Western Newspaper Union. Finally, the League took advantage of offers of free radio time wherever it could.

The NRA, Alphabet Agency playing cards deck was a Grass Roots bid for poplar attention. The American Liberty League were not content with urging Congress to pass legislation cancelling the National Rehabilitation Act (NRA) and the new laws that created an unheard-of minimum wage of 40 cents an hour, along with Social Security. They were going for the jugular.

They sought retired U.S. Marine Corps Major General Smedley Darlington Butler, to lead an army of 500,000 veterans in a march on Washington, D.C. These were the Veterans' Bonus March people in the Hooverville shacks outside D.C. and across America. There were good reasons why someone seeking to overthrow the U.S. Government would have wanted Butler involved. He was a powerful symbol to many American soldiers and veterans — "an enlisted man's general." Butler spoke out for their interests while on active duty, and after retirement. He would have attracted men to his cause who would not otherwise have participated in any march on Washington.

Butler made radical proposals no one else dared to, like … "all workers in defense industries, from the lowest laborer to the highest executive, be limited to $30 a month, the same wage as the lads in the trenches got." He also proposed that any declaration of war should be passed by a plebiscite in which only those subject to conscription would be eligible to vote.

"I spent 33 years and four months in active military service and during that period I spent most of my time as a high class muscle man for Big Business, for Wall Street and the bankers. In short, I was a racketeer, a gangster for capitalism."

General Smedley Butler

The veterans had made camp in the Anacostia flats while they awaited the congressional decision on whether or not to pay the bonus. The motion was decisively defeated, but the veterans stayed in their camp. The newspapers reported that Butler had arrived with his young son, Thomas, in mid-July the day before the official eviction by the Hoover administration. He

walked through the camp and spoke to the veterans; he told them that they were fine soldiers and they had a right to lobby Congress just as much as any corporation. He and his son spent the night and ate with the men, and in the morning Butler gave a speech to the camping veterans. He instructed them to keep their sense of humor and cautioned them not to do anything that would cost their public sympathy.

On July 28, Army cavalry units led by General Douglas MacArthur (with Major Dwight D. Eisenhower at his side) dispersed the Bonus Army by riding through it and using gas. During the conflict several veterans were killed or injured and Butler declared himself a "Hoover-for-Ex-President-Republican."

In 1934, General Butler testified in secret before two Representatives of a special committee on Un-American Activities, John W. McCormack of Massachusetts, and Samuel Dickstein of New York. In 1934, they investigated Communist and Nazi propaganda and recruitment efforts in the United States prior to World War II. Dickstein was subsequently revealed as a paid agent of the Soviet NKVD. McCormack maintained a consistently liberal voting record throughout his Congressional career, including support for the New Deal

At the upper levels of Washington there are no secrets. Roosevelt no doubt knew what Butler had testified. He knew of the existence of a plot in 1934, Butler told the committee members that one Gerald P. MacGuire, a Wall Street bond salesman, made him an offer. The *New York Times* reported that Butler had told friends that General Hugh S. Johnson, former head of the National Recovery Administration, was to be installed as dictator, and that the J.P. Morgan banking firm was behind the plot. Butler told Congress that MacGuire had told him the attempted *coup* was backed by three million dollars, and that the 500,000 men were probably to be assembled in Washington, D.C. the following year. All the parties alleged to be involved publicly said there was no truth in the story, calling it a joke and a fantasy.

In its report, the committee stated that it was unable to confirm Butler's statements other than the conversations with MacGuire. No prosecutions or further investigations followed. The reason most of us have never heard this story is that historians have not reported any independent evidence apart from Butler's testimony. The news media dismissed the plot, with a *New York Times* editorial characterizing it as a "gigantic hoax."

On the other hand, when the committee's final report was released, the *Times* said the committee "purported to report that a two-month investigation had convinced it that General Butler's story was alarmingly true" and "... also alleged that definite proof had been found that the much publicized Fascist march on Washington, which was to have been led by Major. Gen. Smedley D. Butler, according to testimony at a hearing, was actually contemplated." The individuals involved all denied the existence of a plot, despite evidence to the contrary. Though the media ridiculed the allegations, a final report by a special House of Representatives Committee confirmed some of Butler's statements.

Part of the reason for the lack of prosecution of the alleged plotters may have been the untimely death of the only man who could have testified against the rest: Gerald MacGuire. He died at age 37 from complications of pneumonia.

The fact remains that Butler claimed he saw through their supposed concern for Roosevelt. He testified before Congress that he told MacGuire he saw it all to be a plot to replace Roosevelt with a "Secretary of General Welfare." He deduced that the real goal was a coup d'état to take Roosevelt captive, and force reinstatement of the gold standard, the loss of which many wealthy Americans feared would lead to rapid inflation. Roosevelt would remain as a figurehead until he could be "encouraged" to retire.

Excessively dramatic as it all sounds, it is more believable than FDR having the Secret Service suppress a deck of cards because he didn't want to see his picture on the Kings in a poker deck. He saw it as a "clear and present" personal danger.

If you want to know more of the details of this lost chapter in American history, I urge you to Google *An attempted American coup d'etat: 1934*.

2010 FAKE FLAGS

When I was conducting a Welfare-to-Work program in 1992, one of the interactive activities for the 15 women in each class was to draw an American Flag. The result; 95% of the people who tried got it wrong — I was one of them.

Just about everybody knew it had 13 stripes, but the sequence of red and white stripes suffered a bit. The positioning of the stars was everybody's downfall. When you look at it, 6-5-6-5-6-5-6-5-6 is apparent. It's sort of like the kid who says, "I know how to spell BANANA — I just don't know when to stop."

What difference does it make? There is a very real side to where the stars on the American Flag are placed. During the ten-year period from 2001 to 2010, the U.S. Census Bureau reported that Americans purchased over $69 million dollars worth of illegal copies of Old Glory from Communist China. (No later figures are available). In the year following 9/11 alone, the Chinese cashed in on our national grief. They sold us over $29.1 million dollars worth of them. That also translates into thousands of lost American jobs.

Adding insult to injury, most of the flags were incorrect copies. Many had from 40 to 55 stars and from 12 to 15 stripes.

To those of us who are dead serious about the authenticity and sanctity of the Flag of the United States there is no document more important than President Dwight D. Eisenhower's Executive Order 10834, dated August 21, 1959.

The design is not a suggestion or a guideline — it is a legal definition of what constitutes the official Flag of the United States of America. Minor

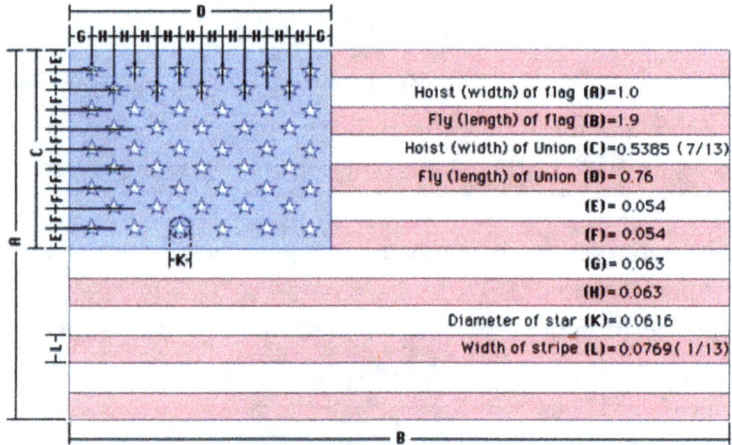

details like the spacing between the individual stars is specified.

Even the colors are rigidly specified by law. Red, White and Blue? Yes, but Government Spec DDD-F-416F, dated 31 March 2005, identifies them as Old Glory Red, White and Old Glory Blue on the International Pantone Matching System. Chinese flags sometimes vary from vermillion to near purple.

The key to spotting illegal flags at a glance is really quite simple. Look at the position of the five-pointed star in the lower right hand corner of the blue field. When the line between the fourth white stripe and the fourth red stripe is extended to the left it should just barely touch the top points of the six stars in the bottom row on the blue field … Like this.

By this measure alone, the vast majority of those flags made in China are *illegal*. But a quick Google trip shows that even some American Flag makers are also getting it wrong.

Executive order 10834 was issued by a United States President and has the full force of law, based on the authority derived from the Constitution itself. Executive Orders do not require Congressional approval to take effect and they have the same legal weight as laws passed by Congress.

Some commercially available flags almost meet the requirements. But, *almost* only counts in horseshoes and hand grenades.

The Flag Code states, "No disrespect should be shown to the Flag of the United States of America." Intentionally disregarding the legal design and colors of the Flag of the United States in its manufacture is "disrespecting" it.

Many American politicians and Government officials have unwittingly contributed to the general acceptance of fake flags. However, I must say that they are generally victims of circumstances. They assume that the responsible parties — usually aides or art directors — check out the flags they pose with. Unfortunately, they probably didn't know the difference either.

Here are some familiar faces with phony flags you may have seen on TV:

Donald Trump   *HillaryClinton*

Bernie Sanders   *Barack Obama*   *Jimmy Carter*

George W. Bush *Nancy Pelosi* *Mitch McConnell*

All the flags you saw in the above photographs violated the Law of the Land. The problem obviously cuts across Party lines.

Allen Hicks and I had worked out the details of publicizing our discoveries when I had a minor stroke in 2011 and had to withdraw from the activity. We had not succeeded in interesting the Boy Scouts, schools, or politicians in joining our program.

2013

Dielman Inn Project, Community Empowerment Through Education. Conceptualization By The Messenger Foundation

Around January of 2013, Will came up with a brilliant idea — we would buy the Deilman Inn in New Windsor, MD and establish a multi-faceted project. It would be aptly named THE DIELMAN INN PROJECT.

It would serve many functions. Using federal financing through grants and loans, it would be a residence for homeless veterans, and a training venue for certifying veterans in such skills as restoration carpentry, electrical installation and repair, and commercial painting. We had lined-up professionals in all those areas to teach and monitor the training. The students-in-training would actually be refurbishing the building at a cost far below what outside contractors would charge.

The ground floor would be occupied by commercial enterprises such as antique or gift shops. The corner shop would be a "Welcome to Historic New Windsor" tourist office. Will, Margaret and I would occupy the brick-walled portion of the building as our residence.

Will devoted scores of hours researching and developing the mechanics and details of the project, and had pretty much persuaded us that it was a successful idea. Our mistake was to have lunch with the town's mayor, Neal Roop, and one of his aides. Roop, it turned out, has a family connection in the ownership of the property. Will told them too much, enabling them to bypass us and pull the rug out from under us.

The following Monday night, Allen Hicks went to the New Windsor Town Council meeting representing us. He was the only person there besides the town officials. To make a long story short, they had no intention of selling the Dielman Inn. They wanted to control every facet of what goes on there and were not interested in a Veterans program of any sort. They wanted the place to be a commercial establishment. The death knell was the fact that they expected to spend $450,000 on lead paint removal, which would raise the price of the building into the never-never land. Will had

planned to take a state lead-containment certification program costing a few hundred dollars, not $450k.

Using Will's research on the government grants, they claimed his ideas without any credit. However, there is no Veterans connection. I heard that one of the reasons they were worried about a Vets program was because some of them will be black and New Windsor is a lily-white community. Some of the vets might have wanted to live there later.

Under their plan the Inn would be limited to private commercial enterprises. With the price tag they have put on the idea, I doubt it will ever see any measure of completion. Where will they get another person like Will to manage all that needs to be done?

Will and I had a long discussion over coffee on the deck. We agreed that the Inn Project was over. The local politicians did not even acknowledge Will's bid (or return a phone call).

At this writing (11/15/17) there have been no further developments concerning the property.

FRIENDS

Some of the most important events in life are only visible in the rearview mirror. They happened. They couldn't have been forced to happen. We didn't even know they were there. They were spontaneous.

Consider friendships. We think we have chosen our friends, but in reality, any number of chances might have kept us apart ... a few years' difference in the dates of our births, employment choices, the accident of a certain topic being raised at a first meeting. I don't question the fact that some people entered my life at the exact point of need, want or desire ... Call it a Coincidence or Fate if you like, but whatever it is, I am certain it formed a stitch in my personal fabric of life.

In *Synchronicity, Part One*, I discussed the influence Rich Herink had on my early life. In later life I feel compelled to recognize two other friends ... Allen Hicks and Marcia George. Without them the whole trip would have been quite different. Both are strong personalities who should write books of their own. ...Who am I to say they won't? They are only in their sixties and seventies — I'm writing this at 85!

Following are a few words about them:

ALLEN HICKS

In looking back on slightly more than eight decades of living, I have identified a number of what I will call "synchronous people." These are people who have had an influence on the pathways of my life. Among them, one stands out... Allen Hicks. When my retail stores folded, I desperately needed a job to pay the monthly home mortgage. One possible source was a friend, Edie Donohue, the Registrar of the Catonsville Community College, whom I met when I arranged company contracts for Westinghouse managers to take specialized courses.

Edie told me she was leaving the registrar's job and asked if I was interested in applying for her vacancy. We agreed that my early involvement with the Rutgers Bursar's Office and my running a Management Development program should have qualified me for it.

However, when I went to her office expecting to be hired she told me there was a non-negotiable block to my employment — I did not have a Masters Degree. No one could be hired as a teacher or administrator for CCC without one. It made no difference what it might be in, you just needed a MS or MA after your name.

I was in near panic. I had no idea what to do next. As a consolation prize, Edie offered me a ticket for a dinner that evening being held by ASTD, the American Society of Training Directors. I went. A free meal was better than nothing. After eating, we broke into discussion groups. I chose to go to the one about employment discrimination, being moderated by Allen Hicks.

I said I was the victim of Age Discrimination. I couldn't get an interview when it was clear I was in my late 50s. I got a lot of sympathy from the others, but no suggestions. Allen told me to hang around after the meeting. His employer, Arbor, Inc., ran a "Welfare to Work" program under a contract with Anne Arundel County. There was an opening, but the problem was that no one but black women had ever held the job. The assumption was that an old white guy could not win the hearts and minds of the largely black clients. Ninety-five per cent of the enrollees were young women. Allen convinced program management that I could do the job. I kept it for three years.

The broad description of the course content was "Life Skills." It dealt with items most middle-income people learn while growing up without realizing it. We discussed such things as having a checking account … what is insurance? … using a library … paying taxes … basic sex education … and how to apply for a job. My job was to act as a facilitator, allowing professionals in any given field to give talks on their respective subjects.

I was new to the game, and took their objectives literally … I tried to get the students jobs. The basic assumption at the county government level had been that their clients were beyond being helped. Their job was to keep the registry rolls overfull for future classes. This gave the illusion that such a program was needed, providing county employees jobs as a result.

Nobody ever really tried to get the welfare clients jobs. When they finished the two-week class of Life Skills, they simply returned to their previous welfare status. After a year of unsuccessful job searches, they were re-enrolled in the class for another two weeks. After a year on the job I began to see familiar faces. Many women enjoyed the adventure as a social event.

The jobs of the trainers and administrators depended on a cadre of welfare recipients to fill the classes (15 at a shot for two weeks). I found many of them jobs, some before the end of the second week.

What I didn't know was that the program was funded on the basis of $8,000 per student per week. I persisted in making contacts for job interviews and candidates getting hired.

The president of the training company quickly learned the benefits of not being a governmental operation. She discovered the joys of corporate living, and held a long-weekend off-site conference in Ocean City, MD. One of the sessions boiled down to "What to do about Schroeder?" I was undermining their funding with my subversive hiring program. To make up the difference, the program was re-cast as a three-week session.

Furthermore, the critique sheets filled out by the students on the last day of the second week indicated that the students liked me. It had been assumed that only a black woman could run the class successfully.

One said, "If I had Mr. Schroeder in high school. I wouldn't have quit."

I did such unpredictable things as having my left ear pierced for an earring on my 60th birthday. They each came up to my desk to see for themselves that it was real.

I was getting bored with the curriculum myself, so I brought in some pre-historic stone tools left over from my Washington natural history store. We had a lively discussion about the basic needs of life never changing.

I broke the class down into three groups of five, with a problem of a plane crash in the desert. What do you save? Do you wait to be rescued or leave the crash site?

I found interesting speakers like Marcia George who really rattled their cages by admitting that she once considered suicide. Almost all of them admitted they had considered it at least once. When she told them of her journey from being a Playboy Bunny to becoming a minister they were profoundly moved.

Some refused to believe she was 50 years old because of her youthful appearance. Their mothers at that age were washed-out. She had to show them her driver's license to prove it.

I had a psychologist friend who covered the desk with 50 different Matchbox toy cars. He asked them to chose the one car that appealed to them most. From their choices he proceeded to give them pop-psych insights to their personalities.

I was warned by one of the other trainers that the president's solution to my annoying hiring program was to find a reason to fire me.

Synchronicity once more to the rescue. One of the corporate types that had been hired as the Finance Manager attended the off-site meeting and learned that salaries were to be frozen, while also thinning out the herd of administrators. He worried about some of his friends losing their jobs. He confirmed that I was on the list of bye-byes.

He and one of his friends invited me to lunch, when they made a proposition. They knew I was well-versed in Labor Union behaviors and proposed that I organize a union election for the group.

I analyzed the problem and worked out a timetable. If undertook a union organization campaign, Maryland law said Management could not fire me or lay me off in retribution for a year. That would give me enough time to plan an alternate career of some sort.

I contacted the local IUE-CWA Local president, who knew me from my earlier Westinghouse days. At that time I was generating anti-union propaganda … the reverse side of the coin. He was delighted to walk me through the initial procedural steps if it would achieve a mutual objective. He had tried unsuccessfully to organize the same body of people when they worked for Anne Arundel County.

The company president was notified that I represented the IUE-CWA in a petition for union recognition. She shot herself in the foot when she identified only three employees as management. Calling the others professionals reduced the amount she would have to pay them. That left 25 employees who were eligible to be represented by a union.

During the weeks that followed, I managed to persuade a potential majority to cast their votes for unionization. The weak spot was the lead accountant. She was an alcoholic, hired (in a written contract) conditionally to stay sober or resign. When she missed three days after a bender, she was convinced by the president to vote against the union.

We lost election by one vote. When I was called into the president's office to receive the news, I finalized my new plan. I would back off in my zeal to find employment for students (who still had a cash value as long as they were participating in the classroom training). In return, I would agree to being laid off on a certain date, becoming eligible for unemployment payments. I would stay on unemployment until I became eligible for Social Security on my 62nd birthday.

Thus, in November 1994 I became a full-time eBay and Flea Market Entrepreneur.

Two of my children were also hired by their association with Allen while I was still teaching there. Howard taught computer basics to officers at the Naval Academy in Annapolis and went on to establish his own company. His sister, Melanie, worked in a youth training program where she ultimately met her husband, Paul. She has since blessed me with two gifted and talented grandchildren, Kelly and Eric.

Allen became my best friend and we partnered in various business ventures. He is a rare human being with a mind that adapts to virtually anything. Since he is not likely to write his own biography, I will take this opportunity to tell what I know of it. It is fascinating. Although this book is a memoir about me, I feel compelled to give credit to the friends who enhanced my quality of life — Allen Hicks and Marcia George.

First let me talk about Allen. It is not as though he is unaware of his talents; it's more like he is busier living an interesting life than talking about it. In 1972, he posed a photographic question … "Madman or Genius?"

My evaluation favors Genius, with a slight leaning toward Madman.

In June 1972 Allen graduated from St. Mary's of Maryland with a Masters degree in Political Science and History. However, his expansive soul was not content go off to teach somewhere. Even though he did not speak the local languages, he wanted to experience the world. So he hitchhiked across Europe, working as a day-laborer for six months until February 1973.

He says, "I know it sounds corny, but I wanted to really observe the culture and the art of each country. Not as a tourist — not an *Ugly American*. I wanted to see their art work -- meet people — experience different worlds."

When I met Allen 27 years ago, his artistic talents were submerged in the work-a-day world of training people to get into the mainstream of society. He worked on the difficult process of helping people find themselves and their worth to society. He did a pretty good job, and it is impossible for him to go anywhere in the Inner City of Baltimore without running into someone whose life he has affected positively.

But politics and budgets being what they are, welfare assistance lost a lot of its funding. The program was eliminated. Not to be stopped by the mere loss of a job, Allen took advantage of the very principles he was teaching — he learned a new field of work by signing up for computer training. Using his new skills, he became a supervisor in a computer department of the Maryland State Government. However, he felt he was surrounded by poorly motivated and untrained people on his staff. He moved on.

But life for Allen has never been a straight line between two points. His next stop was Maryland Public Television.

Early in 2007 I had lunch with Allen when he asked me to be a part of "The Big Read," a project for MPT. They gave out hundreds of copies of Harper Lee's famous book *To Kill a Mockingbird* to Seniors. Then, in March 2007, they held a luncheon to discuss the book.

The idea was to have a local author discuss *To Kill a Mockingbird*, and facilitate the discussion. ... Allen's recommendation was me. It turned out to be a satisfying ego trip, and extended into my giving a talk to members of the MPT staff about Guiteau. I almost got them interested in considering *The Innocent Assassin* put on TV, but internal politics ended that possibility when he left them.

That summer, Maryland hosted the *Antiques Road Show*. Since I have been a follower of the show for years, Allen got tickets for Melissa, Will and me to get some of our artifacts evaluated. We didn't agree with their appraisals, but it was fun for all of us.

When I tried to explore his feelings as a modern sculptor, I thought of the story about the famous sculptor, August Rodin. He was asked by a student how he could be expected to turn a granite block into a figure of an elephant, the Master said, "Chip everything away that doesn't look like an elephant."

But at the core of the problem, the student needed to have an idea of what an elephant looks like. As a modern day sculptor, Allen defines art as "a man's attempt to interpret what he thinks life and the world look like." When he is successful, he creates a work that captures the essence of a unique perception of an item in the everyday world.

I have seen him work his personal magic on gourds and pieces of wood. In fact, he discovered what secrets lie hidden in wood when he was still teaching for the Welfare program. He told me, "When I took a bunch of teenagers to the American Visionary Art Museum. I became enamored with benches made into animals. I said, 'Hey I can do this!' That same week a neighbor cut down a tree in his back yard. I asked him for a 6-foot section that weighed 400 pounds. I winched it into my yard and set to work with my chainsaw, shaping it into various objects.

"Once I had the wood, things took off. The muse moved me."

Allen grew up in Anne Arundel County. His parents were survivors of The Great Depression with roots in North Carolina. He wrote a TV script (2012) about their struggle titled *Death by a Thousand Cuts*. It was part of a Television Production course he earned at a local college as payment for managing a community Urban Farming Program.

In high school he did detailed anatomical sketches for a friend of his sister who was in nursing school. He found he could do good renditions of bone and skeletal structures.

Illustrative of his random and diverse skills, he went to Barber School, and worked his way through college cutting hair. The barbershop where he worked was robbed three times and closed down after the last one. As a reminder of those days, Allen had an antique barber's chair in his living room as an armchair. When asked if he bought the chair as a piece of art, he says, "It is existential. I bought it because it was there and it appealed to me."

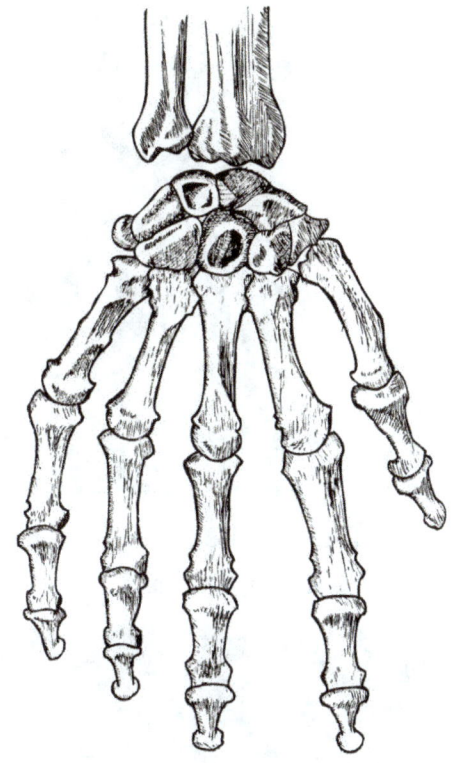

Allen collects art in all forms. … In his words, he likes "natural formations, gourds, from pop art to Folk and representational pieces from modern sources and driftwood. Art just drifts into my life." — He has an eclectic taste in self-expression.

We found a grove of trees next to Route 83, where a wild vine strangles trees, leaving them with an odd corkscrew shape. We cut down a bunch of saplings that Allen fashioned into *Hicks Sticks*. He sold them at the Baltimore Art Fest. We sold one on eBay for $100. We billed them as "Witchstix" from a secret grove on his family's property in North Carolina. I still have a cane he made from one of them.

In 1987, I made a staff from one to make my magic staff as a prop for my role as Merlin in *Camelot*.

King Allen the First posed with a hand-made scepter in his hand-made throne in his backyard. The picture illustrates that there are fences and there are *fences*.

"I hated to leave my home next to Roosevelt Park in Baltimore," he told me. "It was the first house I owned. To me it was my home, not an investment. I couldn't afford structural changes, so I decided to change my home to suit me. I painted murals on walls."

He also founded and ran a community association for residents of the Roosevelt Park neighborhood. He only gave it up when the locals didn't show enough interest to continue its operation on their own.

In recent years he has taken to building furniture from items originally destined for other venues. One of his favorite mediums is books. They become tables, chairs and shelves.

 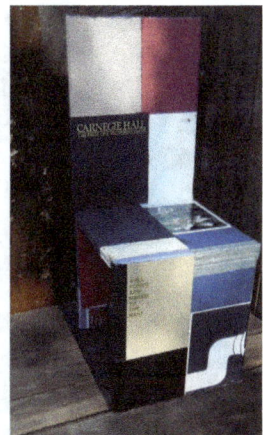

Artful expressions include mosaics and unclassified media.

His experiments with life masks were varied and interesting. I have one covered in gold paint and another designed with playing cards.

Sometimes they were downright spooky. The mask is his, but the hand in this picture was made by Pat.

He briefly experimented with silk scarves.

When I became acutely aware of my mortality after a serious fall in April 2015, I wondered what would become of my large collection of playing cards. My biggest fear was that they would be tossed out in a massive housecleaning event after I died. I decided that their value could be extended by putting them in the hands of someone who might appreciate them. The obvious answer was Allen. In a sense it was a cowardly move on my part … I transferred the burden to someone else's shoulders. I was delighted when he accepted them as his own. I hoped he would do something creative with them. I was not disappointed.

On the following page is a table/desk using rare playing cards as a decorative motif.

Synchronicity 2 • 303

MARCIA GEORGE

Kenny Rogers' song "You Can't Make Old Friends" sums up a feeling that must be experienced rather than described:

> *What will I do when you are gone?*
> *Who's gonna tell me the truth?*
> *Who's gonna finish the stories I start*
> *The way you always do?*
> *When somebody knocks at the door*
> *Someone new walks in*
> *I will smile and shake their hands*
> *but you can't make old friends*
> *You can't make old friends*
> *Can't make old friends*
> *It was you and me, since way back when*
> *But you can't make old friends.*

I recently listened to a discussion on the subject on NPR, citing the loneliness felt by many old people. I could not identify with the problem, as I can honestly say I never feel lonely. Perhaps it is because those I call old friends have not moved beyond a phone call. Maybe after they're gone I will change my perspective.

There are only four or five people I consider "old friends," all of whom I have known for at least thirty years. Marcia George is one of them. She was Marcia Hurt when I met her in 1984, but she subsequently married Eddie George, keeping his name after a divorce.

We met in 1984 at a Psychic Fair in Reisterstown, when we had adjacent tables reading Tarot Cards. We were attracted to each other right away, and believed we were married in a previous life. Shortly thereafter, she did a reading for me at her home in Ellicott City. She warned me of a big storm coming my way for which I had to prepare. The storm turned out to be the closing of the Westinghouse Defense Center. Although she does not remember it, she arranged for me to have a meeting with a retired successful building contractor who counseled me on starting a new life. It was followed by the Westinghouse fiasco and opening the Schrader Scientific store in Washington, DC.

While visiting her and Eddie George at their Berkley Springs, WV, home one weekend, I finished reading *Cows, Pigs, Wars, and Witches: The Riddles of Culture* by Marvin Harris. That led to creating an outline for *John Frum, He come* during the two-hour drive home.

I was greatly impressed by the extreme diversity of her life ... from Indiana farm girl to Playboy Bunny to entrepreneur to psychic to Clergywoman. She presided over the marriages of all three of my daughters, and Pat's Memorial Service.

At this writing (September 26, 2017) she just gave up her summer house rental service in Berkley Springs. I talk with her frequently on the phone and exchange emails often.

In some respects she occupies a place in my life similar to Allen's. They both have a quality I have not found elsewhere ... I trust them with personal emotional information I would tell no one else. Both are totally non-judgmental — very rare indeed. She has been one of the most profound spiritual and intellectual influences on my thinking.

Rather than try to tell her intriguing and complex story, I offer a piece she wrote about herself. It's told in a unique monologue from an extraordinary point-of-view. You can extrapolate many aspects of her life from what she describes in her world travels.

SHOES SAY WHAT WORDS CANNOT

Throughout my life shoes represented where I was at that time, and where I was headed. Looking at the shoes I wore can reveal the path I was on.

Oh! These high heels? Well I wore them for the two years I was a Playboy Bunny. It was grueling to be on your feet for hours on a Saturday night ... Never

Playboy Club

able to rest or sit down. I witnessed more than one Bunny drop to her hands and knees groaning and crawling to the dressing room after finishing a long Saturday night shift.

Standing on my high heels, dyed to match my lavender Bunny costume I met Bob Hope, Judy Garland, Singer Lana Cantrel, Hugh Hefner, of course the Mafia and many other celebrities.

Playboy Club

Usually, I do not reveal that I was a Bunny. Why? Because people sometimes think a Bunny took her clothes off and was photographed. The only women who took their clothes off were the ones aspiring to a centerfold. And disrobing did not insure that she'd make the cut to the magazine. The magazine's Playboy Club publicity photo shoots were often bogus. As Bunnies, we'd grab for the magazine that show-cased our club. It would have pictures of us, stating that Bunny Carol was in college or studying to be a dental hygienist or the like! What tomfoolery this was. We'd laugh our heads off to see what was said we were doing. In fact, many were divorced mothers desperately trying to make a living. Or working to put husbands through law school.

Working at the Playboy Club introduced me to money. I'd thought I'd found the pot of gold at the end of the rainbow. Yes, we worked hard, running in our high heel shoes to wait on customers, but the earnings were incredible. Today it would be like earning $80,000 a year. I bought a black sexy Corvette, and with money I saved, I made the down payment on my first house.

I grew up living on the Indiana Prairie with my family of farmers. Remembering my youth as a first grader … as a family off we would go to the shoe store to buy new school shoes. We were required to place our feet

Indiana

in the x-ray box and I would peer down to see my greenish, bony feet. Dad grinning at me, as he purchased those sturdy Buster Brown Oxfords. Dad's father gave him a team of work horses … King and Princess … as a wedding present. Dad would swing me up on to the back of Princess, as she was more trustworthy than King. My Buster Brown-shod feet and legs would stick straight out because the back of Princess was so broad. Oh, the thrill of sitting up so high on her back, like I was an Indian princess riding on a gaily caparisoned (decorated) elephant!

Teen Years

By the time I was a young teen, saddle shoes were the rage, right along with Chuck Berry and Elvis. Jitterbugging, twisting and twirling. First dates? Well then I wore black soft leather Cappizzio flats. Oh my, how sexy and lovely they were. I felt like a pampered princess wearing those luscious slippers. For me, a huge plus wearing these flattest of flat shoes was that I probably would not tower over my date, who hadn't gotten his full manly height just yet.

College

Penny loafers carried me through college years. Oh, I was so cool. Partying with the fraternity guys, dancing the twist to Ray Charles and trying out alcohol for the first time. Singapore Sling was my beverage of choice ... I thought it was an exotic, sophisticated drink. Now I remember, I was just an Indiana farm girl, ignorant about much of life.

High heels went out the window. In came flip-flops, wearing these while living in Coral Gables, Florida. With my first child, Bridgette, a dark-eyed beauty, Oh, God! I fell in love with her. Wearing shorts and flip-flops, hoisting her around on my hip was a time of deepest pleasure and fulfillment as a young mother.

Now divorced, nightlife for me was wearing sexy boots or strappy platform heels as I caroused the bars of Fells Point on the Baltimore waterfront with my best friend, Mary. Mary looked as though she just got off a Viking sailing ship with her long blond swinging hair. Boy, did she draw the men to us for spontaneous night sailing on the Chesapeake Bay. We had wild and fun times and maybe a bit reckless too. Hell, I was like a Sarah Palin on the campaign trail.

Baltimore

My second child, Jamie Talbot, was born at the same time I birthed Coffee Hostess, an office coffee service that friends and family thought was doomed to failure. Driving my Volkswagen Bus with coffee kits, a playpen, with babies chattering and playing, I grew Coffee Hostess into a profitable enterprise. I would cold call on companies, asking to speak to the office manager. At first I thought having my kids in tow would be a deterrent to selling the office coffee service. However, those midwestern women office managers loved it.

Coffee Hostess Service

What shoes did I wear? I would wear sandals, flats and muck-a-lucks when it snowed. Muck-a-lucks? Brushed natural leather knee-high sheep-lined fur boots incredibly comfortable, which I wore until they were falling apart. Oh, how I loved those old boots.

Mukluks

TRAVEL

Time marches on and I traveled the world in walking tennis shoes. Europeans asked me "Why do Americans always wear those white, ugly gym shoes? They have no style"

However, white walking shoes brought me to Paris, touring the Louvre museum.

Le Louvre

It is overwhelming when I recount all the places I have traveled to ... Moscow and Lenin's tomb on Red Square. Do you know I saw Lenin's corpse? Preserved all these years. It was challenging, surreal actually, for me to realize who I was looking at under glass in the mausoleum.

A night train to St. Petersburg brought a visit to Katherine The Great's glittering Summer Palace. The Nazi's destroyed a lot of the Palace near the end of WWII. However, today it is a restored marvel. Viewing the gaudy, gold-gilded walls and huge mirrors and the unthinkable luxury the royals lived in caused me to realize, *no wonder there was a Russian Revolution*. The majority of Russians lived in poverty or very close to it.

Standing in my American white tennis shoes in front of the famous Mona Lisa painting, I was in a state of awe that I could be so close to this eternally famous work of art. Walking in Paris, Notre Dame, the Eiffel Tower, the Seine, The Opera, the 12th Century Le Marais where we had an apartment on my second honeymoon.

Michelangelo's David in Florence, Italy was a moment of breathtaking beauty and wonder! And, Michelangelo's Sculptured Pieta, looking nearly alive! Pompeii, a stunning site to walk through. Looking at the paintings remaining on the walls, walking where the Pompeii citizens walked, all in my tennis shoes.

Travel
Europe

Strolling along the streets of Calcutta, India had such an impact that I am still psychically marked from the experience. Overwhelming humanity living in conditions I could not have imagined! It was exotic, mysterious and dusty, and I hope to return someday wiser and more experienced.

Maturity has brought me to orthopedic inserts for my tennis walking shoes. The adventure of moving to Texas finally satisfied a long dream to own a pair of cowboy boots. These are honeys.

What do you think? No boring brown or black ones for me, but spankin' red. When I was younger, thinner, and lovely looking, heads would turn admiringly. Now that attention is a past memory. Today these boots bring looks and praise and even envy sometimes. Yeah, I do strut with them a little with them on. But, hey, wouldn't you?

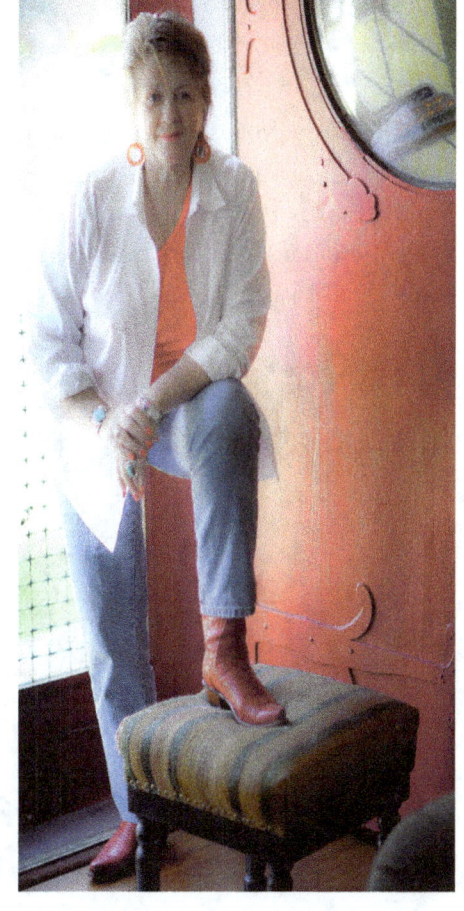

NOVEMBER 2008

The week following Pat's death I invited all the kids to a *remembrance meeting*. Each made a comment on their "memories of Mom." This photograph records the last time we were all together in one place. Without Pat the cohesiveness of the family went into a steep decline. The focus was on individuals rather than family.

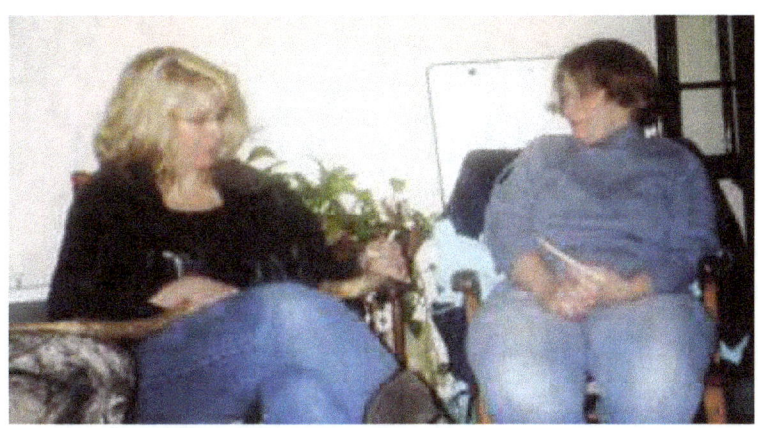

Epilogue

"The time has come," as the Walrus said, "to talk of many things." In this case, what I believe is the end of the book. One theory of writing suggests that every paragraph in a memoir should really begin with: "And then ..." If you have gotten this far, you realize that I was guided by this principle, even if I did not literally say so. For the sake of my own sanity, I have to put an end to it.

I began *Part One* with thoughts from Robert Frost's, *The Road Not Taken*, then I tossed in a little Ralph Waldo Emerson to give it some depth: "Do not go where the path may lead, go instead where there is no path and leave a trail."

I think it appropriate to round it out with another Frost goody, *Stopping by Woods on a Snowy Evening:*

> *"The woods are lovely, dark and deep,*
> *But I have promises to keep,*
> *And miles to go before I sleep,*
> *And miles to go before I sleep."*

At the risk of being considered maudlin, I have only few miles to go before I sleep. The main promise to be kept is to myself in the publication of this book. As I said at the beginning, *This is an Ego Trip.*

All the while I have not lost sight of a vital guidepost; "If you don't write it down, it didn't happen. There were scores of people who were part of the stories I have told in this book (maybe even you, the reader)… but *I* wrote it down.

My prime motivator is the public celebration of the achievements of the Schroeder family, underscoring that there are few "one-trick ponies" in our herd. Life for us is not a spectator sport … we are more into *being watched* than watching. Hence, we are likely doing something creative like writing, teaching, painting or acting. It's hard to find most of us ever being on a sports team, but we are often involved in the leadership of active or creative groups of people.

When I started writing *Synchronicity, Part One,* I thought I knew where I stood on the subject of Free Will. Now I am not so sure. However, reviewing some of things that have unfolded in the past eighty years, I have shifted from denial to realizing I may simply have not completely understood. That is not to say I have achieved totality, just that the jury is still out.

I do find it hard to accept the idea of simply being caught up in the cogs and gears of the Universal Machine. That would imply that there is only one timeline. I am more inclined to think there are infinite pathways. Being a strong believer in The Concord Gang (Emerson, Hawthorne and Thoreau), I respect many of their observations. They saw our role in the Universal Game as interactive, like the Lottery, "you gotta play to win."

If I knew then what I know now, would it make any difference? Perhaps Fate distills the essence of what's truly important (and allows us the illusion of Free Will). So we go ahead and play the hand dealt.

One simplistic way of seeing things, is to imagine you are seated in a game of Five-Card Draw Poker. Deuces are wild and you can get four new cards by showing you have an Ace. Anything can — and will — happen. Maybe it's time to invoke Willy Nelson:

"You've got to know when to hold 'em ...
Know when to fold 'em...
Know when to walk away ...
Know when to run ...
You never count your money ...
When you're sittin' at the table ...
There'll be time enough for countin' ...
When the dealin's done."

Emerson offers a more optimistic prospect:

"What lies behind you and what lies in front of you, pales in comparison to what lies inside of you... Dare to live the life you have dreamed for yourself...
Go forward and make your dreams come true."

When I was teaching Management classes at Westinghouse, one of the most successful aspects of self-help programs was visualizing your objective as having already taken place. However, the line between visualizing and pipe-dreaming is a very thin one. I think the mainspring of success is believing that it can happen. What often happens is that our subconscious mind guides or pushes us into situations that improve the probability of achieving our objective. Emerson describes it well: "Once you make a decision, the universe conspires to make it happen."

I still persist in my belief that *The Innocent Assassin* will be screened as a movie or TV program. It will be after I die, and the result of somebody who can make it happen will say, "How come this story has never been told in the mainstream media?" At that point Melanie, as the Executor of my Intellectual Properties, will have to see it through.

If I had stayed in Bill's Gulf Station pumping gas, instead of taking a job in New York as an office boy, the probability of ever becoming a Public Relations Manager for four different Dow Jones Blue-chip companies would have been infinitely reduced.

As we all know well, sometimes the pivotal factors in our lives occur in areas beyond our control. In my own case, the two elements that made life-sized impacts on my story were totally unrelated … (1) learning to type and (2) collecting playing cards.

Because of injuries to motor-control centers from a childhood accident, I could not master writing legibly, in spite of long practice sessions. (Even today, I can't read notes I wrote to myself yesterday.) Salvation came at Fort Dix Clerk-Typist School … at last I could type almost as fast as I thought. When I went to Stenographer's school my notes were nearly illegible. When it came to transcribing them, I relied heavily on my better-than-average memory skills.

The payoff was being able to type my schoolwork at Rutgers (higher grades), and writing legible ideas on communication jobs later.

Unrelated to my writing skills, in later life discovering the world of playing and Tarot cards opened a world of financial independence. That, in turn, allowed me the time to write seven books by employing my typing skills again.

LOOSE ENDS

Assuming this is the last book I will go through the trouble of publishing, I guess I need to tie up the loose ends of things I touched on along the way. Anything I think of after *Part Two* has been printed will be found in a file titled *Bill's Extra Stuff*.

Even if you haven't been paying close attention, you know I am obsessed with Synchronicity. In more simplistic terms many call it "coincidence." I prefer to interpret things in Jungian terms. Looking at the big picture, it is hard to deny there is something going on and we don't know what it is. Einstein gave it some thought and said, "Coincidence is God's way of remaining anonymous."

Pre-life

Another puzzle that I expect to solve in the near future — What happens when I am finished with the physical body I now occupy? Sorry, but I don't expect to share the answer with you after it happens. Undoubtedly, you will eventually find out for yourself. Everybody talks about the *Afterlife*. But those of us who believe in reincarnation realize there is probably a *Pre-life* as well. One name for it is *Limbo*. That's where we go between lives.

Death

My only fear of Death is that it may be a boring state of consciousness of a dark, empty void (which might explain why some people reincarnate — sheer boredom). What I hope for is a creative consciousness in what is, for lack of a better term, an *Afterlife*. Several thousand years of thinkers have not come up with a clear picture of Limbo, except that it is somewhere between Heaven and Hell. You don't get a roadmap until you are on your journey. I have explained earlier in this book my view of the relationship between Time and Consciousness.

It would be presumptuous for me to insist I have the answer. The closest I can come is that you will *most likely find what you expect to find*. If all this *consensus reality* is just a temporal illusion, those of us with more creative imaginations may have something more favorable to look forward to. I'm happy with thinking this world is but a canvas for our imagination.

As for the vacated carcass, to illustrate the firmness of my beliefs, I paid in advance for direct cremation by a local undertaker (including pick-up and delivery). No phony and expensive ceremony. Regarding the burial of a body in a cemetery, I can't think of anything more grisly, gruesome or ghastly.

I have a wooden box I picked up somewhere that is decorated with skeletons. I used it in my Tarot reading days to create a spooky atmosphere, implying a connection with the spirit world. It is an ossuary — a container into which the bones of dead people are placed. Supposedly, they would be available for re-animation at the Second Coming of Christ. I have suggested to my children it be used to temporarily hold the cremated ashes of Pat and me until someone gets around to putting them in a hole at the foot of our favorite tree. Mother Nature will then have a chance to recycle the chemicals therein as fertilizer.

TRUTH

One of the subjects that captured my attention along the way is *Truth*. Here's another subject that vast amounts have been written about. Unfortunately, as an absolute, it simply does not exist. Its real name is Perception. Hamlet summed it up for Rosencrantz and Guildenstern: "… for there is nothing either good or bad, but thinking makes it so."

Four hundred years later, in *A Few Good Men,* Col. Nathan R. Jessup (Jack Nicholson) gives a memorable 20th Century view of the subject to Lt. Daniel Kaffee (Tom Cruise):

Kaffee: I want the truth!
Jessup: You can't *handle* the truth!

Over a few drinks, twenty years ago, I had a very frank discussion with another, older writer who had just retired from a Public Information Officer's job. He had spent six months in Antarctica — obviously a good place to do some serious thinking and writing a definitive book on propaganda.

"Bill," he said, "do you know what we do for a living?"

"We are professional communicators," I cheerily responded immediately.

"*Bullshit!*" he said emphatically. "I really expected a lot better answer from you. … We are Professional Liars. And you just committed the worst sin in the book … you believe your own propaganda."

"Oh!" I said.

"We come with a host of labels … advertising copywriters, speechwriters, public relations reps, government spokesmen, propagandists, and just plain politicians. But we have a special talent for telling *just enough* of the truth to get a desired response from the poor, dumb bastards who are our targets."

We had another drink and we talked for an hour. When I digested the thoughts, I realized he had nailed it, explaining my encounters with the Truth in so many instances. For me, the most impactful situation had to be as executive speechwriter for Honeywell Computers.

While headquartered in Phoenix, one of the Division's most critical operations was a factory in San Diego. Competition with Silicon Valley for one hundred scarce (think 1974) IT techs threatened the operation. Word had gotten out to the employees that the contract they were fulfilling for the DOD would not have a follow-on. The plant would close when the current work was done — everybody would be on the street. Management's primary concern was that computer geeks with state-of-the-art knowledge would jump ship before we were ready to throw them over the side.

I sat in on a conference headed by Human Resources Manager Del West and two Vice Presidents. My job was to develop a communication program assuring the California employees that confidential follow-on contracts were in the works in Washington. But, due to the National Security nature of the project, details could not be shared on other than a need-to-know basis.

We barraged employees and managers alike with stories full of confidence and innuendoes. No one had anything to fear for the future. The crescendo was a catered all-employee dinner meeting, six weeks before the contract was to end. There would be three Vice Presidents addressing the group (Division Operations, Defense Contracting, and Manufacturing). They had convinced me, now I had to see that they convinced the California employees.

I wrote three 15-minute after-dinner speeches and programmed the event. It took on the aspect of a play with me as the author and director. I joyfully followed their talks as they dutifully read their scripts. Even Del West was pleased with the show. We successfully kept from hemorrhaging vital employees before the contract deadline.

I never officially found out what became of the plant because of what happened to me next.

I joined the VPs for a lobster dinner that evening at a posh restaurant. We complimented ourselves on the smoothens of the operation, but I soon picked up on the fact that I was the only one who did not know that the plant would, in fact, be shut down the week after the final production run … *there never was a follow-on contract.*

Feeling I had been taken, I excused myself from the table (but not without finishing my lobster first). On the subject of seafood, I began this chapter with a quote from Lewis Carroll's *Walrus and the Carpenter*. Few people recognize that the Walrus is the Patron Saint for Propagandists. He fills the oysters' heads with cute irrelevancies and winds up devouring them in return for listening. John Lennon much later admitted that when he said, "I am the

Walrus," he did not know he was the villain of the piece (He was high on acid).

I was told to take the next day off and stay at the seaside motel, I was checked into. I slept poorly and the next morning I decided to spend the day at the beach, reading.

The book I chose to bring along was *Mother Night* by Kurt Vonnegut, Jr. This was synchronistic on two counts; He had once held my job at GE and he was writing on the subject of propaganda and lies.

I became aware that my three VP speeches were nothing more than carefully constructed Lies.

I strongly recommend reading the book, if for no other reason than his explanation for the main character's defense for his writing Nazi propaganda … he couldn't believe anyone could be so stupid as to believe it.

The influence of mental stress cannot be discounted. I believe I was so stressed over what an idiot I had been, that I allowed it to influence my health. You can read that episode in the section of this book where I contracted San Joaquin Valley Fever.

There are four or five of my friends in their 70 and 80s who talk on the phone regularly. We are all in relatively good health. We all the same question — Why me? How come our spouses (and even children) have died? Some have been alcoholics or heavy smokers. No one has behaved in any extreme fashion. The consensus is genetics … We just inherited the right genes.

If there is an area of agreement among us, it is faith in moderation — don't sweat the small stuff. We all recognize anxiety as the common enemy. I can safely say we are guided by the famous Serenity Prayer by philosopher Reinhold Niebuhr:

God grant me the serenity
to accept the things I cannot change;
courage to change the things I can;
and wisdom to know the difference.

www.ingramcontent.com/pod-product-compliance
Lightning Source LLC
Chambersburg PA
CBHW070047080526
44586CB00013B/943